Snapshots of Forgotten Adventures

Cover image provided courtesy of the Schomburg Center for Research in Black Culture.

Permission for musical examples and quotations
  kindly provided by Karen Hilliard-Johnson.

This work © 2024 Sarah Masterson
        All rights reserved, including the right to reproduce this book
        or portions thereof in any form whatsoever.

Book and cover designed by Midge Wood

 Tyger River Books
A division of TigerCo Industries, LLC
Pomaria, South Carolina

ISBN 979-8-9881887-5-9 (hardcover)
ISBN 979-8-9881887-6-6 (casebound)
ISBN 979-8-9881887-7-3 (paperback)

Library of Congress Control Number: 2024904357

Snapshots of Forgotten Adventures

Rediscovering the Piano Music of Philippa Schuyler

by Sarah Masterson

TYGER RIVER BOOKS

to my parents,
Keith and Connie,
without whom this book would not have been possible

Table of Contents

List of Figures and Musical Examples	ix
Acknowledgements	xv
Prologue	1
Chapter 1: Schuyler as Storyteller: A Search for Identity	5
Chapter 2: Roaches, Religion, and Romance: An Overview of Schuyler's Piano Music	15
Chapter 3: Kyagambiddwa's Uganda: *African Suite*	39
Chapter 4: A Mutapa Ruler and a Nobel Prize Winner: *African Rhapsody*	53
Chapter 5: A New Movement: Dennis Gray Stoll and the *White Nile Suite*	64
Chapter 6: Religious Devotion: Arranging *Uganda Martyrs*	81
Chapter 7: Strong Friends and Strong Enemies: *Seven Pillars of Wisdom*	91
Chapter 8: Professional Success and Personal Disillusionment in Cairo: *Nile Fantasy*	122
Chapter 9: Composing Africa's Independence	135
Epilogue	145

Notes	151
Appendix A: List of Schuyler's Compositions	175
Appendix B: Source Texts in *Uganda Martyrs* and *Untitled*	191
Bibliography	198

List of Figures

Figure 1.1: Astrology Symbols and Musical Pitch

Figure 1.2: Tarot Cards and Musical Pitch

Figure 1.3: Emotions and Musical Pitch

Figure 3.1: Map of Schuyler's African Tours

Figure 7.1: Notes on 1964 Concert Program

Figure 7.2: Schuyler's Musical Alphabet

List of Musical Examples

Example 2.1: *Song of the Machine*, mm. 1-4

Example 2.2: *Christmas Eve*, mm. 13-20

Example 2.3: *Fairies Dance*, mm. 1-8

Example 2.4: *The Jolly Pig*, mm. 1-6

Example 2.5: *Cockroach Ballet*, mm. 1-6

Example 2.6: *Cockroach Ballet*, mm. 15-22

Example 2.7: *Cockroach Ballet*, mm. 84-95

Example 2.8: *Voodoo Festival*, mm. 8-12

Example 2.9: *The King of France*, mm. 1-6

Example 2.10: *Carnival in Languedoc*, mm. 6-10

Example 2.11: *Carnival in Languedoc*, mm. 55-62

Example 2.12: *Carnival in Languedoc*, mm. 63-70

Example 2.13: *Patagonian Triste*, mm. 4-11

Example 3.1: *Sanga*, mm. 1-6

Example 3.2: *Fumitta Embogo*, mm. 33-36

Example 4.1: *African Rhapsody*, mm. 1-10

Example 4.2: *African Rhapsody*, mm. 41-44

Example 4.3: *African Rhapsody*, mm. 118-119

Example 4.4: *African Rhapsody*, mm. 194-197

Example 5.1: *Legend of the Mahdi*, mm. 1-4

Example 5.2: *Legend of the Mahdi*, mm. 26-29

Example 5.3: *Legend of the Mahdi*, mm. 64-67

Example 5.4: *Legend of the Mahdi*, mm. 146-147

Example 5.5: *Legend of the Mahdi*, mm. 218-222

Example 5.6: *Alexandria*, mm. 1-6

Example 5.7: *Alexandria*, mm. 22-27

Example 5.8: *Port Said*, mm. 1-4

Example 5.9: *Port Said*, mm. 23-24

Example 5.10: *Port Said*, mm. 64-67

Example 5.11: *Fall of Babylon*, mm. 15-18

Example 5.12: *Fall of Babylon*, mm. 31-32

Example 5.13: *Fall of Babylon*, mm. 98-99

Example 5.14: *Fall of Babylon*, mm. 177-178

Example 5.15: *Fall of Babylon*, mm. 204-207

Example 5.16: *Fall of Babylon*, mm. 287-294

Example 6.1: *Uganda Martyrs*, mm. 1-13

Example 7.1: *Seven Pillars*, Prologue, mm. 5-15

Example 7.2: *Seven Pillars*, Prologue, mm. 29-32

Example 7.3: *Seven Pillars*, Prologue, mm. 1-2

Example 7.4: *Seven Pillars*, Prologue, mm. 24-25

Example 7.5: *Seven Pillars*, Prologue, mm. 33-36

Example 7.6: *Seven Pillars*, Prologue, mm. 37-40

Example 7.7: *Seven Pillars*, Prologue, mm. 176-181

Example 7.8: *Seven Pillars*, Part I, mm. 1-4

Example 7.9: *Seven Pillars*, Part I, mm. 9-10

Example 7.10: *Seven Pillars*, Part I, mm. 13-16

Example 7.11: *Seven Pillars*, Part I, mm. 72-73

Example 7.12: *Seven Pillars*, Part I, mm. 171-178

Example 7.13: *Seven Pillars*, Part II, mm. 7-12

Example 7.14: *Seven Pillars*, Part II, mm. 26-28

Example 7.15: *Seven Pillars*, Part II, mm. 54-57

Example 7.16: *Seven Pillars*, Part III, mm. 1-2

Example 7.17: *Seven Pillars*, Part III, mm. 37-44

Example 7.18: *Seven Pillars*, Part III, mm. 53-56

Example 7.19: *Seven Pillars*, Part IV, mm. 5-8

Example 7.20: *Seven Pillars*, Part IV, mm. 55-56

Example 7.21: *Seven Pillars*, Part IV, mm. 57-63

Example 7.22: *Seven Pillars*, Part IV, mm. 117-118

Example 7.23: *Seven Pillars*, Part IV, mm. 133-136

Example 7.24: *Seven Pillars*, Part IV, mm. 165-171

Example 7.25a: *Seven Pillars*, Part I, mm. 128-129
Example 7.25b: *Seven Pillars*, Part V, mm. 1-6

Example 7.26: *Seven Pillars*, Part V, mm. 46-47

Example 7.27: *Seven Pillars*, Part V, mm. 81-84

Example 7.28: *Seven Pillars*, Part V, mm. 241-245

Example 7.29: *Seven Pillars*, Part VI, mm. 1-10

Example 7.30: *Seven Pillars*, Part VI, mm. 44-49

Example 7.31: *Seven Pillars*, Part VI, mm. 93-98

Example 7.32: *Seven Pillars*, Part VI, mm. 168-173

Example 7.33: *Seven Pillars*, Part VII, mm. 3-4

Example 7.34: *Seven Pillars*, Part VII, mm. 32-37

Example 7.35: *Seven Pillars*, Part VII, mm. 38-40

Example 7.36: *Seven Pillars*, Part VII, mm. 43-50

Example 7.37: *Seven Pillars*, Epilogue, mm. 1-2

Example 7.38: *Seven Pillars*, Epilogue, mm. 9-10

Example 7.39: *Seven Pillars*, Epilogue, mm. 99-108

Example 7.40: *Seven Pillars*, Epilogue, mm. 313-316

Example 9.1: *Untitled*, mm. 1-2

Example 9.2: *Untitled*, mm. 43-44

Example 9.3: *Untitled*, mm. 47-49

Example 9.4: *Untitled*, m. 50-51

Example 9.5: *Untitled*, mm. 52-53

Example 9.6: *Untitled*, mm. 79-80

Example 9.7: *Untitled*, mm. 81-82

Example 9.8: *Untitled*, mm. 83-84

Acknowledgments

"It takes a village" has been overused to the point of cliché, but that makes it no less true. The pandemic made virtual research a necessity, and this book has only been possible with the help of friends, family, colleagues, and, sometimes, even strangers who have been willing to help research, proofread, search archives, and serve as sounding boards throughout this process.

I am grateful to Newberry College for helping to fund my research for this book, and to our campus librarians for tracking down rare books, musical scores, and articles for me.

Thank you to the archivists and researchers at the American Music Research Center at UC Boulder, the Center for Black Music Research at Columbia College, and the Schomburg Center for Research in Black Culture, who went above and beyond to allow me to complete this research almost entirely long distance.

Thank you to Dr. Kathryn Talalay for her willingness to revisit her research on Schuyler and for sharing invaluable advice on this project.

Thank you to my research assistants, Sasha Doster of New York University, who helped inventory and prioritize the many recordings in the Schuyler Family Audio collection, and Paul Johnson of Newberry College, who transcribed three lost scores from aging audio recordings.

Thank you to Jodie Peeler and Tyger River Books for continual encouragement and seeing the potential in Schuyler's story and this book.

Thank you to Karen Hilliard-Johnson for providing permission for my virtual research in the Schuyler Family Papers and for copyright permission to include the many musical examples and quotations found in this book.

Thank you to my graduate school friends Thaddaeus Bourne, Jen Wanner, and Leann Sanders, for their research help and advice. Thanks also to Sarah Burns, for not only answering my numerous and widely varied history questions, but also taking time out of a vacation to help take notes on Schuyler's audio recordings.

Thank you to Donna Thompson, who has been a friend, copy editor, and writing coach throughout this process.

Most importantly, thank you to my parents, Keith and Connie. They have been there for every step of this process, from hearing my first attempts at learning Schuyler's music to traveling to New York to help with my research. They sorted through archive boxes, read Schuyler's letters, took countless photos and notes, and even discovered a new piece...and along the way, I think they became almost as taken with Schuyler's story as I have been. Their confidence in me allowed me to believe my pursuing a project of this scale was possible.

All quotations from Schuyler's letters, personal papers, and publications are included as written, with their original misspellings, grammar issues, and occasionally strong language, in order to remain as faithful as possible to their original intent.

Prologue

There is so much to learn, and so little time in which to learn it.
– Philippa Schuyler, *Adventures in Black and White*[1]

While countless pages and recordings have been devoted to the great male composers, music by Black women has largely been ignored by the classical music community for well over a century. Recent years have seen the rediscovery of several such composers, with music by historically marginalized composers being performed and researched more frequently, although significant disparities remain today.

Surveys such as Helen Walker-Hill's 2007 *From Spirituals to Symphonies: African American Women Composers and Their Music* and Nathan Holder's 2020 children's book *Where Are All the Black Female Composers?* have started helping to bring these forgotten composers their deserved recognition.[2] The music of Florence Price is now being widely performed, recorded, and studied. Quite successful in her lifetime, Price wrote numerous works and was the first African American woman to have a composition performed by a major orchestra. Her music was almost entirely forgotten after her death, but its revival over the past decade has led to her current reputation as one of the great twentieth-century American composers.

At the same time, her contemporaries such as Nora Holt, Margaret Bonds, and Julia Perry are also beginning to receive more attention. In 2020, the first biography of Price was published, with the first biography of Pulitzer Prize-winning composer Tania León following soon after, in 2022.[3] October of that same year marked the orchestral premiere of Helen Hagan's piano concerto by Dr. Samantha Ege and the Yale Philharmonia, a staggering 110 years after its composition. An accomplished composer and pianist, Hagan was the first Black woman to earn a bachelor's degree from the Yale School of Music, and the first movement of her piano concerto remains her only surviving composition.[4] In both 2022 and 2023, the Grammy for Best Orchestral Performance went to albums featuring works by Florence Price,

Jesse Montgomery, and Valerie Coleman, with several other landmark recordings released during that period.*

Despite this increase in recording and scholarly activity, somehow the music of Philippa Schuyler has continued to be overlooked. When mentioned at all, Schuyler tends to be discussed as a child prodigy, pianist, or journalist, with book chapters devoted to everything from her mixed-race heritage to her parents' unique diet regimen.[5] Her compositional career was surprisingly extensive, particularly given the brevity of her life, yet it comprises barely a footnote.

Sometime in 2016, I stumbled across one such footnote in the form of a short two-paragraph biography of Schuyler. Instantly hooked, I began searching online to learn more, but only uncovered a handful of blog articles, a single 1995 biography by Kathryn Talalay, and references to a planned 2004 movie that never materialized. After reading Talalay's excellent book, I began trying to track down Schuyler's piano music with hopes of programming some of it. I expected to do a quick search and order some scores through inter-library loan; instead, I found an assortment of handwritten manuscripts in special collections with varying degrees of organization. Thus, I began what became a years-long process of researching and studying Schuyler's piano music. My efforts became partly a treasure hunt and partly a puzzle, but no matter the obstacles, it was always a story I could not leave behind.

As a pianist, my original intention was simply to learn and perform Schuyler's music, so I began by requesting scans of the manuscripts. Very patient librarians guided me through the process of getting copyright permission, kindly provided by Karen Hilliard-Johnson, and making access requests. It soon became clear, however, that some scores were incomplete, while others seemed to be preliminary drafts. Movements were not necessarily in order, and pieces were not always in their expected location. Schuyler's handwriting was often difficult to read, with multiple omissions and alterations penned into the manuscripts. In between semesters and class sessions, I perused the pages and created typed versions of the scores to use for performances and study. School breaks were used to travel to the Schuyler Family Papers and Audio collections at the Schomburg Center for Research in Black Culture in New York.

Studying Schuyler's music ultimately required extensive additional

---

* In 2022, the award for Best Orchestral Performance went to The Philadelphia Orchestra's recording of Price's first and third symphonies, and the 2023 Best Orchestral Performance was awarded to the New York Youth Symphony's album featuring works by Price, Montgomery, and Coleman.

research. In composing, Schuyler pulled from her seemingly encyclopedic knowledge of Africa in particular, leading to side quests about topics as varied as T.E. Lawrence, Haitian Vodou traditions, sixteenth-century African rulers, medieval French folk songs, the 1960s Congo crisis, and the late Dr. Albert Schweitzer. Along the way, many people helped with my research, and I am particularly indebted to Dr. Phil Dorroll of Winthrop University for his assistance in understanding more about the Qur'an, Dr. Heather de Savage for her help searching for those medieval French folk songs, and Sarah Burns for her guidance and reading recommendations on a wide variety of history topics.

Ever the journalist, Schuyler tended to include some sort of narrative in her pieces, and thorough research in her archived papers helped reveal her sources and intended plotlines. The fifty boxes comprising her portion of the Schuyler Family Papers include countless programs, correspondences, handwritten notes, and other ephemera that illuminate the inspirations and compositional processes which produced her music. The recordings in the Schuyler Family Audio collection include lecture recitals on Africa and other topics, radio interviews, performance and practice recordings, and even a session with a clairvoyant. Hearing Schuyler talk about her compositions in her own words proved invaluable, and the assorted music recordings helped confirm details of some of her less finalized manuscripts.

The more I delved into Schuyler's compositions, the more it became clear that these works were significant in their scope, complexity, and global approach. While biographical information on Schuyler is readily available, details of her compositions, or even an accurate and complete listing, are not, with the bulk of her works remaining unpublished or even completely unknown, and rarely programmed. As I began performing Schuyler's works, I soon realized that her music and story resonated with many audience members. Piano students, teachers, and even non-musicians all asked where they could learn more, and I was always disappointed to share that almost nothing except Talalay's biography was available outside academic journal paywalls.

In developing this book, one of my priorities has been providing accessible information to anyone with interest in Schuyler's compositions, regardless of their musical or academic background. While there is certainly much to investigate in terms of ethnomusicological and theoretical approaches to Schuyler's music, I strongly believe this type of general introduction to her compositions is equally valuable. Furthermore, the lack of published scores and resources on Schuyler's compositions makes it difficult for researchers to even know what possible fields of inquiry exist. In writing this book, my goal is to initiate a conversation about Schuyler as a composer, hopefully inspiring further interest in and publications of her music.

> Since I had to learn about life on the run, the form would have to be looser than a sonata, yet held together...This book is a series of snapshots of adventure, of exotic people, ideas, and scenes caught swiftly in passing.
> – Philippa Schuyler, *Adventures in Black and White*[6]

Although she was writing about her 1960 autobiography *Adventures in Black and White*, these words could just as easily describe Schuyler's piano compositions. Composed during her continual national and international tours, Schuyler's mature music draws extensively on her experiences across a wide variety of cultures. From her unconventional life as a child prodigy, to an adulthood spent trying to find her place in the world, Schuyler's life was filled with contradictions, triumphs, tragedies, and an unflagging determination to learn all she could about the diverse people she encountered. From her first attempts at composition when no more than a toddler, to writing pieces amid world tours and war zones, she always tried to share what she learned through her first and last love – music. Pulled from folk melodies given to her and collected in her own field recordings and notes, her musical inspirations range from Haitian Vodou melodies to medieval French folk tunes to Ugandan hunting songs, and even an oratorio about Catholic martyrs in Africa. Rather than forcing these tunes and styles into standard Western formal structures, Schuyler creates a variety of miniatures and mosaics that reflect her perceptions of the cultures and people she met.

In focusing on Schuyler's identity as a composer and musician, this book in many ways resembles Schuyler's own autobiography of vignettes, telling the individual stories of her compositions rather than creating another full biography of her life. Schuyler fit a truly impressive amount of living into her thirty-five years, and it is inevitable some events will be left out. She filled many roles in her brief life, including child prodigy, journalist, outspoken anti-Communist, devout Catholic, champion of women's and children's rights, and world traveler. Despite her multi-faceted life, Schuyler's core identity always remained that of a musician and composer, and this closer examination of her compositional output reveals a highly intelligent woman searching for identity and belonging but seeming to find it only in her music.

Chapter 1
Schuyler the Storyteller: A Search for Identity

> My God, there is so much fighting in the world...But I prefer the piano. Music, the international language speaks to the soul. Words are dangerous swords. No matter what you say, someone is always going to disagree with it.
> – *Letter to Andre Gascht, undated*[1]

Who was Philippa Schuyler? Was she a lonely child prodigy with a complicated relationship with her mother, or an intrepid journalist reporting on violence and wars abroad...or perhaps she was a naive romantic searching for fulfillment in a string of ill-fated love affairs? She spent her childhood working under immense pressure from a mother who adhered to a disciplinary parenting philosophy which favored punishments and whippings over physical affection. Even as a toddler, Schuyler called her parents by their first names, never by any terms of endearment.

Conceived in part as a social experiment, Schuyler's progress was documented religiously by her mother, Josephine, who rigidly controlled her daughter's raw food diet and schedule. In public, Mrs. Schuyler presented the image of a relaxed parent catering to her remarkable daughter's needs and whims; privately, she expected her daughter to be beautiful, intelligent, accomplished, and financially productive from an early age. Schuyler's father George was a writer who traveled frequently, leaving his family at home, and, in many aspects, this domestic arrangement led to mother and daughter becoming one another's entire world.[2]

Aside from a few years of partial days at the Convent School at Manhattanville College of the Sacred Heart and Father Young S.J. Memorial High School, Schuyler typically studied at home or with private tutors.[3] The close but contentious relationship with her mother continued throughout Schuyler's life, with Mrs. Schuyler serving as her manager. In their frequent correspondence, Schuyler not only confided in her as a close friend, but also continued to feel extreme pressure to make money and find a romantic match of whom her mother approved.[4]

As she grew older, Schuyler's love life made headlines in society pages, with magazines like *Jet* speculating on her romantic liaisons and marriage prospects.[5] Her archived papers are overflowing with love letters from a wide array of men, often with several writing her at the same time. Marriage proposals, professions of love, sketches of her, and even a request for a bra size fill the pages. Schuyler compared notes on each possibility with her mother, even getting background checks on some. Nevertheless, her more serious relationships tended to end badly, and she never married.[6]

In her professional life, Schuyler traveled the world as both a pianist and journalist, visiting some of the most unstable and dangerous areas possible. She investigated widespread rapes and war crimes in the Congo in 1960, covered violence in Angola and Nigeria, and spent most of the final months of her life in Vietnam.[7] Seemingly fearless, she charmed and finagled her way onto military flights and into hot zones, at one point writing her friend Father Lyons that she was disguising herself as Vietnamese to avoid mandatory evacuations in Hue, so she would not have to leave "at the very moment that Hue [was] becoming interesting."[8] Despite all the far-flung travel, danger, and personal drama, Schuyler was, first and foremost, a musician. In one of her last letters to her mother in March 1967, she wrote from the Joan of Arc Convent in Hue:

> Here I am, hundreds of miles from anywhere – right at the end of the world. And what am I doing? Practicing, performing, and associating with priests and ministers! Just as I do everywhere.[9]

Even during a war, Schuyler was still planning programs, practicing repertoire, and writing music, with her final works, both complete and incomplete, likely composed sometime in 1966. In the last three years of her brief life, her unique and fully formed compositional voice began to develop, giving us a tantalizing glimpse of how her future musical career might have looked.

> I want to compose music that reflects the world we live in today. I do not want to imitate the past. - *Philippa Schuyler, age 10* [10]

Although Schuyler's compositional style certainly evolved from ages four to thirty-five, two aspects remained constant – her interest in both narratives and folk music. In her early works, the stories she incorporated within her compositions could be as simple as the life cycle of the roaches that lived in her kitchen (*Cockroach Ballet*) or the death of her pet bird (*Death of the Nightingale*).[11] Later compositions showcased complicated and extended narratives, while her folk music arrangements explored the stories of the people and regions from which they came.

Schuyler's interest in folk music and non-Western traditions began at a young age, and, beginning with her first compositions at the age of four, Schuyler was fascinated with unusual melodies and dissonances. While those first works were understandably short and simple, many still explored tone clusters, modal tunes, and unusual topics.[12] Her personal childhood music scrapbooks reveal an early interest in non-Western music, even including an essay on ancient Egyptian music that attempted to convert a Coptic music parchment into Western notation.[13] One of Schuyler's later undated scrapbooks from the 20th season of Young People's Concerts criticized a United Nations-themed concert program for its lack of diversity, and several of her handwritten pages described all the music they could have included from Brazil, Mexico, Indigenous cultures, and American musicians of color. Her central thesis asserts: "Music has always been a unifying force among men, for sincere music is always international."[14]

Despite her youthful goal of creating relevant, innovative music, Schuyler ultimately drew extensively on older folk music traditions in her compositions. Rather than avoiding imitation in general, she instead sought musical relevancy outside the Western classical music canon, drawing on sources that include traditional Ugandan songs, Haitian Vodou melodies, and Arabic music. Because she traveled widely and internationally from quite a young age, Schuyler's vision of her contemporary world was one of a uniquely multicultural sound rooted in the people she met and the places she explored.

Despite a thorough, if haphazard, education, Schuyler never attended college; instead, she referred to her world travels as her college education.[15] She spent her adolescence touring the globe, visiting thirty-five countries by the age of twenty-three.[16] Along the way, she listened to people's stories, read everything she could, and wrote all of it down. The need to record what she learned led to her work as a freelance writer, and also inspired her musical career as a performer and composer. We can hear her visits to Sudan and Egypt in *White Nile Suite*, learn about her research on T.E. Lawrence and Islam in *Seven Pillars of Wisdom*, listen to a Haitian Vodou ceremony in *Voodoo Festival*, and experience her favorite African folk songs in *African Suite* and *African Rhapsody*.

Schuyler's compositional style varied based upon her inspiration, with her adaptations of African music sounding quite different from her arrangements of medieval French chansons. In general, her earlier folk music works tend to be short and straightforward, presenting the melody in a simple, style-appropriate setting, often with variations on a second or third "verse."[17] In her late twenties and early thirties, she began experimenting with longer, more intricate compositions, incorporating aspects of African and Arabic music traditions into her pieces rather than simply arranging melodies. These later works explore narratives in increasingly complex ways, using named themes, musical alphabets, and melodic transformations to convey not only the plot, but also her reflection on the more abstract meanings and implications of it. Despite these complicated, almost cryptographic designs, her music often has an improvisatory feel, at times including explicitly *ad libitum* sections.[18] In her tribute to Schuyler on WLIB's memorial radio broadcast, music critic and composer Nora Holt commented: "Her composing was so natural it was difficult to decide where the improvising began and the academic prevailed."[19]

As she spent more time in Africa and the Middle East, Schuyler grew increasingly familiar with regional musical traditions, folk songs, and folklore. Her lecture recordings reveal her wide-ranging knowledge of the variety of cultures, languages, history, and music across the continent of Africa, as well as in the Middle East and South America.[20] Given her extensive research and focus on folk music, comparisons between Hungarian composer and musicologist Bartók and Schuyler are perhaps inevitable, but Schuyler's approach to incorporating folk music is fundamentally different in that she exclusively arranged and studied music of other cultures and regions – never American, African American, or North American Indigenous sources. When she traveled for her concerts, Schuyler made a point of listening to local music whenever possible, jotting down melodies as she heard them. Local musicians and researchers gave her collections of folk tunes to arrange for piano, with several remaining unused at her death.[21]

This focus on the music of other cultures was born from her search for identity, as well as the influence of her extensive international travel in adulthood. She wrote about her frustration with the "racial situation" in the United States, asserting in her 1960 autobiography that "we cannot uphold liberty and equality abroad, while permitting racial segregation and discrimination here."[22] A 1966 interview quotes Schuyler on demonstrations against racism and apartheid: "How patient can you be after several hundred years of waiting?"[23] Letters to her mother from the 1960s describe her sense of isolation in the United States due to her biracial heritage.[24] Schuyler instead sought a sense of identity abroad, at times passing as white or hoping to gain European citizenship through marriage.[25] In exploring other cultures' musical traditions, she seems to have been seeking the sense of belonging that proved elusive in her home country, but that search appears to have been only intermittently successful. While some of her writings and letters about Africa show Schuyler finding a sense of meaningful connection there, other personal notes reveal the continuing loneliness she felt:

> Awful isn't it. Wounds and hurts. I am a beauty – but I'm half-colored – so I'm not to be accepted anyplace. I'm always destined to be an outsider, never, never <u>part</u> of anything. I hate my country – and no one wants me in any other country.[26]

Her search for meaning and identity also led Schuyler to religion and the occult. As a child, she studied singing and composition at the Convent Music School on the Manhattanville College campus, and she continued to correspond with the school's director for many years afterwards, eventually converting to Catholicism in her late twenties.[27] Letters with her mother and romantic interests alike make frequent references to the Catholic Church and her faith.[28] Even her writing career became at least partially focused on Catholicism, resulting in articles for Catholic publications as well as her 1963 book, *Jungle Saints*, about Catholic missions throughout Africa.[29]

Despite her personal beliefs, Schuyler was always curious about the religions practiced in other parts of the world. Her non-religious parents suggested young Schuyler study all the options before deciding on a faith, so she explored Hinduism, Islam, and even Rosicrucian before converting to Catholicism as an adult.[30] Over the years, she spent time in Islamic majority regions like Sudan and the Middle East, becoming more knowledgeable about Islam through personal study and conversations with locals. Several of her later letters to her mother even end with "Inshallah!", meaning "If Allah wills it!"[31] She integrated that familiarity with the Islamic faith into her Arabic influenced works, particularly in developing the narrative for *Seven Pillars of Wisdom*.[32] Her tours in Haiti introduced her to Vodou traditions, inspiring her settings of Vodou melodies.³³ She added her own English lyrics for the Vodou song "Erzulie Malad'oh," which include these somber verses:³⁴

> Erzulie Eh!
> The child of a troubled land-
> Where destiny's call-
> Is savage and wild.
>
> Her heart is bleeding for her people-
> Her eyes are weeping for her people.
>
> Erzulie Eh!
> Erzulie! Come to me!
> Oh! -------
>
> Ouai! Erzulie come to me!
> Her heart is still and silent-
> Her eyes are closed and weary.
>
> Erzulie Eh!
> Erzulie weeps no more!

Despite its seeming contradiction with her devout Catholic faith, Schuyler also maintained a lifelong fascination with astrology, tarot, and numerology. She compulsively checked her horoscope and would get tarot readings as often as possible. Letters exchanged with her mother are filled with discussions of her cards – what they said about her recital programs, the men she met, and even the larger socio-political situations she investigated.³⁵ After one of her visits to Africa, she described a vivid and, at times, morbid, African version of tarot, with cards like "Revolution: 'Maison-Dien'. Fire burning a palace (temple?), explosion, two corpses bleeding" and "La Mort: corpse, pieces cut out of it, the heart half dragged out, two men with knives looking furtive in a clearing in the jungle."³⁶

Interestingly, her archived papers reveal that this obsession also extended to Schuyler's approach to composition. Horoscope symbols and Roman numerals are scribbled in the margins of letters, programs, business cards, and any other piece of paper she could find. Sometimes they are paired with note names or numbers, but they also accompany all sorts of questions, from the mundane to the professional. On some, she asks what piece she should play on her next recital, or whether she should travel to a particular city.[36] Others include more troubling questions and answers like "Who is my friend? Nobody."[38]

An October 1964 letter to her mother helps clarify the meaning of Schuyler's sketches when she mentions her "Horoscope-Numer-Tarot-Music system" and implies that this was a method she used for composing. She excitedly tells her mother about a game she devised that combines that system with chess, writing: "This means I can use a chess game for a musical piece. That is, they have books of great chess games – and I could use part of one, translated in musical terms, a rapid way of arriving at a musical passage or section of a piece." In the rest of the letter, she goes on to describe an elaborate game involving a board painted with tarot symbols and alternate chess pieces representing tarot and astrology concepts like The Empress, The Woman with the Scales, The Sun, The Magician, and many more.[39] It is unclear if Schuyler ever fully generated a musical piece with this game, but her detailed notes indicate she used her Horoscope-Numer-Tarot-Music system in some way. In this system, each of the twelve horoscope symbols and their ruling planets are paired with one of the twelve chromatic pitches, as shown in Figure 1.1. Roman numerals representing the twenty-two major arcana tarot cards are also paired with pitches (Figure 1.2).[40]

While some practitioners align astrological signs with specific tarot

Figure 1.1

Astrology Symbols and Musical Pitch

Pitch	Astrology Sign	Planet
C	Leo	Sun
C#	Virgo	Mercury
D	Gemini	Mercury
Eb	Taurus	Venus
E	Libra	Venus
F	Aries	Mars
F#	Aquarius	Uranus
G	Sagittarius	Neptune
Ab	Pisces	Neptune
A	Cancer	Moon
Bb	Scorpio	Pluto
B	Capricorn	Saturn

Pitch	Tarot Card	Tarot Card	Tarot Card
C	I (The Magician)	XI (Justice)	
C#	V (The Hierophant)	XXI (The World)	
D	V (The Hierophant)	XIX (The Sun)	
Eb	III (The Empress)	XVII (The Star)	
E	III (The Empress)	VIII (Strength)	
F	VII (The Chariot)	XII (The Hanged Man)	
F#	XIV (Temperance)	XVI (The Tower)	
G	IV (The Emperor)	VI (The Lovers)	
Ab	IX (The Hermit)		
A	II (The High Priestess)	XVIII (The Moon)	
Bb	XV (The Devil)	XX (Judgment)	0 (The Fool)
B	X (Wheel of Fortune)	XIII (Death)	

Figure 1.2: Tarot Cards and Musical Pitch

cards, that is not the case here. Hypothetically, a person's birth chart or a specific tarot draw could be used to generate a short melody or theme; some of Schuyler's notes also pair the letters in people's names with horoscope symbols and note names.[41] In other sketches, she assigned pitches to the numbers 0 through 63 and used those to create a variety of matrices.[42]

Cryptographic musical designs seem to have fascinated Schuyler later in her life, and the more complicated her personal life became, the more elaborately she tried to encode narratives into her music, finding a sense of order in the only medium she truly controlled. Part of her Horoscope-Numer-Tarot-Music system likely included a version of numerology, and some of her final works use her own musical alphabet to spell the names of musical themes, discussed in detail in Chapter 7. In sketches of her unfinished *Sonata diabolique*, Schuyler also pairs note names with colors and emotions (Figure 1.3), possibly indicating the beginnings of yet another strategy for encrypting a story into her compositions.[43]

Ultimately, Schuyler's musical alphabet is the only cryptographic design appearing in her surviving manuscripts, although it remains possible that sketches detailing the use of her Horoscope-Numer-Tarot-Music system are simply missing. Because of her early death, the ideas she had for generating music with horoscopes, tarot cards, and colors were likely plans for future

Pitch	Color	Emotion
B	Black	Hatred and malice
Bb	Deep flashes of red on black	Anger
F	Sanguine red	Sensuality
C#-	Dull brown	Avarice
F#	Gray brown	Selfishness
Bb	Green brown	Jealousy
A: B: F#	Gray	Depression and fear
Eb	Crimson	Loving nature
D	Orange	Pride and ambition
C	Yellow	Intellectual
C#-:F#	Gray-green	Deceit and cunning
E	Emerald green	Versatility and ingenuity
C#	Pale delicate green	Sympathy and compassion
G	Dark blue	Great religious feeling
--	Light blue	Devotion to noble ideals

Figure 1.3: Emotions and Musical Pitch

pieces which unfortunately remained unused. These elaborate systems for embedding names, symbols, and emotions into musical works provide important insight into Schuyler's mature compositional approach, which combined these relatively rigid designs with occasional improvisation and folk music elements.

Schuyler also began experimenting in later works with ways to merge aspects of African and Arabic musical traditions with the piano, a traditionally Western instrument. Different tuning systems can make the endeavor difficult, but she tried to incorporate their approaches to melody, structure, repetition, and dissonance, along with a distinctly non-Western sense of musical form. Tone clusters and split-note chords attempt to mimic quarter tone tuning, and scales tend to be either major, pentatonic, or modal. Schuyler uses minimalist building blocks, typically based on folk melodies or her named musical themes, to generate the larger structures. Short melodies slowly evolve over percussive bass patterns, with sections often delineated by sudden changes in the melodic content.[44]

At performances of Schuyler's late works, the pervasive use of repetition often stands out to listeners. Criticisms of the music tend to focus on that constant repetition and lack of formal structures; despite some merit to this observation, these critiques tend to be somewhat Western-centric in their idea of what "good" music is. In actuality, her compositions are not necessarily devoid of formal structures, but they often lack Western musical forms. Schuyler was well educated from a young age in composition and music theory, as shown in her archived papers, which are filled with composition and counterpoint exercises, notes on other composers' works, and her teachers' critiques.[45] In these African and Arabic inspired works, she was consciously choosing to compose outside Western traditions, drawing instead on the music she heard and loved in her travels and translating it to her own instrument. Repetition and ostinatos are key features of African and Arabic music traditions, and musical structures tend to be built through aspects other than traditional Western harmony. Most importantly, Schuyler always fit the musical style and formal design to the story she wanted to tell.

Musical alphabets, programmatic designs, and folk music elements certainly are not unique to Schuyler's compositions, but a firsthand knowledge of the cultures from which she borrowed, along with her varied compositional output and unusual background, sets Schuyler apart from many of her contemporaries. Each of her African inspired works was deeply personal, having evolved from her own adventures, relationships, and intellectual passions. After an overview of her early works, the remaining chapters of this book explore the stories of these compositions crafted by a composer just beginning to find her own identity and voice.

Chapter 2
Roaches, Religion, and Romance
An Overview of Schuyler's Piano Music

As a child prodigy dubbed "Harlem's Mozart" in the press, Schuyler's musical talent and eccentric upbringing were the subject of many interviews and puff pieces.[1] One of her mother's favorite stories to share in those features involved Schuyler's *Cockroach Ballet*. Not long after composing it, Schuyler excitedly played the piece for Mother Stevens, head of the music department at the Convent School where Schuyler studied composition and theory. Mother Stevens complimented her work but asked why she would want to write about roaches instead of angels. Schuyler replied, "But dear Mother, I've never seen an angel, but I've seen many cockroaches."[2]

In her childhood works, Schuyler did indeed focus on writing what she knew – books she read, special events in her life, and, of course, the roaches in her kitchen. As a teenager, she experimented with composing for orchestra in well-received, competition-winning works, but her focus continued to be on telling her story.[3] World travels led to an interest in an eclectic array of music traditions, expanding her well of knowledge and influencing her compositions and performance repertoire. By her early twenties, that meant a growing interest in romance and the music of Spain and Latin America as she less frequently performed her childhood and adolescent works.[4] By the time she turned thirty, her focus had shifted to Africa and the Middle East, with her compositional style following suit. Her recitals consistently featured her own music, particularly pieces composed after 1958.[5] In her final works, Schuyler arrived at her mature compositional style, with its focus on elaborately programmatic music inspired by Arabic and African music traditions.

Even in her rudimentary early compositions, elements of Schuyler's musical style consistently appear, especially her interest in creating a musical narrative and her love for dissonance. In a 1938-1939 scrapbook from the

Example 2.1: *Song of the Machine*, mm. 1-4

Example 2.2: *Christmas Eve*, mm. 13-20

Young People's Concerts series, she writes extensively about program music and the various composers who used or avoided the genre. According to eight-year-old Schuyler, program music was less respected than abstract music, "but audiences like program music most." She was aware most of her compositions at that point would qualify as such, amusedly noting that "Mother Stevens does not like program music."[6]

Schuyler's scrapbook for the 1941-1942 season explored modern composers as varied as Igor Stravinsky, Roy Harris, Harry Burleigh, Marc Blitzstein, Aaron Copland, and Deems Taylor. Ten-year-old Schuyler especially

Example 2.3: *Fairies Dance*, mm. 1-8

enjoyed the music of Stravinsky and other modernists, commenting: "I like the rigor and originality of modern music. It expresses our life today and I find it very satisfying."[7] She admired composers who used dissonance to stretch the definitions of tonality without fully venturing into atonality, and her own works share a similar approach. Even in her childhood compositions, dissonances appear frequently, notably when portraying an aspect of the music's plot as in *Cockroach Ballet* and *Song of the Machine* (Example 2.1).[8]

These early works show Schuyler's compositional skills progressing from rudimentary pieces to longer compositions telling more elaborate stories. In *Christmas Eve* (composed at age 5), she alternates between simple chromatic motives and diatonic triads, frequently writing in unison (Example 2.2).[9] *Fairies Dance* is undated but was most likely written around the same time, based on the handwriting and its style. As seen in Example 2.3, this brief work is similarly repetitive, with a single chord repeated for several measures in the left hand and modal patterns in the right hand.[10] Composed at age 6, *The Jolly Pig* explores more tonal writing, but remains relatively simple. Basic D major patterns repeat in the bass, while two-note motives appear in the treble. Sudden dynamic contrasts depict the pig's merriment (Example 2.4, page 18).[11]

Also composed at age 6, *Cockroach Ballet* marks one of Schuyler's first attempts at more extended narratives. Much longer than her earlier pieces, *Cockroach Ballet* tells a detailed story, often included in recital programs for performances of the piece: "The cockroaches are dancing and feasting when suddenly the human beings appear and tragedy results. However, there are

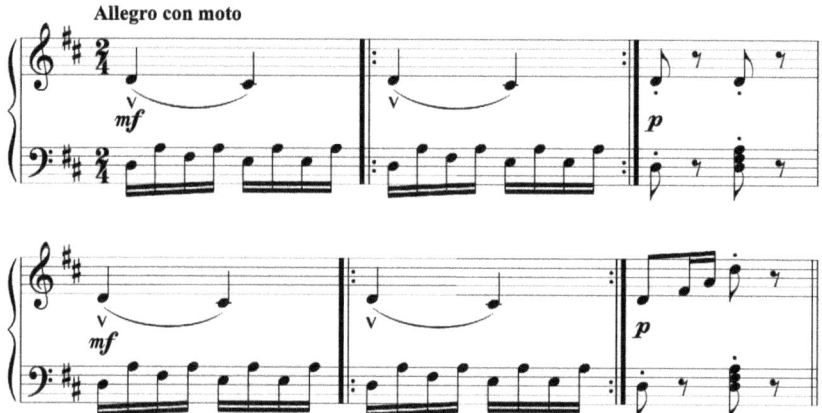

Example 2.4: *The Jolly Pig*, mm. 1-6

some survivors whose escape from death promises the continuation of the race."[12] In the opening measures, strong dissonances mark the beginning of the roaches' dance (Example 2.5). Schuyler labels the human beings' entrance in the score; their theme repeats a simple accompaniment in the bass, with busy chromatic eighth notes in the treble (Example 2.6). As the piece concludes, the surviving roaches quietly scurry away, with patterns recalling their opening dance (Example 2.7).[13]

Of special note among Schuyler's childhood works is her *Suite from the Arabian Nights*, completed by 1938 with an additional movement added later. Conflicts between the dated handwritten manuscript (transcribed on February 21, 1939) and the suite's appearance in a recital program two months prior (December 8, 1938) make establishing an exact date of composition challenging.[14] Inspired by her favorite book, *1001 Tales of the Arabian Nights*, the programmatic suite's movements feature evocative titles: *Camel Race*; *The Sandstorm*; *The Caravan*; and *Streets of Damascus*.[15] A few months later, Schuyler added a fifth movement, *Dance of the Forty Thieves*.[16] Musically, *Suite from the Arabian Nights* shares similarities with Schuyler's other compositions from that time period, specifically in the repetitive left-hand patterns and simple triadic harmonies. The piece's importance stems from its inspiration, which foreshadows Schuyler's lifelong fascination with Arabic topics.

Most of Schuyler's earliest pieces were transcribed by her piano teacher Arnetta Jones, a Harlem native who had studied piano at the Juilliard School of Music. In a letter to New York University during Schuyler's third year of study, Jones attested to their authenticity, noting that Schuyler never "per-

Example 2.5: *Cockroach Ballet*, mm. 1-6

Example 2.6: *Cockroach Ballet*, mm. 15-22

Example 2.7: *Cockroach Ballet*, mm. 84-95

mitted me to change one note in a pattern, motive, phrase, period, etc."[17] Although Jones notated Schuyler's first compositions for her, she did not specifically teach her composition. In summer 1937, Schuyler enrolled in her first formal composition classes at the Convent School on Manhattanville College of the Sacred Heart's campus. She continued to study there for several years, entering the Convent's Annunciation School in September 1938.[18] Moving quickly through grades, she began attending partial days at Father Young S. J. Memorial High School in fall 1942. Around the same time, her mother attempted find a private composition instructor for Schuyler. After well-known Mexican composer Carlos Chavez indicated he was not accepting students at the time, she turned to local New York composer Otto Cesana.[19] Schuyler's lessons with Cesana continued until she was fifteen; once those studies concluded, her travels became her education.[20]

While studying with Cesana, Schuyler's compositional focus shifted to the orchestra, and she wrote her first two works in that medium. Her first orchestral piece, *Manhattan Nocturne* (ca. 1943-1945), was inspired by her relief to arrive home from one of her concert tours. Its exact date of composition is difficult to ascertain, due to contradictory accounts from Schuyler. Program notes indicate that Schuyler wrote the piece when she was twelve, which would have been in 1943 or 1944, but her autobiography claims she began the composition in 1945.[21] Schuyler recounts that she had intended to write a piece inspired by her impressions of Mexico during a 1945 visit. After a variety of unusual and unsettling experiences, including attending a particularly bloody bullfight, she instead began *Manhattan Nocturne*, a "tone poem expressing [her] longing for home."[22] Possibly intended to be paired with the piece, a poem of the same title can be found buried amid assorted poetry in Schuyler's archived papers. Although no author is listed, the handwritten corrections imply that Schuyler herself wrote the following lines:

> Silver towers, golden skies,
> In falling snow or dark disguise
> Street-lights glowing like bright fire-flies,
> Or dim at dawn when the fog horn cries.
> Forget the traffic; the tyrant clocks,
> Evening crushes or noisome docks –
> George Washington Bridge at night
> Is like a topaz chain of lights;
> Visit the Park a day in spring
> When the blossoming trees wear festive white;
> Or see Times Square with the taxi fleets,
> The running signs and fragrant sweets;
> Mid-town at dusk will make you sing,
> Manhattan at night has everything.[23]

Premiering at Schuyler's thirteenth birthday party, *Manhattan Nocturne*'s piano transcription was first reviewed by Nora Holt in the *Amsterdam News*. Holt described the piece as "a creation of a mind young in theoretic pronouncement but mature in conception."[24] Although she performed it frequently in her earlier tours, Schuyler rarely played the transcription in recitals after 1958, aside from a 1964 youth program on her West Indian Tour.[25]

Other works composed during Schuyler's teenage years include an untitled piece with seven short movements and a piano arrangement of her orchestral scherzo *Rumpelstiltsken*. Although undated, the untitled multi-movement work was likely written relatively early in Schuyler's career, based on the handwriting and compositional style. The majority of its seven movements span less than a page, and the full set resembles her other early works stylistically. Only movements three and seven include titles – "Hallow'een" and "Little Valse," respectively. Compared to Schuyler's later music, the narrative is practically nonexistent, but the set still shows a young composer exploring more extended structures.[26] Of more significance in her career, the original orchestrated version of *Rumpelstiltsken* appeared as the second movement of her *Fairy Tale Symphony*. Composed in 1944-1946, the scherzo won second prize in the Grinnell Foundation's 1946 composition competition, with the orchestrated version of *Manhattan Nocturne* simultaneously placing first.[27] One of her only published pieces, *Rumpelstiltsken*'s piano transcription was a favorite of Schuyler's, appearing frequently in her recital programs through 1960.[28]

As a young adult, Schuyler began to chafe under her mother's constant supervision. In late 1950, she set forth on her first concert tour without her mother, traveling throughout the Caribbean.[29] Her newfound freedom from parents and teachers allowed the composer to focus on writing music to perform herself. As a teenager, she had been guided to work on pieces for orchestra as the next step in her development as a composer. While touring alone, she gained more independence and was able to pursue her own musical interests exclusively. The resulting pieces are almost entirely for the piano, and they reveal her interest in folk music traditions from surprisingly diverse regions. Beginning in her earliest international tours, Schuyler had been investigating the culture and music of the areas she visited, and we can hear the results of that study in these short sets.

Embarking on her first solo tour, Schuyler flew to Haiti alone to perform her *Rhapsody of Youth* for President Magloire's December 1950 inauguration. While there, she spent her free time exploring far beyond Port-au-Prince. Among the sites she visited was a Vodou sanctuary, which proved quite memorable for the young composer. In her autobiography, she later wrote:

> I recalled the frightening painting of Baron Samedi, the spirit of death, and the jumbled collection of weird, shabby, exotic and prosaic objects on the *pé*, or altar, of a small voodoo sanctuary, with its grisly bloodstains from the previous night's ritual, and the huge grimacing black cross on the wall, lugubriously clad in a top hat and frock-coat, the flocks of cocks and hens gamboling flirtatiously outside the *humfo*, unaware that they would soon be rent apart in a horrible and repulsive ceremony.[30]

Near the end of her visit, she met Professor Werner Jaegerhuber, a Haitian composer who devoted much of his career to documenting and studying traditional Vodou songs.[31] Jaegerhuber had spent his early adult life in Germany before fleeing Nazism in 1937; upon returning to Haiti, he began his study of Vodou music.[32] His 1945 collection *Complaintes Haitiennes* (*Haitian Folklore Songs*) arranged six of these Vodou melodies for voice and simple piano accompaniment.[33] He also incorporated those melodies into his compositions, including his *Messe Folklorique Haitienne*, a Catholic Mass derived from both Gregorian and Vodou traditions.[34] Upon meeting Schuyler in 1950, Jaegerhuber gave the young pianist a set of Vodou themes to arrange for piano. Schuyler simply called them "voodoo peasant themes," making it unclear whether Jaegerhuber provided her with a copy of his original research notes or his published collection of arrangements.[35] At some point, Schuyler did obtain her own copy of his *Complaintes Haitiennes* (*Haitian Folklore Songs*), which can be found in her archived papers.[36]

One year later, Schuyler included a set titled "Vodun Chants" in three recital programs, with no mention of Jaegerhuber or specific song titles.[37] She may have decided to continue working on her arrangements, as Schuyler did not perform them again until 1958, when their finalized versions began to appear on her recital programs. In those programs, she credited Jaegerhuber with collecting and transcribing the melodies, which she described as "chants to Erzili, Goddess of Love, Damballah, the Snake God, Marassa, the God of Twins, Legba, the God of Roads, and Ti-Jean-Petro, the tree-dwelling spirit."[38] Based on that list, some scores have been lost, but a chant to

Erzili appears in *Voodoo Festival*, and the chant to Damballah corresponds to Schuyler's missing manuscript *Damballa*, which can be heard on her 1965 LP *Pianologue*. Her 1958 recital programs include additional Haitian folk works titled *The Goddess of Love*, *The God of the Sea*, and *Festival in Port-au-Prince*. By December, Schuyler began programming *Damballa* rather than *The God of the Sea*, and her 1960 programs change the title *Festival in Port-au-Prince* to *Voodoo Festival*.[39]

Establishing the deeper meaning of these songs proves challenging, due to the fluidity of spirits (or *lwa*) in Vodou, as well as changes and improvements in our understanding of Vodou traditions since Schuyler's lifetime. Schuyler's interpretation does not always fully match Jaegerhuber's, and neither corresponds exactly to more recent literature. Adding to the issue of possibly changing titles, the scores for *The Goddess of Love*, *The God of the Sea*, and *Damballa* are all missing. *The Goddess of Love* was likely an arrangement of Jaegerhuber's transcription of "Erzulie Malade." As previously mentioned, Schuyler wrote additional English lyrics for this song, which Jaegerhuber described as a "song of mercy to Erzulie, Great Goddess of Love in the Voodoo Mythology."[41] A more detailed understanding of the Èzili family of Vodou *lwa* complicates matters, because there are many different embodiments of Èzili.* Of possible relevance here and to Schuyler personally, Èzili Freda is typically presented as mixed race, luxurious, and sexual. In Vodou lore, she tends to have a tragic love life, and her only son is lost at sea.[39]

Along with her arrangements of *Sakura* and *Arirang*, *Damballa* is a special case among Schuyler's missing manuscripts. While all three scores are lost, they can be heard on Schuyler's 1965 LP *Pianologue*. So that I could better study and perform these works, my research assistant, Paul Johnson, transcribed all three pieces from an aging copy of Schuyler's album. Performed with a very flexible tempo, *Damballa* is short and fairly simple, with a singing melody suspended over continually shaking bass tremolos.[40] Its source material initially seems obvious given its title; Jaegerhuber describes his transcription as an invocation to Dambala, "God of great power of Olympian character, Dispenser of Life, coming from the Kingdom of Allada whose symbol is a serpent."[41] That matches Schuyler's description of Damballah as "the Snake God" and aligns relatively well with Hebblethwaite's more extended explanation of the Danbala *lwa*. The song's repetitive lyrics invoke

---

* Jaegerhuber, Schuyler, and Hebblethwaite all spell *lwa* names differently. I have used each writer's original spelling here.

Example 2.8: *Voodoo Festival*, mm. 8-12

Danbala's "sacred name."[42]

While listening to Schuyler's recording and examining Johnson's transcription, a problem with these interpretations becomes obvious. The melody in Schuyler's arrangement does not match Jaegerhuber's "Dambala" transcription, but instead corresponds to "M'agué Ta Royo," a song to the "God of the Oceans."[43] In all likelihood, Schuyler originally labeled this *The God of the Sea*, although her reasons for changing the title to *Damballa* remain opaque.

Listed in earlier programs as *Festival in Port-au-Prince*, *Voodoo Festival* combines two melodies from Jaegerhuber's collection, "Gros Loa Moin" and "Erzulie Oh! Erzulie sa!"[44] Schuyler makes few alterations to Jaegerhuber's version of the first melody, simply adapting its asymmetrical meter into cut time with syncopation and accents (Example 2.8).[45]

"Gros Loa Moin" does not correspond to any of the spirits in Schuyler's list of topics; Jaegerhuber describes the song as symbolizing a business owner whose failing business is due to not fulfilling his duties to Simbi, "divinity of the Water."[46] More recent scholarship by Hebblethwaite describes Simbi as a healing *lwa* associated with water and Saint Christopher, with the following updated translation:

> My great lwa, my great lwa,
> Simbi in the water.
> My great lwa, my great lwa,
> Papa Simbi.
> My boat is sitting in the bay,
> It can't cross over.
> I'm asking what is this thing?
> I can't talk about it.
> Oh I can't talk about it.[47]

The second section of the piece adapts "Erzulie Oh! Erzulie Sa!", which follows immediately after "Gros Loa Moin" in Jaegerhuber's *Complaintes Haitiennes* as well. Although the Erzulie of "Erzulie Malade" was considered the Goddess of Love, here Jaegerhuber calls the song's topic Erzulie Sa, the "spirit of the Ocean wife of Agué."[48] The various manifestations of Èzili have many lovers, but Metrès Èzili is known as the mistress of Agwe Tawoyo, the *lwa* of the sea.[49] Hebblethwaite's English translation of "Erzulie Oh! Erzulie Sa!" reads:

> Oh Èzili! That Èzili!
> Hey Èzili! That Èzili! Oh yeah!
> On the sea my canoe wants to flip over.
> We have to pray to God
> so that people won't drown.
> Hey Èzili! Good luck woman, that Èzili!
> Mother Èzili, good luck woman,
> That Èzili! Oh yeah!
> On the sea my canoe wants to flip over.
> We have to pray to God
> so that people won't drown.[50]

Not long after completing her Vodou arrangements, Schuyler's compositional interests traversed the globe to Asia. After her first visit to Hawaii to perform at the 1958 Gershwin Festival in Oahu, Schuyler received a collection of Asian and Polynesian folk music from musician and environmental activist John M. Kelly, Jr.[51] Schuyler's archived copy includes a handwritten note of dedication: "A modest gift in tribute. To Philippa Schuyler – One who shares a deep respect for the peoples' music of the East."[52] The son of Hawaiian artist John M. Kelly, Sr., Kelly had studied music at the Juilliard School of Music before teaching at Palama Settlement's music school in Honolulu.[53] His interest in the traditional music of his multicultural students led him to collect, transcribe, and arrange a variety of Hawaiian, Korean, Japanese, Chinese, and Filipino folk songs for the Palama Settlement Children's Chorus to perform, and he eventually published many of his transcriptions in *Folk Songs Hawaii Sings: A Collection of Songs from Polynesia and Asia for Piano and Voice* in 1962.[54]

Soon after sending Schuyler his folk music collection, Kelly corresponded with her mother to set up a performance at the Palama Settlement's music school in Honolulu.[55] Schuyler returned there in December 1958, staying at the Kellys' home and performing his arrangements of *On Koto* and *Arirang* on her concert the following day.[56] In her autobiography, she wrote glowingly of her brief time there, seeming particularly enchanted with meeting Kelly's parents. While she admired his father's artworks, the Kellys' marriage made even more of an impression: "Truly, I felt, this is the way life should be, the way marriage, the way old age, the way happiness should be."[57]

In addition to the two pieces she performed in Honolulu, Schuyler's other Asian folk music settings include *Sakura*, *New Moon*, *Wanchai Road*, and *Khanghai*. Although the connection can be difficult to discern, all six pieces take their melodies from Kelly's folk music collection. Unlike Schuyler's other folk music arrangements, several of these were completed before she traveled to their source countries, with those written first also proving the simplest. Composed before her first visits to Japan, Korea, and Hong Kong, *New Moon*, *Arirang*, and *Sakura* all correspond closely to Kelly's versions. *New Moon* (copyright 1960) is described in its manuscript as being arranged by John Kelly, then elaborated upon by Schuyler.[58] A very straightforward adaptation, *New Moon* sets the melody of a Chinese folk song from Kelly's collection, "New Moon Over Kangting" ("Kang-Ting Suing Yueh"). Kelly notes "New Moon" originated in Kangting, capital of Sikang, and indicates the song describes the hope and renewal associated with the new moon.[59]

Two of Schuyler's lost manuscripts from her LP *Pianologue* also arrange Kelly's melodies – *Sakura* and *Arirang*. As heard in Schuyler's recording, the two arrangements faithfully follow Kelly's versions, with some elaboration on later verses.[60] Given Schuyler's tendency to improvise on her own compositions and arrangements in performance, it is possible that both works were more ornate when heard live. Of the two, *Arirang* seems to have resonated the most with Schuyler; she spends a full page of her autobiography on its meaning and emotional effect. According to her, *Arirang* originated two thousand years ago in Korea:

> One legend says it originated when the crushed people rose in revolt against a despotic emperor. The rebellion failing, the people were slaughtered by the imperial soldiers, and thousands of patriots were led across the primeval Arirang mountain to be executed – this was the song that rose spontaneously from their hearts, to send their message, their feeling of unconquered love for humanity to the world for all time![61]

Kelly was less effusive, merely noting that many versions of its origin have been told, but that the words "crossing the hills of Arirang" had "come to mean that one must surmount life's many vicissitudes and meet squarely the challenge to happiness."[62]

At first, the score for *On Koto* appeared to be lost as well. Further investigation revealed, however, that Schuyler based *Wanchai Road* on Kelly's "On-Koto" melody, despite no reference to folk music of any kind in the score. In some programs, Schuyler describes it as a folk song arrangement from China, but the liner notes for *Pianologue* make no mention of that, instead claiming that it "depicts the teeming alleyways, sidewalk vendors, jostling crowds and overcrowded slums of Hong Kong's Wanchai District, where Richard Mason's 'World of Suzie Wong' took place."[63] Mason's 1957 novel tells the story of the romance between a British artist and a Hong Kong prostitute, and its popularity inspired adaptations for the stage and silver screen.[64] Nonetheless, *Wanchai Road*'s main theme in fact matches "On-Koto" from Kelly's collection.[65] In all likelihood, Schuyler's *On Koto* and *Wanchai Road* are the same piece, with revisions. Schuyler performed *On Koto* for several months before changing the title between two different drafts of the program for her May 1959 recital at Carnegie Hall.[66] *Wanchai Road* is a bit longer than her previous Kelly elaborations, and Schuyler takes more liberties in arranging the tune, probably making changes to the score when she updated the title.[67]

Adding to the intrigue, references to a Japanese folk song called "On Koto" are difficult to find outside Kelly's collection, so Schuyler may have learned that the melody originated in Hong Kong or China...or decided that *Wanchai Road* would make a more marketable title, given the popularity of the 1960 movie version of *The World of Suzie Wong*. Around the same time, Schuyler began corresponding with a Hong Kong journalist who visited her in New York in 1959. According to Schuyler, they planned to collaborate on a series of short pieces to be titled *Hong Kong Days and Nights*. In her autobiography, she calls the reporter Victor Fung, but his actual identity was likely Ernie Pereira.[68] The subject of numerous discussions with her mother, Pereira exchanged love letters with Schuyler, although their tone often implies more of the love was on his side. Their surviving archived letters do not give the impression they were collaborating on any compositions, but their correspondence could have provided additional influence for *Wanchai Road*'s title change.[69]

While her liner notes describe *Khanghai* as depicting "the proud nobility of Mongolia's greatest mountain range," they also claim that it develops themes given to her "by a Chinese refugee in Hong Kong."[70] While that may be the case, the main theme of *Khanghai* matches another folk song in the John Kelly, Jr. collection, "Blue Flower" ("Lan Hua-Hua"). According to Kelly, the song tells the story of a young girl who rejects being sold in marriage to an older man in favor of love.[71] Like *Wanchai Road*, *Khanghai* may have undergone an evolution in title and content. Schuyler's 1959 programs include a work from the John Kelly Collection called "Love Song from North Shenshi," and Kelly notes that "Lan Hua-Hua" originated in North Shenshi.[72] One year later, *Khanghai* first appeared as part of Schuyler's copyrighted *Around the World Suite*, and "Love Song from North Shenshi" disappeared from her programs. Since both pieces were likely based on the same folk song, this change suggests that Schuyler may have retitled and rewritten her earlier arrangement to create the longer and more elaborate *Khanghai*.[73] Although still based entirely on a single folk song, *Khanghai* includes a much wider variety of textures, moods, and virtuosity, showing Schuyler beginning to reflect on her own interpretation of the folk inspirations.[74]

While these folk song arrangements do show more of Schuyler's mature compositional style and interests, they are still the product of a relatively young and sometimes naïve personality. Schuyler was in some ways a lifelong romantic, but in her teens and twenties she was especially interested in finding love. Her 1950s letters to her mother often described her newest crush or complained about his failings, and she also tended to romanticize many of the places she traveled, particularly Latin America.[75] While life experience and reporting on war crimes dampened that enthusiasm as the years passed, she never fully lost her appreciation for romance, despite growing cynicism about men.

One lecture recital recording in the Schuyler Family Audio collection exemplifies the way Schuyler romanticized the culture and music of Latin America. Although the recording is not dated, Schuyler goes by the name Felipa Monterro, which provides a clue as to when the performance happened.[76] In the early 1960s, Schuyler and her mother devised a plan for her to build a career under that name, hoping to pass as Iberian and be able to arrange more performances for white audiences in the United States. She first performed as Felipa Monterro in April 1963, so this lecture recital must have occurred sometime afterward.[77]

Titled "The Latin Gift to the World: Music and Romance," Schuyler's lecture traces the concept of romantic love from fifteenth-century France to

Portugal, Brazil, Spain, Latin America, and Italy. She includes remarks on her own experiences in those regions, claiming that "life in Brazil was a constant state of lovemaking" and "Portuguese are the greatest lovers."[78] After citing numerous musical examples like Portuguese *fados*, Bahian folk dances, Spanish *jotas*, and compositions by Albeniz and de Falla, Schuyler spends the second half of the tape performing at the piano. Many of the examples come from composers she favored in her recital programs at the time, such as Augusto Casanovas, Alberto Ginastera, Manuel Infante, and Manuel de Falla. Of her own arrangements, Schuyler includes her settings of fifteenth- and seventeenth-century French chansons.[79]

Of these, the undated *Carnival in Languedoc* arranges seventeenth-century French songs, while *Suite de Normandie du Moyen-Age* (by 1960) is based on fifteenth-century chansons.[80] In later programs, Schuyler began to refer to this set by the shortened title *Normandie*.[81] Frequently performed by Schuyler in the last three years of her life, the suite is described in her program notes as variations on fifteenth-century French songs, with ornamentation "typical of the influence of Arab music on early European music."[82] The recorded versions of its two surviving movements, *The Poet's Love* and *The King of France*, are straightforward settings of their tunes with basic accompaniment patterns.[83] Both manuscripts are short with little variation; when she retitled the suite, Schuyler also revised and combined them to create a more complex, single work. While some performances of the first version of the suite included a missing third movement, *Flowers of Death*, it remains unclear if Schuyler included it in *Normandie*, particularly since she only recorded the first two movements in *Pianologue*.[84] Unfortunately, the revised score for *Normandie* is also lost, referenced only in recital programs and a 1965 letter from Dennis Gray Stoll* in which he suggested that Schuyler rerecord her album *Pianologue* to replace the individual movements with her updated version.[85]

The King of France takes its theme from the late fifteenth-century chanson "Le Roy Engloys." In the liner notes for *Pianologue*, Schuyler simply calls this "a gay song sung after the English withdrawal."[86] Found in the Bayeux Manuscript, the short chanson tells the story of English King Henry V unsuccessfully trying to take over France in 1450.[87] According to those same liner notes, *The Poet's Love* is also from medieval France, with words attrib-

---

* Composer and conductor Dennis Gray Stoll met Schuyler in 1964, and they began a professional and eventually personal relationship that continued for some time. Chapters 5 and 8 discuss their collaboration in more detail.

Example 2.9: *The King of France*, mm. 1-6

uted to Francois Villon, although its actual source remains unknown.[88] Unlike much of Schuyler's music, these settings of French folk songs are very consonant and tonal, with simple textures and rhythms. As seen in Example 2.9, the often-repetitive left-hand patterns call to mind her frequent use of ostinatos, but her characteristic dissonances, asymmetrical meters, and non-Western scales are all absent.[89]

In *Carnival in Languedoc*, Schuyler begins to experiment with creating more elaborate stories in her music. Where her childhood works often had vague descriptions, this much longer piece includes a very detailed, written-out plot. While she does not yet use her musical alphabet to spell the names of characters or ideas, she does label each event with Roman numerals in the score. Quite the melodramatic tale, the script tells the story of Janeto, a woman in an unhappy marriage who embarks on a doomed affair with Pierre. After Pierre is killed in a duel with Janeto's husband, things take a turn toward the supernatural with witches, ghosts, vampires, and an implausibly happy ending, complete with the resurrection of Janeto's dead lover. Schuyler writes:

> *Adieu, Pauvre Carnival*: Janeto, unhappily married to Antoine, meets Pierre at the Carnival. She falls in love with him but does not know if she will ever see him again.
> *La Troumpuzo* (*The Faithless One*): (I-V) She does encounter him again. He returns her love. They are in ecstasy. They have a passionate romance. (VI) Carrying on their romance without her hus-

band suspecting requires much elaborate intrigue and furtive deception. (VII) Despite all their precautions, her husband finds out, and raises a storm of fury. (VIII) What shall she do? She feels so alone in her grief and loss. (IX-X) Antoine, in his fury, does not let any grass grow under his feet. He challenges Pierre to a duel. They fight vigorously. Antoine kills Pierre and flees. (XI-XII) Janeto weeps by Pierre's coffin in the mausoleum where he has been interred. Its ghostly atmosphere strikes fear into her heart. It is chill, damp and dark. Night has fallen. In the cemetery, the ghosts, vampires and skeletons leave their graves and dance on them. It is a hideous, terrifying sight to watch their wild dancing and orgy. (XIII) Screaming, she flees through the wood. She trips over a root and faints. (XIV) She falls into a delirious dream in which she relives the ecstasy of her romance with Pierre. (XV) The witch of the forest sees her lying outside her door, lifts her, and drags her into her hut. The witch gives the still unconscious girl some of the brew she has been preparing and says an incantation over her. (XVI-XVII) The girl arises in a trance and begins to dance wildly. Then she collapses again seemingly dead. She lies there still and lifeless. (XVIII-XIX) The witch continues with her hocus-pocus and incantations. Suddenly there is a strange feeling of another presence in the room. Little by little, the ghost of the dead Pierre is summoned up, and begins to take human form. (XX) The girl stirs, little by little, both resume life, recognize each other. Eagerly they embrace. They are both alive again! (XXI) The whole village celebrates with joyous dancing. News arrives that Antoine has been killed by highwaymen as he fled through the dark roads of the province. The young couple, now free to marry at last, joyously embrace as the villagers merrily celebrate..."[90]

In the process of depicting that narrative, *Carnival in Languedoc* also incorporates three seventeenth-century French chansons. Its first section, "Adieu, Pauvre Carneval" (Example 2.10, page 32) quotes a traditional Occitan song of the same title that was typically sung at the end of the carnival celebration.[91] After this introduction, the much longer second section includes variations on two other French chansons, "La Troumpuzo" (Example 2.11, page 32) and "Digue, Janeto" (Example 2.12, page 32).[92] The variations begin simply and grow increasingly virtuosic, with chorales, counterpoint, a waltz, and other settings along the way. Schuyler ends with a challenging

Example 2.10: *Carnival in Languedoc*, mm. 6-10

Example 2.11: *Carnival in Languedoc*, mm. 55-62

Example 2.12: *Carnival in Languedoc*, mm. 63-70

Liszt-like finale played as fast as possible.

Like most of Schuyler's mature works, the manuscript for *Carnival in Languedoc* does not include a date of composition. Several clues to its approximate date can be found, however, in Schuyler's archived papers. Although its title does not appear anywhere in Schuyler's recital programs, she did perform a medley of Languedoc folk themes in her 1961 and 1962 concerts. Most of those programs do not include details about the medley, but one program from a 1962 recital in Nairobi mentions specific folk songs that match those arranged in *Carnival in Languedoc*.[93] In each program, the medley is credited to Ludovic Cassan; in all likelihood, Cassan's 1948 *Vieilles chansons de la terre d'Aude* was Schuyler's source for the seventeenth-century melodies she used.[94] The manuscript's compositional style and handwriting share many similarities with Schuyler's other works of the 1960s, and early sketches show a much more detailed musical plan than typically found in Schuyler's earlier works. Those sketches include notes on the three folk themes and ideas for how to develop them, including variations that would imitate other works Schuyler performed at the time – a Turina sonata, De Falla's *Fire Dance*, and a *vidala* rhythm. At the top of the page, she indicates the piece should have "a puckish, yet grave and archaic impertinence."[95] Based on all these clues, *Carnival in Languedoc* was likely written after *The King of France* and *The Poet's Love*, sometime in 1960 or early 1961.

As evidenced by her lecture recital on romantic love, Schuyler was especially enthralled with the music of Spain and South America. Her performance repertoire included a wide variety of Spanish and Latin American music, often by less well-known composers like Padre Antonio Soler, Leopoldo Montenegro, Augusto Casanovas, and Juan Riperda.[96] In her archived papers, even more scores can be found, many of which seem to have been sent to her in hopes that she would program them. In preparing these pieces for performance, she often made her own edits, penciling and taping in different introductions, endings, omissions, and even adding chords for effect.[97] Perhaps as part of her memorization process or to reduce the number of scores she traveled with, Schuyler also transcribed other composers' works by hand, both in full notation and her own shorthand.[98] This habit made the process of establishing a list of her own Spanish and Latin American inspired compositions less straightforward than expected. Complicating the matter further, the specifics of how pieces were listed varied significantly from program to program and from year to year. Considering the challenges in communicating the details of recital programs, which she mailed or telegraphed to her mother from remote locations, these differences may have been the result of communication issues rather than carelessness. Still, she certainly seemed to view her titles as fluid. Schuyler's programs after 1961 often included a *Danzas Argentinas*, *South American Dances*, or *Latin American Dances*, without mentioning individual movement or piece titles.[99] Her programs at times listed the set as composed by her, as folk music arranged by her, or with no composer listed at all.[100] Based on the arrangements of other composers' music found in her archived papers, most of the pieces in these sets were probably not by Schuyler.

In a folder of assorted musical fragments and drafts, two sketches are

Example 2.13: *Patagonian Triste*, mm. 4-11

labeled simply as "Argentina," a title previously included in lists of Schuyler's original compositions.[101] Upon further examination, the first piece appears to be her own arrangement of Julián Aguirre's *Triste No. 3* from his collection *Aires Nacionales Argentinos*; the main differences from Aguirre's published score are the key and the way some rhythms are notated.[102] Known for his folk nationalist compositional style, Aguirre incorporated traditional *gaucho* and *triste* melodies into much of his music.[103] As such, Schuyler included this piece in the South American folk music section of her album.[104] The second unfinished sketch is a piano transcription of Ginastera's *Canción al arbol del olvido*, which she performed frequently under the title *Milonga*.[105] Given their prominent use of Argentinian folk tunes, these works were likely included in Schuyler's *Danzas Argentinas* set.

Of the surviving manuscripts and pieces listed in her recital programs, the only example of South American music that Schuyler truly considered her own is *Patagonian Triste*. According to Schuyler, *Patagonian Triste* arranges musical themes from "Chile's sad, desolate southeast region…given to her in Santiago;" its title references the Patagonian region at the border of Chile and Argentina.[106] This brief, one-page piece imitates the traditional instrumentation of guitar and voice, with a syncopated, repetitive guitar-like pattern in the left hand combined with a melancholy, *cantabile* melody in the treble (Example 2.13).[107] Despite its title, the style more closely resembles a *milonga* than the traditionally slow and plaintive *triste*. Given that the *triste* is an Argentinian dance form, Schuyler may have performed *Patagonian*

Triste as part of her *Danzas Argentinas* set, despite its Chilean source.

In the early 1960s, Schuyler's focus as a journalist shifted almost entirely to Africa, with her books *Who Killed the Congo?* and *Jungle Saints* being written about a bloody revolution in the Congo and Catholic missions in Africa, respectively.[108] At the same time, her concerts began to consistently program her African inspired compositions, often as part of lecture recitals related to her work in Africa. She further documented her research on African folk music in the 1960 article "The Music of Modern Africa," and she quoted folk songs in her *African Suite* and *African Rhapsody*.[109] Like most of Schuyler's scores, their manuscripts are not labeled with a date, but given the timing of her African tours and article on African musical traditions, they were likely composed in the late 1950s or early 1960s. *African Suite* appears in programs as early as 1960.[110] *Chisamharu the Nogomo* premiered on September 13, 1964; in later programs, it appears under the title *African Rhapsody* with a dedication to Dr. Albert Schweitzer on his ninetieth birthday.[111] Detailed discussions of these works appear in Chapters 3 and 4.

Labeled in its manuscript as being composed by Kyagambiddwa-Schuyler, *Uganda Martyrs* arranges Joseph Kyagambiddwa's *Uganda Martyrs African Oratorio*, which was written for the 1964 canonization of the Uganda Martyrs at St. Peter's Basilica.[112] This connection places the undated *Uganda Martyrs* as one of Schuyler's later works, likely composed in late 1964. A more detailed discussion of *Uganda Martyrs* can be found in Chapter 6.

In her final pieces, Schuyler advances from simply arranging folk songs to exploring a complicated, almost cryptographic narrative style. Inspired by the Arabic music of North Africa and the Middle East, these works mark an important, conscious shift in her compositional style. Her *White Nile Suite* (by 1964), *Seven Pillars of Wisdom* (1964), and the piano concerto *Nile Fantasy* (1965) all reflect Arabic influences, albeit in less obvious ways than in Schuyler's earlier folk-inspired works.[113] In these compositions, Schuyler uses features like non-Western scales and rhythmic patterns, ostinatos, and occasional folk tune quotations to create longer and more complex structures. Detailed discussions of *White Nile Suite*, *Seven Pillars of Wisdom*, and *Nile Fantasy* appear in Chapters 5, 7, and 8, respectively.

In examining Schuyler's piano music, some special issues related to her later compositions become evident. Her archived papers are only partially organized, and several works initially appear incomplete. I spent many months and archive visits searching through fifty-five boxes to try to locate and reconstruct as many as possible. Her earlier pieces – those written while she was young enough for her mother to preserve them at home – are more legible and complete. Her later works, written during her whirlwind world tours and coverage of wars in the Congo and Vietnam, are much more scattered. Several of those compositions now appear to be lost, although they certainly could be sitting undiscovered in the back of a library or private collection.

Adding confusion to the issue of lost works, Schuyler viewed the titles and sometimes even the content of her compositions as malleable. Many of her 1960s compositions changed titles frequently, and she continued editing them after their premieres. In some instances, this caused works to be classified as missing when, in fact, the titles had been changed, as with *Nubian Legend* and *Legend of the Mahdi*.[114] Schuyler's tendency to alter and improvise on her own pieces as she played further blurs the issue; for consistency, I have focused on her written scores as the authority.

Schuyler's copyright filings also complicate the issue of compositions and titles, particularly regarding her folk music arrangements and *African Suite*. Although no surviving recital programs include this specific piece, Schuyler obtained a copyright for *Around the World Suite* on January 27, 1960. The original manuscript is missing from the Schuyler Family Papers, but the Library of Congress stored the copy Schuyler submitted when filing for the copyright. That copy shows that the *Around the World Suite* included the following folk song arrangements:

    I. Patagonian Triste
    II. Voodoo Festival
    III. Khanghai
    IV. Wanchai Road
    V. Sanga
    VI. Tweyanze
    VII. Fumitta Embogo
    VIII. Poet's Love
    IX. King of France[115]

A similarly-titled set appeared in a single program from a recital in Boston on October 25, 1959, labeled "Adventures in Black and White – Music of the People (Around the World works – edited by Miss Schuyler)," capitalizing on the upcoming publication of her autobiography *Adventures in*

Black and White. That set included notably different folk song arrangements, including works by other composers, and they appear in a completely different order as well.[116] In fact, Schuyler continued to perform all these pieces on their own and under their original titles for some time after filing the copyright for *Around the World Suite*. *African Suite* (containing *Sanga*, *Tweyanze*, and *Fumitta Embogo*) appeared in recital programs until May 1964, while *The Poet's Love* and *The King of France* were included in *Suite de Normandie du Moyen-Age* until at least February 1962, with later programs featuring their revised and consolidated version *Normandie*. Similarly, Schuyler performed *Voodoo Festival* until at least April 1962.[117] Her 1965 album *Pianologue* also featured most of these works under their own separate titles, with no mention of an *Around the World Suite*.[118]

All this confusion raises some interesting questions. If Schuyler never performed *Around the World Suite* under that title, what was the purpose of combining separate works into this one suite? I suspect that Schuyler may have been planning (or hoping) to publish some of her scores, and a suite related to her world travels timed to coincide with the 1960 publication of her autobiography and travelogue may have seemed particularly marketable. The exclusion of the more faithful John Kelly, Jr. arrangements, *Sakura*, *Arirang*, and *New Moon*, adds credence to that theory, as she would not have had sole copyright of those works. In fact, she filed for a shared copyright of *New Moon* two months later in March 1960.[119] Although the fact that the suite was never actually published seems puzzling at first, Schuyler may have struggled to find a publisher, or she simply became so busy with traveling, reporting, and her personal life that she procrastinated. Regardless, the existence of a combined version of these works creates another decision for the performer – namely, which version to program. Because Schuyler never actually performed *Around the World Suite* under that title, I have chosen to discuss the included works separately.

After sorting through changing titles and evolving movements, a few of Schuyler's works are still missing. As previously mentioned, three lost manuscripts have been transcribed from her LP *Pianologue* - *Sakura*, *Arirang*, and *Damballa*. Several childhood pieces listed in her early recital programs are also missing, as noted in Appendix A. Of her truly lost mature compositions, the earliest is from December 1950, when she composed and performed *Rhapsody of Youth* for Haitian President Magloire's inauguration.[120] Two of her last compositions are also missing or incomplete – *Rhapsodie togolaise* and *Sonata diabolique*. Partial sketches for *Sonata diabolique* were found in a large, archived box of miscellaneous papers and sheet music, but if Schuyler ever completed the work, the manuscript has not been preserved. The sketches show Schuyler planning a three-movement, programmatic sonata, in which each movement is based on a novel with dark, supernatural elements: *La Bas*, *Carmilla*, and *The Burning Court*.[121] Joris-Karl Huysmans's controversial 1891 *La Bas* (*The Damned*) follows a novelist who becomes entrenched in Satanism and the occult after researching Gilles de Rais, the fifteenth-century serial killer of children.[122] Predating Bram Stoker's *Dracula* by over twenty years, Sheridan Le Fanu's 1872 *Carmilla* follows lesbian vampire Countess Karnstein (Carmilla) in one of the first examples of vampire fiction.[123] Finally, John Dickinson Carr's 1937 novel *The Burning Court* tells a locked room murder mystery involving suspected witchcraft.[124] Schuyler's plans for *Sonata diabolique* include a detailed list of musical themes spelling the names of important characters, items, and topics from these three books using the same musical alphabet as in *Seven Pillars of Wisdom* (see Chapter 7).[125]

After such an extensive planning process, it seems strange that Schuyler never completed *Sonata diabolique*, but a possible explanation can be found buried in a June 1965 letter from fellow composer and romantic suitor Dennis Gray Stoll. In reply to a now lost letter from Schuyler, Stoll calls Carmilla's story "at this day and age a subject for Peter Sellers" and implores Schuyler not to associate her music with it, asking, "Why a story at all? Just let it stand on its own beautiful legs!" Later in the letter, Stoll teasingly calls Schuyler his "diabolical witch girl," feeling she empathized a bit too much with the vampire Carmilla and might need one of her Catholic priests to exorcise her.[126] Although Schuyler wrote back with a typically fiery response, it is unfortunately possible that such criticism from a close confidante led Schuyler to abandon her rather fascinating plans for *Sonata diabolique*.[127]

The only reference to *Rhapsodie togolaise* comes from a recital program for its premiere in Togo on February 2, 1966, just one year before Schuyler's death.[128] Sketches or manuscripts of the work have not been found, but if these were indeed her final pieces, they demonstrate Schuyler continuing to compose while enduring personal strife and pursuing an increasingly demanding reporting career. From age four until her death at thirty-five, she remained faithful to her first love - music.

Chapter 3
Kyagambiddwa's Uganda: *African Suite*

> It is a mistake to speak of 'the African personality,' for Africa has more variety than any other continent in the world. Africa's music has the widest dissimilarity, but it is always original, refreshing, ingenious, colorful and fascinating.
> – Philippa Schuyler, "The Music of Modern Africa"[1]

Africa fascinated Schuyler, drawing her back repeatedly, despite the upheaval and violence she observed on some of her trips. The number of nations gaining their independence gave her hope for the future; in her 1960 autobiography, she called it "the most exciting continent in the world today."[2] Between October 1955 and December 1960, she traveled to at least twenty-one African countries: in northern Africa, Egypt, Morocco, and Sudan; in central Africa, Cameroon, Republic of the Congo (then French Congo), Democratic Republic of the Congo (then Belgian Congo), and Gabon; in eastern Africa, Burundi (then Urundi), Ethiopia, Kenya, Madagascar (then the Malagasy Republic), Rwanda (then Ruanda), Tanzania (then Tanganyika), and Uganda; in western Africa, Benin (then Dahomey), Ivory Coast, Ghana, Liberia, Nigeria, Senegal, and Togo (then French Togoland).[3] In later years, she added the southern African countries of Zimbabwe (then Southern Rhodesia), Mozambique, Zambia, Angola, and South Africa (Figure 3.1).[4]

Schuyler was captivated by Africa's incredible diversity of cultures, music, languages, landscapes, and wildlife. Traveling through the continent, often alone, came with numerous challenges that were unusual for a concert pianist. Overwhelming heat extended across all her African tours, and Schuyler wryly observed that somehow, no matter what time of year she visited, locals told her she had just missed wonderful weather.[5] Giant roaches, swarming ants, and other insects abounded.[6] Not only was tap water unsafe

Figure 3.1: Map of Schuyler's African tours

to drink in many areas, but Schuyler experienced a water shortage in Ghana. Very small amounts of water came out of the taps in the middle of the night, when families collected it to conserve and use for the entire day.[7]

Sometimes, simply getting from one concert to the next proved to be a surprising challenge. Roads tended to be unpaved and at times borderline impassable, with drivers needing to carry machetes in the truck to clear vegetation or cut down branches to create makeshift bridges. Flights, often on small or aging planes, were sporadic, undependable, and uncomfortable. In her writings and lectures, Schuyler tells of flying on miserably hot cargo planes delivering bananas, taking lengthy canoe rides, and even being stranded after discovering she had been sold a plane ticket for a nonexistent flight.[8] During Schuyler's tours, Africa's phone service was quite limited, and timely receipt of mail was also an issue due to her continually changing location. As a result, communication with the outside world could be intermittent at best.[9]

Despite all the travel difficulties, Schuyler continued to be enthralled by Africa. After a particularly challenging 1959 tour, she was asked if she would return to the continent. In her autobiography, Schuyler recounts her reply: "Yes. I am called by its deserts and forests, streams and sandstorms, as by a hypnotic drug, lured by its mystery, so new, yet so old…I will always want more."[10]

Schuyler's lectures, writings, and personal correspondence reveal a vast knowledge of the regions she visited – their history, cultures, politics, and music. While she surely did quite a bit of personal research, her archived papers do not include detailed notes where she wrote the resulting information. Schuyler had a good memory, but such notes likely existed at some point. Surviving notebooks from her tours of Vietnam and investigations in the Congo show that Schuyler typically scribbled down everything she saw and heard.[11] Her earlier notes on African music may have been lost due to her chaotic life of constant travel, or they simply were not preserved after her death.

In the absence of her personal notes on the topic, examining Schuyler's surviving lecture recordings and published writings helps create a better picture of her research on African music. Her 1960 article "The Music of Modern Africa" describes several African musical traditions in more detail, explaining specific scale patterns, dances, and instruments. Given the brevity of the article, however, her discussions do not include nearly as much depth as more current texts on African music.[12] As a speaker, she frequently lectured on African topics, typically including facts and sometimes her own opinions about the local music.[13] Additionally, her 1963 book *Jungle Saints* mentions each region's music traditions while surveying Catholic missions throughout Africa.[14] Field recordings in the Schuyler Family Audio collection are a bit more mysterious, given the collection's limited catalog information. With no narration and vague labels like "Arabic Music" or "African Theatre," these recordings' dates and origins have proven impossible to establish. While Schuyler could have recorded them herself, they just as easily could have been given to her by other researchers. At the least, these recordings indicate the scope of Schuyler's interest in music throughout the continent of Africa, as they include music from several different regions.[15] Considered together, her recordings and writings provide us with a better understanding of the music Schuyler heard and studied, along with her personal reflections on some of the styles. Her research certainly lacks the rigor of modern ethnomusicology, and her writings often include her personally subjective opinions in potentially problematic ways. Nevertheless, Schuyler's firsthand experiences and extensive travel in Africa provided her with a unique perspective among American composers of the mid-twentieth century. While this book is a general introduction to her compositions, a more thorough study of her use and appropriation of African music would provide an extensive avenue for future ethnomusicological research.

Schuyler's first introduction to Africa came with an October 1955 tour beginning in the country's northern region. After performing in Egypt, she presented concerts in Addis Ababa, Ethiopia, including a Command Performance for Emperor Haile Selassie.[16] She returned for another concert tour in late 1957, spending Christmas with local hosts. Schuyler seemed enchanted with the experience, calling it "one of the nicest Christmases I have known."[17] Between concerts, she found time to see the paintings of a local artist, Afewerk Teklé, which she felt reflected Ethiopia's centuries-long history of Coptic Christianity:

> I found here the soul of Ethiopia, one of the most religious nations I had ever visited, where mysticism was not tainted by the skepticism of the twentieth century, there were no buts as to whether saints and miracles can or cannot exist, but rather an unstudied crystal-clear acceptance of the wonders and glories of Divine Justice and the Spirit.[18]

As a devout Catholic, Schuyler seemed to feel more at ease in historically Christian Ethiopia than she did in predominately Muslim countries nearby. She especially appreciated women's status in Ethiopia, considering the Amhara women to be "the freest in Africa."[19] Of their music, she wrote that "Amhara music is pentatonic, repetitious…It is dry, arid, completely non-sensual, stylized, without personal emotion, and sounds like the music of biblical Arabia, from where many Ethiopian tribes originally emigrated. Flutes are used, playing many embellished trills."[20]

Further north lies Sudan, where Schuyler first traveled in December 1958. The rigid gender segregation shocked her, as did the widespread practice of female circumcision.[21] She found the experience of performing for a "males only" crowd to be overwhelming, explaining that "being alone among thousands of men is fascinating at first, then appalling, for social situations become formidably difficult."[22]

A return trip the following year included a visit to Khartoum's university, where she was told of the improvements to women's education – the entire country now had four schools for girls, and twenty-four women attended the university.[23] Despite these statistics, she observed relatively little change in the status of women, evidenced by her visit to a harem:

> Last May, I entered a harem in Khartoum, the capital, where a bride was being prepared for a wedding with the groom she had never seen. One girl beat a funereal accompaniment on a round drum, another wailed like a banshee, while the fifteen-year-old bride, whose hands and feet were painted black, and whose head was covered with an impenetrable black wool veil, shuffled back and forth lethargically, without lifting her feet.[24]

While Schuyler considered the women's music to be relatively unemotional and their dancing to be sluggish, she saw men display more energetic movements while dancing together to lively music. She inferred the extreme differences between men's and women's music and dances resulted from what she considered to be the stiflingly limited nature of women's lives there.[25]

Although Schuyler's writings imply a lack of affinity for it, the music of North Africa had a significant influence on her compositional style, and her later works drew extensively on Arabic music. As Schuyler would have been aware, Arabic music traditions include the music of Sudan, Egypt, and Morocco, due in large part to the Arab conquest of the region in the seventh century. In fact, the final movement of her *White Nile Suite* depicts an important event in that military campaign - the fall of the Egyptian fortress of Babylon, located near present-day Cairo, in the year 641.[26] Despite her revulsion toward the treatment of women in Sudan, Schuyler returned to the region on multiple occasions and later included North African themes and topics in *White Nile Suite* and *Seven Pillars of Wisdom*.[27]

After leaving Sudan, Schuyler flew to Uganda in January 1958. Her hosts, the Basudde family, had another houseguest – Joseph Kyagambiddwa (1928-1978), whom Schuyler described as a musician "trying to record and transcribe Baganda music in its pristine, uncontaminated form, lest European influence corrupt its purity."[28] Kyagambiddwa was a Ugandan composer and musicologist who studied at Xavier University and Manhattanville College of the Sacred Heart, Schuyler's childhood alma mater, after attending seminary in Uganda. Like Schuyler, Kyagambiddwa was a faithful Catholic most of his life, primarily composing religious and liturgical music. His music was initially controversial with Catholic clergy because he wrote in a traditional Baganda style, and his texts were in the Luganda language. Furthermore, the melodies used traditional scales and rhythms, and he specified the use of Baganda instruments for accompaniments.[29] Of more relevance to Schuyler's research, Kyagambiddwa was also the first Ugandan to attempt transcribing traditional Baganda music in Western notation, culminating in his 1955 book *African Music from the Source of the Nile*.[30]

On her first morning in Uganda, their host brought Schuyler and Kyagambiddwa to mass at St. Thomas Aquinas Seminary. Afterward, the monks and priests performed a cappella Baganda music outside, singing "Obusolu Bwa Lubale" ("God's Little Animals"), "Mmomboze" ("Wanderers"), and "Ssanya" ("Destructive Famine"). Kyagambiddwa conducted the latter two, noting that all three songs were included in his *African Music from the Source of the Nile*.[31] According to Kyagambiddwa, "Mmomboze" depicts "Galla peoples marching down from Ethiopia, southward, to become great Ganda people here," while "Ssanya" tells the story of the Blessed Martyrs of Uganda.[32] Kyagambiddwa concluded the performance by conducting two African American spirituals and works by Palestrina.[33]

Later that night, Schuyler performed to a packed house in a Hindu movie theater, and the next day, King Mutesa's private musicians performed a *gnoma* (dance-drama) there in her honor. Kyagambiddwa served as the event's host, introducing each musical piece by explaining the instruments used and the meaning of the lyrics. The concert included: "Nkwagala Kuyinga" ("We Love You Exceedingly Much"), "Akaliga" ("The Lamb Who Smoked a Pipe"), "Ensejjere Kawomera" ("Eating Delicious White Ant"), and "Obwato Nakawolele" ("Extraordinary Boats"), all accompanied by traditional dancing. Schuyler found the experience transformative, with her autobiography describing the music's physical effect on her.[34]

In a more measured account, Schuyler's discussion of Baganda music in her article "The Music of Modern Africa" draws extensively on Kyagambiddwa's book.[35] Her descriptions of the Lower Lutambas and Higher Lutambas scales, instruments, rhythmic patterns, and types of songs are nearly identical to Kyagambiddwa's, suggesting that his book was likely her main source on Baganda music.[36] Elements of Baganda music appear throughout Schuyler's African inspired works, particularly in *African Rhapsody*, *Uganda Martyrs*, and, of course, her *African Suite*. Part of the appeal for Schuyler was not just in the music itself, but in the role of the musician in Baganda society:

> The music is exciting, many-voiced, disciplined and without personalized sentiment...The African musician or artist is not a rebel against society, or a Bohemian on the fringe of society, as is so often the case in the West. Rather, he is an integral part of society, and an expressor of its collective traditional values.[37]

Continuing her tour, Schuyler ventured to West Africa, where she heard the music of Dakar, Senegal. She felt it resembled Arabic music in some ways, with dry, repetitious melodies and quarter tone tuning. Further into central Africa, the music of Cameroon obviously impressed her, as she pronounced it "the greatest music of West Africa."[38] Schuyler especially admired the compositions of Albert Mouangue, who added a Western popular music sensibility to his arrangements of traditional music.[39] Like Mouangue, Schuyler aspired to combine Western styles with African traditions in her own specialization of classical music.

Schuyler returned to Uganda in 1959 and 1960. During the 1960 tour, she had the opportunity to visit the kingdom of Toro in western Uganda, where she was the guest of King George III and one of his sons, Prince Christopher. She was able to hear local music, including a little girl performing the very lively Cow Dance.[40] Another royal son, Prince Daniel, introduced her to Fort Portal noblewomen who performed their own songs, accompanying themselves on lute-like instruments and *entimbo* drums.[41] The songs sounded incredibly sad to Schuyler, and she felt they indicated the women were unhappy in their polygamous marriages.[42]

According to Schuyler, the music of Toro used a seven-tone scale in major and harmonic minor.[43] In all her travels, Schuyler only heard the harmonic minor scale used in authentic, traditional African music there.[44] Its melancholy expression captivated Schuyler: "Worlds apart is the sad, melancholy music of Toro, in the rain-drenched blue-green Mountains of the Moon, in Western Uganda. It is the only music I ever heard in Africa that expressed personal sentiment and profound individual feeling."[45]

During her travels in central Africa, Schuyler spent a significant amount of time in the Congo, and, even before reporting on the 1960s Congolese civil war, she presented concerts throughout both the former French Congo and the former Belgian Congo.[46] While there, she observed the customs of some of the estimated two hundred tribes living in the country and wrote of their music's "astonishing variety."⁴⁷ On the way to Léopoldville (now Kinshasa) for her 1960 Independence Day concert, Schuyler performed in Elisabethville (now Lubumbashi) and Lusambo. While in Lusambo, her hosts took her to a particularly lax Belgian jail, where the prisoners were free to leave and work in town during the day. In the courtyard, a prison band performed for her on homemade percussion and wind instruments.⁴⁸ She seemed especially taken with Congolese music, speaking of its "unforgettable lyricism" and the great artistic expression involved.⁴⁹ In lectures on Africa and the Congo, she often mentioned Joseph Kiwele's Copper Cross Choir's work in preserving local chants before they disappeared.⁵⁰ When Katanga seceded from the Democratic Republic of the Congo in 1960, Kiwele was named Minister of National Education, composing Katanga's national anthem in the same year.⁵¹ According to Schuyler, his choir performed frequently in Katanga during that time.⁵²

Given her appreciation for Spanish and Latin American music, it should not be surprising that Schuyler loved the music of former Portuguese Africa, which included the modern countries of Mozambique, Madagascar, and Angola. In a lecture recital on the music of that region, she traced its Portuguese and Arabic influences, playing examples of both a traditional Arabic song and a Portuguese *fado*, as well as a Brazilian piece she claimed was influenced by African slaves creating a new musical style.⁵³ Madagascar was of personal interest to Schuyler because her father's side of the family partially traced their ancestry to that country.⁵⁴ An island located over two hundred miles across the Mozambique Channel from the eastern coast of Africa, Madagascar's music and dance differ in significant ways from other parts of Africa. Schuyler wrote that women enjoyed "complete equality" there, with men and women dancing and performing music together. She described the local traditional music as using seven-tone major scales and featuring string instruments and the accordion.⁵⁵

On a later visit to South Africa, Schuyler met John Blacking, a professor of anthropology at the University of Witwatersrand in Johannesburg. As part of his research, Blacking had collected field recordings from throughout South Africa, and he played some of those tapes for Schuyler during her stay. Schuyler ultimately elected not to use South African music in her compositions, commenting, "I found it a bit dry. Perhaps dry regions produce dry music."⁵⁶

It is also possible Schuyler avoided setting South African music because of her feelings about the country's politics. Horrified by apartheid and racism there, she commented on the topic in interviews and devoted several pages of *Jungle Saints* to the subject. Apartheid in South Africa began in 1948, several years before Schuyler's first visit to Africa, but after the 1960 Sharpeville massacre of protesters, apartheid policies became even more brutal. 1963 and 1964 marked the arrest and trial of Nelson Mandela, resulting in Mandela's life sentence. Apartheid policies continued long after Schuyler's untimely passing, only ending in the early 1990s.[57] For obvious personal reasons, Schuyler was especially troubled by the treatment of mixed-race South Africans, writing in *Jungle Saints*:

> Jobs, homes and social privileges have been taken away from these people, with many resultant tragedies. It is impossible to understand why. There is no logical reason. This fanaticism is not ridiculous, it is melancholy. It drives one to a profound and saddening despair. Is there anything about South Africa that does not drive one to a feeling of despair?[58]

Of all the varied music she heard across the continent, Ugandan and Ethiopian music inspired Schuyler's first African-based composition. She began work on *African Suite* soon after her first 1958 visit to Uganda. Completed by 1960, the composition includes three movements that incorporate Ugandan and Ethiopian folk melodies into a somewhat more complex musical fabric than that which is heard in Schuyler's previous folk arrangements. From 1960 to 1964, Schuyler frequently performed *African Suite* in her concerts, until she reworked portions of its material into her 1964 *African Rhapsody*.[59]

The second and third movements, *Tweyanze* and *Fumitta Embogo*, both take their main themes from melodies found in Kyagambiddwa's *African Music from the Source of the Nile*.[60] *Sanga*'s inspiration was a bit more difficult to determine, partly due to the frequent changes in how it was listed in Schuyler's recital programs. In fact, there are significant discrepancies in all the movement titles across different programs, an issue that extends to many of Schuyler's other works as well. As Schuyler's manager, her mother typically arranged her concerts and sent her programs to the venues. Schuyler wrote her mother complaining about mistakes in piece titles, translations, and program order; even a few letters from others to Mrs. Schuyler correct the titles of pieces and spellings of composer names.[61] While these errors could simply be carelessness and a lack of familiarity with some of the music, there were also significant challenges in transmitting the information. Schuyler sent program information to her mother by telegram or mail, often from remote and ever-changing locations. That information would then be sent to concert venues, potentially with another intermediary along the way; such a chain of letters and telegrams could easily result in mistakes.

While the titles listed in the manuscript score (*Sanga, Tweyanze,* and *Fumitta Embogo*) appear frequently, Schuyler's programs often also label the movements by country or tribe, sometimes with English translations. Strangely, these subtitles vary between concerts. Programs from April 1962 list the movements as "Ethiopia-Uganda-Congo," but a program from May of the same year lists their sources as Ethiopia, Buganda, and Toro.[62] While not fully inaccurate because Buganda and Toro are tribes that reside in Uganda, this mention of the Congo implies a completely different source for the third movement. Another April 1962 program confuses matters even further, listing the movements as: "Ethiopia: Sheperd's [*sic*] Song;" "Uganda: Farewell But Don't Return;" and "Congo: Dance of the Full Moon."[63] Other programs subtitle *Sanga* as "Hero's Song" rather than "Shepherd's Song."[64] Ultimately, the movement titles *Sanga, Tweyanze,* and *Fumitta Embogo* seem to be Schuyler's finalized version of this suite, as evidenced by those titles being used for her 1965 LP *Pianologue*.[65] The original manuscript gives no indication of any other possible titles.[66] For consistency, the manuscript score's movement titles are used here, although the various alternate subtitles do helpfully hint at their possible source folk songs.

The conflicting subtitles of "Hero's Song" and "Shepherd's Song" created some challenges in ascertaining the Ethiopian source for *African Suite*'s first movement. Ethiopian folk songs with titles even remotely resembling "Hero's Song" have little in common with *Sanga*'s musical material, but the subtitle "Shepherd's Song" gives a more useful clue as to the song's origin. *Sanga*'s opening melody (Example 3.1) strongly resembles an Ethiopian folk song called "Shepherd's Flute Song," as recorded by a Waito Shepherd on the Smithsonian Folkways Recordings album *Folk Music and Ceremonies of Ethiopia* (1974).[67] Although Schuyler's version is not a direct transcription, it shares the improvisatory rhythms, phrasing, and tremolos of "Shepherd's Flute Song." While this may not be the exact piece Schuyler heard, she likely was arranging a similar Ethiopian flute song.[68]

In an important divergence from her earlier folk arrangements, *Sanga* incorporates multiple melodies into a larger form, rather than simply imitating the traditional verse structure of a vocal folk song. The opening flute-

Example 3.1: *Sanga*, mm. 1-6

like melody shown in Example 3.1 serves as a recurring refrain and alternates with more aggressive chordal sections. While the opening section's rhythms are written to sound almost improvisatory, the contrasting sections keep a driving beat, with steady yet syncopated rhythmic patterns. The first such section includes flutelike tremolos in the right hand, while the left hand plays short motives imitating pitched percussion instruments. After a return to the opening's six-measure melody, a more lyrical, yet still rhythmically complex, melody enters over percussive downbeat chords in the bass. A final recurrence of the opening's theme then leads into accented, emphatic repetitions of a D major triad to close the movement.

With its extraordinarily fast tempo, *Tweyanze*'s forty measures pass

Example 3.2: *Fumitta Embogo*, mm. 33-36

quickly, with Schuyler creating a joyous atmosphere through its sprightly triple meter and active accompaniment pattern. The entire movement is centered around G, but Schuyler experiments with different modes, using accidentals to shift between major, mixolydian, and the parallel minor. For the source material, she focuses on a single melody of the same name from Kyagambiddwa's collection. Although his book does not mention its specific source, Schuyler labels the melody as originating with the Baganda people. According to Kyagambiddwa, "Tweyanze!" was a ceremonial song written to honor Chief Stanislas Mugwanya, and he translates its lyrics as follows:

> We heartily thank you,
> Generous Mugwanya,
> For all that you've given us.
> Thank you, Mugwanya, thank you![69]

In comparison to Kyagambiddwa's version, Schuyler alters the rhythms and repetitions of phrases to an extent that suggests she might have heard the song in her travels, rather than simply finding it in Kyagambiddwa's book. On later repetitions of each phrase, she also adds small ornaments and trills. The movement is structured like a two-verse song, with the second "verse" repeating the melody louder and in octaves, creating the sensation of more voices joining. The melody remains in the treble throughout, with the left hand playing a lively arpeggiation.

Fumitta Embogo proves more complicated than the first two movements because the titular folk song does not appear until almost halfway through the piece. Kyagambiddwa categorizes "Fumitta Embogo" as a dramatic song, meaning that performances would likely have included actors wearing costumes and dancing or acting out the song's story. According to Kyagambiddwa, "Fumitta Embogo" translates as "Spear the Buffalo;" his translation of the full lyrics reads:

> Spear the buffalo, Ndawula,
> Spear that I may see!
> Your comrades have speared a creature.
> Oh, man! Is it a baby buffalo or a baby hippo?
> They have speared a creature!![70]

Constructed in three distinct parts, *Fumitta Embogo* opens with a syncopated bass pattern that continues for most of the opening section. Short, simple motives recur in the right hand, leading to emphatically repeated chords that use accents to imply an asymmetrical meter. Only at that point does the "Fumitta Embogo" melody from Kyagambiddwa's collection enter, with a sudden texture change. Schuyler presents the tune in a single disjointed line, with the expressive marking "sharp, definitive" (Example 3.2). As this second section progresses, she develops the melody in various ways, first by adding additional voices in counterpoint and then by altering the rhythm. Eighth notes become triplets, and triplets become sixteenths, as the rhythms grow ever faster, leading into virtuosic triplet chords alternating between the hands and a definitive statement of the second half of "Fumitta Embogo." In another sudden shift in texture and dynamic level, the final section begins with that same melodic fragment repeating in the treble, indicated to be played "murmuring" and very softly. Schuyler gradually builds momentum, with the left hand joining the melodic repetitions until fragments of the opening section's melody return, now much faster. These unremitting motivic statements accelerate and grow until the movement abruptly ends. In her autobiography, Schuyler commented that the pieces she heard in Uganda tended to suddenly cut off, which provides a hint as to the inspiration for *African Suite*'s conclusion.[71]

Given that the first and second movements are each based on a single folk song, the opening section of *Fumitta Embogo* seems a bit odd. Its melody does not resemble any part of the "Fumitta Embogo" tune nor any other material from Kyagambiddwa's book, for that matter, so what is its source? A clue can be found in a recital program that indicates this movement originated in the Congo rather than Toro, while another program titles it "Congo: Dance of the Full Moon."[72] Despite today's availability of information, collections of notated folk tunes from the Congo remain difficult to find, and available recordings produced few possible sources. One folk song which bears resemblance to *Fumitta Embogo*'s opening is "Danse de la pleine lune" ("Dance of the Full Moon") from the 1998 album *Musiques et danses du*

Congo Kivu-Uele. Although the pitches do not correspond perfectly, the two songs' style and musical material are quite similar, with the folk song's syncopated bass line in low percussion and constantly moving leaps in higher pitched percussion instruments matching Schuyler's repetitive left-hand pattern and disjunct treble melody.[73] Despite the lack of documentation in Schuyler's notes, I suspect *Fumitta Embogo*'s opening measures are, in fact, based on this Congolese folk song or a similar dance.

While relatively short and straightforward, Schuyler's *African Suite* marks a critical milestone in her compositional development. Here, we see her first attempts at creating larger structures with folk melodies – not only in the movements themselves, but also in organizing them into a larger suite. The suite also marks her first African inspired composition, beginning a new stylistic endeavor that continued through the end of her career. Her later works clearly build upon the ideas originating in *African Suite*, particularly its rhythmic style, repeating patterns, and incorporation of folk melodies. Throughout the remainder of her life, Schuyler continued to be drawn back to Africa and its endless diversity, as evidenced in both her travels and her compositions.

Chapter 4
A Mutapa Ruler and a Nobel Prize Winner: *African Rhapsody*

Dr. Albert Schweitzer has made great accomplishments. There is hardly a corner of the globe where his name is not now a byword for sacrifice, devotion, dedication to Africa's people. But he is not the only one...We dedicate these pages to the vast army of Unsung Schweitzers in Africa today.
-Philippa Schuyler, *Jungle Saints*[1]

At Schuyler's fourth Town Hall recital on September 13, 1964, she premiered both her *White Nile Suite* and *Chisamharu the Nogomo*.[2] Programmed with *Sanga*, these African inspired works were described in an advertisement as East African dances from Mozambique, Ethiopia, Uganda, the Congo, and Tanganyika, which is part of present-day Tanzania.[3] Interestingly, Schuyler performed *Sanga* alone, with no reference to it having been part of her *African Suite*. Her new works were relatively well-received, although a *New York Times* review criticized her compositions for being "rather tiresomely extended," despite their appealing "vigor, color and authenticity."[4] Schuyler's African inspired works do tend to be quite repetitive, with Schuyler herself even skipping some repeats in performance recordings and removing several in later versions of the manuscripts.[5]

Schuyler's titular Chisamharu was Chisamharu Negomo Mupunzagutu, who ruled the Mutapa empire from 1560 to 1589. Encompassing an area including modern-day Zimbabwe and parts of Mozambique, the Mutapa empire remained in power from circa 1250 to 1629. Rich in gold, the empire traded with regions which included parts of coastal East Africa and modern-day South Africa and Zambia. Their Indigenous religion was an important part of how Mutapa rulers maintained their power, because they served as the point of contact with their ancestors in the spirit world.[6]

In the sixteenth century, the Portuguese became quite interested in finding gold in the Mutapa kingdom's lands, with some people believing the empire to be the site of King Solomon's mines. Although Portuguese exploration began in the area as early as 1505, trade missions were not sent to the Mutapa empire until the 1540s, at which point they discovered Muslim traders had already arrived. Because politics and religion were so closely intertwined in the empire, the Portuguese devised a plan to gain control by converting the Mutapa ruler and his court to Christianity.[7]

In 1560, Father Gonçalo da Silveira and two other priests were sent to the Mutapa court, but only Fr. da Silveira made it there safely, after several months of travel. He arrived on December 26 and immediately began his work, asking to meet with Mupunzagutu. The king initially sent Fr. da Silveira bribes of gold, cows, and people, because he expected all outsiders to be in pursuit of wealth and riches, but when the priest declined his gifts, Mupunzagutu was intrigued enough to allow Fr. da Silveira to visit. The king requested that he bring his statuette of the Virgin Mary, whom Mupunzagutu had heard was a beautiful woman. After speaking with him, Fr. da Silveira left the statuette with the king, who later claimed that it spoke to him in a language he could not understand. The priest told Mupunzagutu if he converted to Christianity, he would be able to comprehend what the Virgin Mary was telling him, which led the king to request baptism immediately. After teaching the king and his mother the catechism for four days, Fr. da Silveira baptized both.[8]

The king's conversion seemed well-received by his people, and he presented Fr. da Silveira with one hundred cattle, which the priest then gave to the poor. His selfless act inspired many others to convert, and the priest became well-respected in the community. However, the Muslim traders at the royal court felt that their standing and interests were being threatened, and some of them tried to convince Mupunzagutu that the priest was a Portuguese spy and a sorcerer conspiring against him. After officially hearing the case against Fr. da Silveira, the Council of Mutapa sentenced the priest to death. Despite being warned to flee, Fr. da Silveira remained, believing he had a holy mission. After further debate and challenges to the sentence, Fr. da Silveira was strangled to death in the middle of the night and his body thrown into a nearby river.[9]

Four hundred years later, Schuyler visited the Archdiocese of Salisbury in Southern Rhodesia, now part of Zimbabwe, while researching her book *Jungle Saints*.[10] Renamed the Archdiocese of Harare since then, the area included the site where Fr. da Silveira was martyred; according to Schuyler, he was considered the "founder of Christianity there."[11] She interviewed priests, nuns, and missionaries not only there, but also at other Catholic sites throughout Africa. The pedantic details of the history of Catholicism in Africa interested Schuyler, and she included numerous statistics to provide historical context for each region's Catholic missions. Her writing reveals a somewhat morbid fascination with tales of brutally murdered martyrs; Schuyler recounts stories of the deaths of priests in the Congo in lurid but accurate detail.[12] When discussing Catholicism in then-Southern Rhodesia, Schuyler began with Fr. da Silveira's story, which captivated her enough to inspire a musical composition.[13]

In searching through Schuyler's papers for further mentions of *Chisamharu the Nogomo*, a problem becomes obvious. After its September 1964 Town Hall concert, no other mention of *Chisamharu the Nogomo* can be found in Schuyler's programs. A handwritten manuscript matching that title is in the Schuyler Family Papers, with smaller sections labeled "Monomatapwa," "Tweyanze," "Fumitta Embogo," and "Obwato Nakawolole."[14] The only other reference occurs in Schuyler's recorded lecture recital on the music of Portuguese Africa. In that lecture, Schuyler explains that *Chisamharu the Nogomo* is based, both musically and programmatically, on the music and history of Mozambique.[15]

Shortly after Schuyler's Town Hall concert, in December 1964, the National Council of the Churches of Christ in the USA's Africa Committee wrote to Schuyler on behalf of Columbia Artist Management to ask if she would participate in a WBAI radio broadcast for Dr. Albert Schweitzer's ninetieth birthday. The broadcast would be recorded at Town Hall on Dr. Schweitzer's birthday, January 14.[16] Unfortunately, Schuyler's response was not preserved, but given Dr. Schweitzer's fame and her personal connection to him, it seems likely she agreed to participate.

Younger generations may not be familiar with Dr. Schweitzer, or they may know him as a controversial figure for his prejudiced comments on the African people he served; in Schuyler's lifetime, however, the doctor was renowned around the world for his humanitarian work.[17] Born in 1875, Schweitzer began his career as an organist and musicologist, studying organ with famed French organist and composer Charles-Marie Widor and publishing a landmark study of Bach in 1905. For several years, he simultaneously worked as organist for the Paris Bach Society, lectured on theology at Strasbourg University, published writings on music and theology, and studied medicine.[18] He completed his medical degree in 1913, with specializations in tropical medicine and surgery, areas selected to best prepare him for his planned work in Lambaréné, Gabon. Later that year, he and his wife used their own funds to travel from Bordeaux, France to Lambaréné to establish his hospital. The Schweitzers spent months as prisoners of war in a French internment camp in 1917, returning to Europe for six years after their release. Schweitzer traveled back to Lambaréné alone in 1925 and spent the remainder of his life there, leaving his family in Europe. Over the years, he received many honors, most notably the 1952 Nobel Peace Prize, with the prize money being used to build his hospital's leper colony. By 1965, the small original hospital had grown to include seventy buildings and a leper colony that could accommodate up to two hundred patients. Schweitzer never fully abandoned his love for music, and he frequently raised funds for the hospital through concerts and lectures in Europe.[19]

Schuyler and Dr. Schweitzer first crossed paths in 1959, when Schuyler visited him at his hospital in Lambaréné, making her potentially the only professional pianist to perform for the doctor there.[20] The stop in Lambaréné was not originally part of Schuyler's tour, but she and her mother decided it would be good publicity. Schuyler's mother and, by extension, Schuyler herself, knew the former wife of a Hollywood movie director, Marion Preminger, who had given up her life as a socialite to raise money for Schweitzer's efforts, spending several months each year at his hospital. Schuyler felt that an invitation from Marion was "conspicuous by its absence," and she decided to travel to Lambaréné anyway, explaining to her mother, "After all, I know from experience that everyone ALWAYS wants to see a pretty young girl with charming manners who plays beautiful music and is famous."[21]

Schuyler flew from Brazzaville to Lambaréné in early February, in a tiny cargo plane with four Methodist ministers as her fellow passengers. The flight was miserable, with no food or air-conditioning and frequent stops to unload bananas and pick up more cargo. Seeing an opportunity, Schuyler befriended the ministers on the long flight, explaining that she really hoped Ms. Preminger had gotten her (likely nonexistent) letter communicating the date of her arrival.* Her new acquaintances kindly offered her a ride with them in their pirogue if Preminger had not sent a launch for her, and Schuyler posed for photos with them at some of the plane's stops. As a result, she was able to essentially hitchhike on their jeep ride to the Ogowe River and subsequent canoe trip to Schweitzer's hospital. Between the heat and motion sickness,

---

* In her letter to her mother about the trip, Schuyler tends to use quotation marks when mentioning the letter to convey the deception.

Schuyler described the ninety-minute canoe ride as "hell."[22]

Upon their arrival, the group was met by Olga Deterling, Emma Haussnecht, and Dr. Schweitzer himself.[23] Of this initial meeting, Schuyler later recounted, "My first glimpse of him was unforgettable. He wore white tropical sun-helmet, white trousers, white shirt open at the neck. His face had the kindly, benign look of a practical saint.[24] Of course, no one was expecting Schuyler's arrival with the ministers, and she reiterated her story about the hypothetical letter she had written to Preminger, acting confused at her hosts' surprise. Schuyler then boldly showed Schweitzer one of her more glowing reviews, and he immediately sent someone to fix the piano, saying that Schuyler would be playing for him that evening.[25] With this announcement, she was shown to a small room and given a lantern so that she could be careful to avoid snakes while walking to the outhouse.[26]

After lunch, Schweitzer decided he wanted to hear Schuyler play immediately, and once the piano was ready, Schuyler stacked hymnals on the bench to reach the keys more comfortably. She played Field's *Nocturne*, a Schubert *Impromptu*, and Chopin's *Scherzo in B-flat Minor* before Schweitzer was called away; in relating the tale later, Schuyler remarked that she would have been quite nervous if she had not been so hot and tired. That evening, Schweitzer led a hymn sing and asked Schuyler to perform more. Using the light of a lantern, she played her own *Manhattan Nocturne*, Ravel's *Jeux d'Eau*, and Mussorgsky's *Pictures at an Exhibition*.[27] In her autobiography, Schuyler was uncharacteristically humble about her performance, simply remarking, "Dr. Schweitzer made some compliments to me on my playing that I shall always treasure enormously."[28]

The next day, Preminger took Schuyler on a tour of the hospital and leper village. As they set out to hike there, Schuyler ignored Preminger's advice to "put on sensible shoes," and she simply put "rubbers" over her high heels and grabbed an umbrella, camera, and sun helmet before leaving.[29] Over the course of the morning, they toured the village, hospital wards, pharmacy, and more, with Schuyler taking photos at every opportunity. After dinner that night, Schuyler gave another concert, this time performing for an hour and a half. She played works by Chopin, Griffes, Ravel, and Beethoven, along with Gershwin's *Rhapsody in Blue*.[30] Schweitzer requested the latter piece because he liked "to keep up with what [was] going on in the world."[31]

The following morning, Schweitzer borrowed a boat from a nearby Catholic mission to make Schuyler's return trip a little more comfortable. He posed for pictures with her and said he planned to write Belgium's Queen

Elisabeth to suggest Schuyler perform for her while in Europe. After kissing her on both cheeks to say goodbye, Schweitzer gave Schuyler parting advice to not wear lipstick.[32]

Schuyler was incredibly effusive in describing her time at the hospital and her admiration of Schweitzer. Such enthusiasm could have been either for the good press or simply the product of Schuyler's typically over-the-top writing style. Regardless, Schuyler seemed to truly respect his faith and service:

> I felt broken-hearted at leaving the presence of this magnificent Christian whose lofty devoted heart transcends sectarianism, whose noble example of generosity, heroic stoicism, and chivalrous self-sacrifice, will lend inspiration to humanity for all time. One also regretted leaving the corps of benevolent spiritual self-denying nurses and doctors that assist him in his labors of love and devotion to mankind.[33]

While there is, oddly enough, no official record of Schuyler's participating in the January 14 Town Hall tribute to Schweitzer, it is reasonable to assume Schuyler would have been interested in performing or composing a piece for his ninetieth birthday, given her admiration for Schweitzer and appreciation for the associated publicity. Supporting this assumption is a December 1964 letter from fellow composer Dennis Gray Stoll which congratulates Schuyler on her upcoming participation in Schweitzer's "birthday celebrations," calling her a "splendid girl" for having traveled to his hospital.[34] On the other hand, a *New York Times* review the day after the birthday tribute makes no mention of Schuyler; the concert featured the Esterhazy Orchestra with John Ogdon as the piano soloist.[35] No programs from a January 14 event can be found in the Schuyler Family Papers, although Schuyler did perform *African Rhapsody* the following day in a lecture recital in Powhatan, Virginia.[36] It remains unclear what exactly transpired – did Columbia Artists decide not to feature Schuyler's piece? Or did she broadcast it in a separate event elsewhere? A note from Schuyler to Schweitzer is preserved in her archived papers, and it looks as though it might be a message sent by telegram. The text simply reads:

> Happy birthday. Broadcasting my composition *African Rhapsody* written for your birthday on January 14.[37]

From 1965 onward, Schuyler programmed *African Rhapsody* frequently, including it in several lecture recitals.[38] A recording from one such lecture recital reveals a surprising answer to the question of *Chisamharu the Nogomo* - Schuyler had simply retitled it *African Rhapsody*. Despite the title's change, Schuyler's performance of *African Rhapsody* matches the score for *Chisamharu the Nogomo* almost exactly. In introducing the work, she describes *African Rhapsody* as being inspired by themes from Uganda, the Congo, and parts of West Africa and claims that it premiered in December 1964 at a United Nations reception at the Togo embassy.[39] Indeed, later programs also list *African Rhapsody*'s premiere as occurring at the Togo embassy, so Schuyler probably performed it there under its new title for the first time.[40]

When contacted about the tribute broadcast, Schuyler would have been working intensely on *Seven Pillars of Wisdom*, a composition discussed in more detail in Chapter 7. She recorded practice performances of several movements on Christmas Eve that year, in advance of the February 6 premiere of the complete work.[41] With only one month's notice of the broadcast, Schuyler may have decided to simply repurpose another piece for Schweitzer's birthday celebration.

Interestingly, the title change came with subtle alterations to the piece's program notes, and those alterations help explain why Schuyler selected this specific work to dedicate to Schweitzer. At *Chisamharu*'s Town Hall premiere, the accompanying notes focus on Chisamharu himself, describing him as "the Monomatapwa or Emperor of a huge 16th century domain in East and Southern Africa," with the martyred Jesuit priest seeming to be a bit of an afterthought.[42] Schuyler's later descriptions of *African Rhapsody* shift the focus to Fr. da Silveira, as the first to attempt bringing Christianity to the Mutapa empire.[43] In dedicating the work to Schweitzer, Schuyler also decided to adjust *African Rhapsody*'s narrative to prioritize Schweitzer's fellow missionary more clearly. In fact, Schuyler dedicated *Jungle Saints*, the book in which she tells Fr. da Silveira's story, to those she calls "the Other Schweitzers," meaning the priests, nuns, and missionaries working without recognition.[44]

Despite knowing its original title, *African Rhapsody*'s program is a bit vague since Schuyler's notes do not include any named musical themes or indications of events in the plot. Only her use of a dance from Mozambique connects the music to the story of Chisamharu Negomo Mupunzagutu, because, during his reign, the Mutapa empire had expanded to include parts of Mozambique.[45] In addition to repurposing the entire piece to be dedicated to Schweitzer, Schuyler also recycled parts of *African Suite* within the work, further obscuring any intended narrative.

In the manuscript preserved in the Schuyler Family Papers, Schuyler titles the first section of *African Rhapsody* "Monomotapwa: Chisamharu the Nogomo," in the first and only obvious correlation to the piece's original title.[46] "Monomotapwa" refers to the Portuguese name for the Mutapa empire.[47] While this title can cause modern listeners to infer a colonialist bent, research using the Indigenous name (Mwene Mutapa) may not have been available to Schuyler in the early 1960s, and a later version submitted for her copyright claim omits the descriptor entirely.[48]

"Monomotapwa" draws from the traditional *timbila* orchestra music of Mozambique, which typically features rapid virtuosic patterns on the xylophone-like instruments and performances by groups of dancers.[49] Available recordings show that Schuyler played *African Rhapsody* at an extremely fast, borderline incomprehensible tempo.[50] Even when taken at a slightly less ambitious speed, which makes the notes and rhythms easier to discern, the piece requires a quick tempo and driving beat for its opening section to correctly imitate Mozambique's *timbila* orchestras. Initially, the melody mimics the rolls and drumbeat of *timbila* music (Example 4.1), while using a decidedly non-Western scale. After several continually evolving repetitions, the left hand's drumbeat suddenly changes, now oscillating between clashing minor seconds. Once the groove has been established, short motives begin to repeat in the treble, initially made up of disjointed leaps, then a simple syncopated melody (Example 4.2). "Monomotapwa" continues to build, with descending chromatic triplet patterns leading to syncopated repetitions of a single chord. The section ends with the dramatic sweep of a descending *glissando*, continuing directly into the subsequent portion of the piece.

Next, a transposed version of *African Suite*'s brief second movement (*Tweyanze*) appears, with small modifications to some phrases and ornaments. Perhaps reacting to criticism of the work's repetitiveness, Schuyler drastically cut this section in the version of *African Rhapsody* submitted for copyright. In both versions, *Tweyanze* is followed by the return of the second half of "Monomotapwa." Functioning as a refrain, this part of the opening section returns throughout *African Rhapsody*, always alternating with contrasting material.

After the refrain, Schuyler again recalls part of her earlier *African Suite*, this time a portion of *Fumitta Embogo*. Schuyler alters its opening bass pattern to be significantly more dissonant, now alternating between G-flat and

Example 4.1: *African Rhapsody*, mm. 1-10

Example 4.2: *African Rhapsody*, mm. 41-44

Example 4.3: *African Rhapsody*, mm. 118-119

G harmonies (Example 4.3). Interestingly, the segment of *Fumitta Embogo* that appears here is not based on the actual "Fumitta Embogo" melody, but rather the Congolese "Dance of the Full Moon." Like its appearance in *African Suite*, this section ends with forceful chords that use accents to disguise the beat. Continually repeating, the pounding chords lead without pause into a return of "Monomotapwa."

After a slightly longer repetition of the "Monomotapwa" refrain, Schuyler introduces a new Ugandan folk song, "Obwato Nakawolole," translated as "Extraordinary Boats." Schuyler initially heard the folk song on her 1958 tour of Uganda, as part of the concert performed for her in a Hindu movie theater. Although she seems to have enjoyed all the music she experienced that day, her description of "Obwato Nakawolole" is especially evocative:

> The drummers demonstrated rhythmic, cylindrical and counting drums, and a couple came to the front of the stage – the man in a black Western suit with a leopard skin tied around his waist and posterior, and the woman in a long crimson and scarlet Baganda costume with a black sweater encircling her middle. They began to dance hotly, furiously, frenzied pelvises switching torridly, behinds quivering frighteningly, muscles twitching with orgiastic violence, as the drums beat pounded and boomed with malevolent joy.[51]

As with "Tweyanze" and "Fumitta Embogo," a version of "Obwato Nakawolole" can be found in Kyagambiddwa's *African Music from the Source of the Nile*. Described as "the traditional song of the Ganda fleet on Lake Nalubale (Victoria)," this folk song is classified by Kyagambiddwa as one of the few Ganda work songs.[52] Kyagambiddwa translates its lyrics as follows:

> The boats are roaming!
> You boatmen, swing the paddles!
> (Chorus) Ah! They made the Admiral some canoes
> Wherein to wash ground foods![53]

Schuyler's version of "Obwato Nakawolole" is ultimately quite different from Kyagambiddwa's, although the basic melodic outline remains recognizable. While she may have taken some liberties with it, Schuyler likely heard a longer and more complex version of the song in that 1958 live performance. In her own arrangement, Schuyler develops the four-measure theme in Example 4.4 with rhythmic and ornamental changes, even interspersing her characteristic dissonance in the form of forearm tone clusters. Ending with drumming, dissonant chords, the "Obwato Nakawolole" section is followed by a related transition. Here, Schuyler uses flowing triplet patterns in

Example 4.4: *African Rhapsody*, mm. 194-197

the bass to call to mind the "Extraordinary Boats" of the title. A short bass melody repeats in the right hand, alternating with motives drawn from earlier in the piece, specifically from the second half of "Monomatapwa." These fragments begin to repeat and build in dynamic and tempo as they reach the work's final section, which recalls the abrupt conclusion of Schuyler's *African Suite*. Although not identical, *Fumitta Embogo*'s ending treble melodic fragments return over another bass pattern, accelerating into frantic repeated chords, accentuated by a descending *glissando* to conclude the work.

After completing *African Rhapsody*, Schuyler began programming it frequently, with the piece almost entirely replacing *African Suite* in her performances.[54] By combining a variety of folk melodies into a larger work, *African Rhapsody* demonstrates a step forward in Schuyler's compositional technique. While *African Suite* simply collected three short movements that arranged folk songs, Schuyler attempted to build a larger, more complex structure in *African Rhapsody*. With its inclusion, however vague, of the story of Chisamharu Negomo Mupunzagutu and Fr. da Silveira, *African Rhapsody* marked a refocus on program music and narrative in a more obvious way. Its changing title is just one example foreshadowing Schuyler's loose approach to her 1960s compositions, in which she often borrowed from her own work, altered movement titles, and even changed the musical content at times. Schuyler treated her compositions as malleable, rather than as finished and permanent works. Always tinkering and editing, she could never quite leave her later compositions alone, searching instead for a perfection which forever eluded her.

Chapter 5
A New Movement: Dennis Gray Stoll and the *White Nile Suite*

He likes me because he is terribly interested in his new musical movement – that the only possible future for Western music lies in the Asian and Arab inspiration.
– Letter to Josephine Schuyler, undated[1]

Although Schuyler's *White Nile Suite* premiered at the same September 1964 Town Hall concert as *Chisamharu the Nogomo*,[2] its unofficial London premiere would prove more influential in Schuyler's career. While in London that October for a concert engagement, Schuyler attended a cocktail party, and when the host requested that she play something for the guests, she performed her new *White Nile Suite*, along with several other works. British composer Dennis Gray Stoll, also in attendance that night, was instantly fascinated by Schuyler and her music.[3] Nineteen years older than her, Stoll had primarily worked as a conductor before contracting polio in 1947. Unable to conduct for many years because of his illness, he began to focus on writing and composing, developing an interest in Arabic music.[4]

Stoll and Schuyler began writing one another within weeks of that first meeting, sharing ideas about music and discovering their mutual appreciation for African and Arabic music.[5] Both composers believed, as Schuyler described in an interview, that Western classical music had become "as automatic as our machinery," and that African and Arabic musical traditions offered the only viable way forward.[6] Soon Stoll was introducing Schuyler to such important figures in British social life as Dame Sylvia Thorndike and Sigmund Freud's niece, along with other members of the aristocracy. Using his connections, he began to arrange concerts for Schuyler in England and wrote a glowing review of her first public London performance of *White Nile Suite*.[7] Schuyler expressed enthusiasm for his music, and by November, Stoll was sending her his *Persian Dance*, discussing Arabic and Indian scales with her, and beginning a piano concerto in her honor.[8] According to Schuyler, Stoll needed "a pianist who understands his Eur-Asian-Arab idiom to play his works," and she was delighted to be his protege.[9] Stoll may have had more in mind, as he was quite attracted to Schuyler from the beginning. Schuyler may have assumed their relationship to be strictly platonic, considering Stoll was married to his third wife, Patricia. In fact, she stayed at their home within days of meeting him, getting to know both husband and wife better.[10] Once his romantic interest became more obvious, Schuyler did not appear to reciprocate, but she may have feared the potentially negative impact an outright rejection might have on her career, given all the opportunities Stoll promised.[11] For almost a year after their first meeting, she managed this balancing act, with their professional relationship proving quite productive.

The composition that initially caught Stoll's interest, *White Nile Suite*, was Schuyler's first work to use what she termed "Afro-Arab scales and rhythms."[12] Because of Schuyler's early death, *White Nile Suite* remains one of her longest and most mature compositions. In some ways, the suite can be less accessible than her other works, due to the extensive use of dissonance; in its third and fourth movements, Schuyler rarely includes a melody without adding harsh minor seconds.[13] Although the movements do not seem to depict specific sequences of events, Schuyler still drew on extra-musical inspirations – in this case, the famous Nile River. In explaining the importance of the title's White Nile to Western audiences, Schuyler called it the "lifeline of Egypt."[14] The subject of several nineteenth-century expeditions to discover its source, the White Nile flows north through Uganda and Sudan before combining with the Blue Nile in Khartoum to form the Nile River, extending from there through Egypt to the Mediterranean Sea.[15] Its source remains mysterious even today; Lake Victoria in Uganda is often cited as its source, but recent scholarship traces it to various rivers that feed into Lake Victoria.[16] Each movement of the *White Nile Suite* depicts a specific city on the banks of the Nile River – Omdurman, Alexandria, Port Said, and ancient Babylon. Although the exact movement titles vary sometimes between programs, Schuyler most consistently describes them as:

Legend of the Mahdi (Omdurman) and His Dancing Dervishes
Alexandria
The Water-Front at Port Said on a Hot Night
The Fall of Babylon[17]

White Nile Suite was performed frequently by Schuyler, with its first London public performance at the Westminster Theatre in March 1965; that concert was enthusiastically reviewed by Stoll for the *Music Journal*.[18] It remained a favorite of Schuyler's until her death and was included in her last documented concert on March 22, 1967, at Hue MACV Compound Chapel in Vietnam.[19]

The only movement of the suite to be performed by Schuyler on its own was *Legend of the Mahdi*, which at times went by the alternate title "Nubian Legend" when programmed as a standalone work. Lecture recital and practice recordings confirm that both titles were assigned to the same piece.[20] Schuyler performed the movement on its own frequently enough that she copyrighted it separately from the full suite, but, oddly enough, under its original *Legend of the Mahdi* title.[21] In fact, she first performed the movement on its own only days after *White Nile Suite*'s premiere. Calling it "the Sudanese part of her *White Nile Suite*," Schuyler played *Legend of the Mahdi* for Sudan Day at the World's Fair on September 16, 1964, before a crowd which included both Sudan's United Nations representative and the commissioner-general of the Sudan Pavilion.[22] In some later recital programs and lectures, Schuyler claimed the piece was commissioned by the Sudanese government, usually when calling it "Nubian Legend."[23]

An early version of *Legend of the Mahdi* reveals that Schuyler initially named the movement for the city that inspired it – Omdurman, which she visited on her second trip to Sudan in 1959.[24] From the account in her autobiography, she did not seem particularly impressed, aside from the ivory and gold jewelry she saw at the market.[25] Located on the western bank of the Nile River, Omdurman was briefly the capital of Sudan during the Mahdist State of the late nineteenth century. In 1881, Muhammed Ahmad bin Abdullah of Sudan declared himself the Mahdi, or messiah. Aided by an army of his followers called the Ansār, known by Westerners as Dervishes, the Mahdi led a rebellion against Egypt and, by extension, Britain, which controlled Sudan at the time. After a long siege, they defeated the British to take Khartoum in 1885 and officially established the Mahdist State, with Omdurman as its capital. Six months later, the Mahdi died of an unknown illness and was buried in a sacred tomb in Omdurman. The Mahdist State continued until its defeat by the British army, led by General Kitchener in 1898. On his orders, the British damaged the Mahdi's tomb, threw the body in the Nile, and Kitchener himself took the Mahdi's head as a trophy. The tomb was rebuilt in 1947 and still stands today.[26]

At some point, Schuyler decided to change the title to *Legend of the Mahdi*, at times with the subtitles "Omdurman" and "and his Dancing Dervishes," to make its connection to the story of the Mahdi more obvious. In explaining the movement's narrative, Schuyler recounted the Mahdi's story as follows:

> The magnificent Mahdi, the Sudan's great 19th century leader, held court here. Many of his chief officers were Dervishes. After his death in 1885, his tomb in Omdurman was the object of wide-spread pilgrimage. His devoted followers often substituted pilgrimages to the Mahdi's Tomb for pilgrimages to Mecca.[27]

When performing the movement as "Nubian Legend," Schuyler tended to be more imprecise about the movement's inspiration, omitting any reference to the Mahdi. In those lectures and programs, she merely mentioned that the musical themes were from Sudan and described Nubia as one of the oldest civilizations in the world, claiming that the work depicted "the struggle between Islam and Christianity in the Sudan."[28] In all likelihood, these changes did not signify an evolution in Schuyler's conception of the work; instead, she simply described and titled it to fit the topic of the lecture or themed program being presented.

Like most of Schuyler's compositions, *Legend of the Mahdi* is structured according to her narrative. It can be divided into roughly two halves, with a main theme recurring throughout the work. According to Schuyler, the movement's melodic material is based on themes from Omdurman.[29] Attempting to imitate Sudanese musical style, Schuyler's melodies tend to be repetitive and constantly evolving. Motives recur with slight changes in rhythms, ornaments, and intervals in each iteration, slowly modifying the melodic content, and creating a sense of continuously building music, with few structural divisions. Despite Schuyler's emphasis on repetition, the movement is ultimately transformative, ending with a different tonal center and melodic material than those with which it began.

Legend of the Mahdi opens with the main theme, meandering over a repeated dissonant chord (Example 5.1, page 68). Without any true ending, Schuyler continues into a contrasting segment in which alternating chords accelerate and crescendo, snowballing into a *Presto* section (Example 5.2, page 68). Here, the bass's repetitive pattern moves even lower, now alternating between jarring harmonies in the upper and lower registers that accent

Example 5.1: *Legend of the Mahdi*, mm. 1-4

Example 5.2: *Legend of the Mahdi*, mm. 26-29

Example 5.3: *Legend of the Mahdi*, mm. 64-67

both the downbeat and an offbeat to muddle any sense of meter. As the tempo slows slightly, Schuyler returns to another directionless melody accompanied by a drum-like bass pattern. Parts of the melody repeat, slowly metamorphosing through slight alterations. Again, without any sense of ending, the main theme returns, now set in extremely dissonant minor ninths and gradually accelerating, building momentum as rhythms double and quadruple in speed. The theme eventually breaks down completely into

Example 5.4: *Legend of the Mahdi*, mm. 146-147

virtuosic figuration, until it cuts off abruptly without any cadence (Example 5.3). Suddenly, the opening returns, with the entire first half repeated twice. One of the repetitions is indicated with repeat signs, while the other is written out in the manuscript, with some small omissions and alterations. In performance, Schuyler often omitted the second repeat, as evidenced by her practice and lecture recital recordings.[30]

After the repetitions of the first section conclude with the same cacophonous and abrupt ending, Schuyler again brings back the opening melody. Here, the primary theme is played twice as slowly and an octave lower, with Schuyler indicating that it should sound mysterious. Contrasting material follows, with a sudden shift to the upper register and much quicker rhythms (Example 5.4). This strange-sounding segment alternates with the main theme, each time accompanied by a slightly different left-hand pattern. Each iteration of the main theme builds drama, moving higher and adding octaves; although Schuyler includes very few dynamics, it naturally builds in volume as well. Eventually, a new melody enters, constantly accelerating through shortening rhythms and fragmentation, propelling the music forward into the movement's finale. Schuyler ends *Legend of the Mahdi* victoriously, with several measures of hammering, accented B chords (Example 5.5, page 70) – a half step away from the opening's bass C chords. Over the course of the movement, Schuyler transforms the meandering opening melody into a triumphant ending cadence.

For *White Nile Suite*'s second movement, Schuyler drew inspiration from the Egyptian city of Alexandria. She seemed fascinated with its ancient

Example 5.5: *Legend of the Mahdi*, mm. 218-222

past, from its founding by Alexander the Great to its diverse religious history, at times describing it as a "stronghold of early Christianity in Egypt."[31] Founded by Alexander the Great in approximately 332 BC, Alexandria grew to become an important center of Egyptian commerce, education, and intellectual thought.[32] Conquered by the Romans in 30 BC, the city then became one of the most important producers of grain.[33] Years later, according to Coptic Orthodox tradition, the apostle Mark founded the Coptic Church there in 42 AD.[34] The city remained an important port throughout the Middle Ages, even after being conquered by Muslim Arab armies in 642 AD.[35]

For *Alexandria*, Schuyler focuses on the city's early history, claiming in her lectures and program notes that its main theme is derived from an ancient Macedonian hymn to Apollo, or alternatively, the sun.[36] While few authentic ancient Greek musical works survive today, that description matches the First and Second Delphic Hymns, both written in approximately 128 BC, although the exact dates are still debated. The hymns are two of the earliest and longest surviving musical examples from ancient Greece.[37] Research on them has expanded since Schuyler's lifetime, but an examination of the published versions available to Schuyler reveals some connections. Of the two Delphic Hymns, Schuyler's melody most resembles the second of the three sections of the First Delphic Hymn; although not a perfect match, the similarities in melodic shape and pitches are noticeable enough to confirm that this was her most likely source.[38]

Like several of Schuyler's other manuscripts, the original score for this movement includes no dynamics or tempo markings; in their absence, Schuyler's practice recordings, along with later versions incorporated into her other works, help give the performer some guidance for creating an interpretation.[39] In general, the beginning tempo is ambitiously fast, and dynamics build naturally as textures thicken and melodies ascend. Divided into three sections, *Alexandria* opens with a quick, syncopated bass line repeating a single E-flat. After setting up that pattern, Schuyler begins to introduce short ascending and descending melodic fragments over it (Example 5.6).

Example 5.6: *Alexandria*, mm. 1-6

Example 5.7: *Alexandria*, mm. 22-27

These gestures repeat throughout the first section, each time played as fast as possible, with the motive's final note sustained. Halfway through the section, the bass moves up a fourth to A-flat; otherwise, its pattern drives forward unabated.

Without any pause, the movement's main theme, based on the First Delphic Hymn, appears for the first time, accompanied by a sudden shift in tempo, meter, and accompaniment pattern. Twice as slow, this section's more lyrical melody is broken into two short phrases which repeat several times, while the left hand now steadily repeats fourths and fifths (Example 5.7). As the theme progresses, Schuyler extends later iterations of each phrase while moving ever higher. Finally, a new melody appears, repeated twice to close the section. In performance, Schuyler gradually slowed the last phrase, holding its final chord for several extra beats.

In *Alexandria*'s longer concluding section, Schuyler combines elements of the first two while returning to her opening tempo. At first, the melody is based entirely on the movement's opening section, now with pounding triplet fifths replacing the original syncopated bass. Short melodic gestures repeat as before, ascending higher each time. Part of the main theme from the second section returns, climbing more quickly and adding an octave doubling to the bass as the dynamic grows louder. As the momentum reaches its peak, the melody returns to the short fragments of the opening section, now significantly altered, as the left hand suddenly leaps almost two octaves down to the bass register. To close the movement, its first motives are restored to their original form as the tempo gradually slows. Schuyler repeats the last gesture twice, as the accompaniment pattern winds down, and the movement concludes with a single treble D, sustained as its sound dies away.

The suite's third movement, *Port Said*, is named for what Schuyler called "the world's most corrupt and exciting city," depicted "on a hot night."[40] In some of her programs, the movement is listed by the longer title "The Water-front at Port Said on a Hot Night." One of the newer cities featured in *White Nile Suite*, Port Said was established in 1859 during the construction of the Suez Canal. It was named for the Wāli, Sa'id Pasha, who was ruler of Egypt and Sudan at the time.[41] Because of its location on the Suez Canal, Port Said proved crucial during the 1956 Suez Crisis, when France and Israel tried to invade Egypt while British troops were still guarding the canal.[42]

Interestingly, Schuyler includes a second inspiration for *Port Said*, subtitling it "Hasanun" in her manuscript.[43] In a recorded lecture recital about Portuguese Africa, she plays this movement without any mention of the *White Nile Suite*. Instead, she describes it as a traditional Arabic song called "Hasanun," which she translates as "beautiful boy." Imitating the style of Arabic music, Schuyler uses extensive *rubato* and constantly shifting ornamentation throughout most of the movement, with a lively, syncopated contrasting middle section.[44]

Port Said begins with a strange, brief introduction. Rather than establishing a key or meter, Schuyler instead repeats a short pattern of dissonant chords three times (Example 5.8). The combination of the odd, irregular rhythms and rests with the indicated *rubato* obscures any sense of meter, opening the piece with a sense of mystery and ambiguity.

Maintaining the flexible tempo, the first half of the movement begins with a section of repeated single-measure phrases comprised almost entirely of descending trills, accompanied by a simple bass pattern. These short phrases alternate between emphasizing D-flat and F-sharp, with slight changes in each new iteration. In the last phrase of this section, the continual trills slither down from F-sharp and back up, over and over (Example 5.9). Suddenly, a new melody enters, centered around A-flat and played strictly in time, although the bass pattern continues as before. This melody climbs higher and

Example 5.8: *Port Said*, mm. 1-4

Example 5.9: *Port Said*, mm. 23-24

higher, accumulating slight alterations and ornaments along the way. Schuyler then repeats the entire segment, with the melody in octaves but otherwise unchanged. To conclude the first half, she brings back the final phrase of its first section, with its trills, rubato, and chromaticism. Repeated *ad libitum*, the trills lead directly into the movement's second half.

The style changes immediately, as the syncopation and faster rhythms create a lively, dance-like mood. Although the tempo remains constant, the new, quicker rhythms make this segment feel a bit faster. After a short transition, the true content of the section begins, with a similar but very dissonant melody. Schuyler sets the melody in octaves with an added minor second, perhaps trying to recall the quarter tone tuning of traditional Arabic music (Example 5.10, page 74). This entire section is repeated, and, in performance, Schuyler typically began softly on the repeat, before slowly growing louder into the emphatic, accented chords of the section's end.

Although those chords could serve as a satisfactory ending for the movement, Schuyler instead brings back the opening, repeating the first thirty-nine measures exactly. She does not even bother to write it out in her manuscript, but simply gives the instructions. Then, the last four measures of the first half return, with their winding trills, repeated *ad libitum*. In the absence of an ending cadence, not to mention any dynamic or expressive markings, the performer must determine how to interpret these final measures. In a later version, Schuyler indicates that the pianist should continue without pause into the fourth movement, although, musically, a slight breath seems

Example 5.10: *Port Said*, mm. 64-67

necessary.

As Schuyler noted in her recital programs, there were two Babylons – one, the ancient city mentioned in the Bible, and the other, a later Egyptian fortress near modern-day Cairo. She named the final movement of *White Nile Suite* for the latter, located on the banks of the Nile Delta. Specifically, the *Fall of Babylon*'s title is inspired by the fortress's defeat during the Arab conquest of Egypt in 641 AD.[45] A pivotal event in the history of Egypt, it marked one of the first major Egyptian victories by the invading army. A few years prior, Arab armies had set out to conquer surrounding regions after the Prophet Muhammed's death.[46] Egypt proved more difficult to overpower than expected, with the siege of the Fortress of Babylon continuing for months. Eventually, the ruling Byzantines negotiated a surrender, paving the way for the fall of Alexandria soon after.[47] Egypt and the rest of North Africa were forever altered, with their music and arts heavily influenced by the conquering Arab armies.[48]

Schuyler experimented with alternate titles for *Fall of Babylon*, at times calling it "Fortress of Babylon" or "Egyptian Babylon" in her recital programs. Although the original manuscript included the subtitle "Beni Hashim or the Prophet's Tribe," referring to the clan of the Prophet Muhammed, no references to that subtitle appeared in her programs. Regardless of its name, the narrative for the movement remained the same, and Schuyler considered it to be the climax of the entire suite. Much longer than the preceding movements, *Fall of Babylon* is largely based on a main theme and

Example 5.11: *Fall of Babylon*, mm. 15-18

secondary theme, which are developed in a variety of ways throughout the work. Overall, the movement is highly dissonant, expanding on the use of octaves with added minor seconds from *Port Said*, and almost all the melodic material is similarly written. Although few instances of *rubato* are indicated in the score, tempo fluctuations occur throughout. Some tempo changes are included in Schuyler's manuscript, while others can be found in her practice recordings and in later versions of the movement incorporated into other works.

Fall of Babylon opens with a foreboding introduction that repeats a dissonant pattern of syncopated ninths, set in the low bass register. Beginning very slowly, each repetition of the pattern grows faster, creating the sense of rhythms doubling and quadrupling. When the movement's true tempo arrives, syncopated chords with an added minor second transition into the primary theme (Example 5.11). This main theme alternates with contrasting material throughout the remainder of the movement, typically with the characteristic dissonance of octaves with added minor seconds. As this first section progresses, the melody travels from treble to bass, adding tremolos, trills, and other dramatic gestures in the right hand. The texture and dissonance build to a peak, while sharp *glissandi* punctuate every other measure.

The mood immediately shifts with the entrance of the secondary theme. Although Schuyler does not notate a tempo change in her manuscript score, practice recordings and later versions slow slightly at the beginning of this new section. Like the primary theme, this contrasting melody recurs at several points later in the movement. Following the thick textures of the preceding section, the secondary theme initially sounds relatively simple, with a straightforward climb up and down in each measure over a bass accompaniment pattern (Example 5.12, page 76). After several repetitions, this theme evolves, keeping the same rhythms but allowing a more interesting contour to take over. After some virtuosic figuration, this segment leads to emphatic repetitions of the same rhythm, now comprised solely of A-flats interspersed

Example 5.12: *Fall of Babylon*, mm. 31-32

with one other note per measure. That accented note interrupts each measure, rising ever higher, until it becomes a tone cluster and then a written-out *glissando*. The *glissandi* evolve into fast-moving triplets, naturally growing louder as the music builds. Finally, descending trills recalling *Port Said* slow the momentum, as the accompaniment pattern's rhythms wind down.

After a sustained final trill, the introduction returns, now serving as a transition. As before, each repetition accelerates until the movement's main tempo is reached; this time, each phrase adds an additional dissonant note, thickening the texture. As the movement's lively tempo arrives, the primary theme returns bombastically, now with dense harmonies filled with added minor seconds and ninths. Schuyler begins to transform the melody, first into a single line in the high treble, and then by adding descending *glissandi* as punctuation. She eventually dispenses with the primary theme entirely, with dramatic cross-rhythms between the hands, and the section ends with a short return of the secondary theme, now accompanied by the preceding measures' accompaniment pattern.

In another abrupt change, the texture becomes sparse, and a new melody and left-hand pattern begin (Example 5.13). In contrast to most of the movement, this section remains relatively calm, never really pushing forward or growing in dynamics or texture. Dissonance is introduced at times, but the melody always returns to its secure single line, until a reference to the movement's secondary theme destabilizes its structure. The treble melody begins to fragment, with the motives gradually merging rhythmically. Rhythms double and quadruple, eventually blurring into a trill. As that trill is sustained, the movement slowly reaches a standstill, before the introduction's melody reenters, now in low octaves that evolve into dissonant ninths before adding a dramatic octave leap. As before, the tempo accelerates into a return of the primary theme, again using dense chords with added seconds and *glissandi* interspersed. The melody transforms into huge triplet chords

Example 5.13: *Fall of Babylon*, mm. 98-99

Example 5.14: *Fall of Babylon*, mm. 177-178

Example 5.15: *Fall of Babylon*, mm. 204-207

which abruptly cut off as the return of the primary theme is interrupted by an improvisatory, contemplative section. Ascending and descending scale patterns and dramatically sustained notes end in silence, after which a new melody enters.

With a brand-new bass pattern setting the tone, a serpentine theme begins (Example 5.14), with nothing seeming particularly familiar, until the return of the triplet pattern from the end of the secondary theme's section, now over the new accompaniment. The dramatic *glissando*-like gestures and repeated rhythms that originally preceded those triplets follow, as Schuyler reverses, or mirrors, the secondary theme's section. Rather than ascending, its patterns descend into scale-like, virtuosic figuration that swoops up and down, ending suddenly with sustained Cs.

After those sustained notes die away, a mysterious melody begins to slowly descend sequentially (Example 5.15). Several iterations lead to a rumbling left-hand pattern, with the right hand soon joining with melodic material that recalls an earlier tune. As the phrases repeat and gradually change,

Example 5.16: *Fall of Babylon*, mm. 287-294

the texture thickens through octave doublings and added minor seconds, while both the melody and accompaniment climb higher. Phrases begin to shorten, as these changes occur more frequently, intensifying as the movement's finale approaches.

Schuyler ends *Fall of Babylon* by recalling and summarizing the main events of the movement's plot in its finale. First, the secondary theme returns, now an octave higher and over a dissonant bass pattern. After several measures based on that theme, the primary theme enters with thick textures spread across the far ranges of the keyboard. Its opening repeats over and over, each time ending higher and a bit differently. Sixteenth notes begin to intermingle with the melody, eventually taking over completely. The finale culminates with chords in both hands leaping back and forth two octaves on each eighth note. To conclude, Schuyler restates the beginning of the primary theme one last time, ending in tremolos that descend to an accented bass harmony, again with the movement's characteristic dissonant added second (Example 5.16).

Not only is the complexity of the *White Nile Suite* a fascinating study musically, but the conflicting versions in the Schuyler Family Papers invite several additional questions. Within a folder of mostly unfiled copyright claims, there is a stamped form for Schuyler's copyright on *White Nile Suite*. While this fact is not particularly unusual, it is quite surprising that the form's list of movements does not match Schuyler's manuscript score. Instead, this version combines movements from *Seven Pillars of Wisdom* and the original *White Nile Suite*, listing the movements as: The Arab Revolt; Alexandria; Fortune Favored the Bold Player; Intro: Port Said; and The Fall of Babylon, Egypt.[49] The Library of Congress still has a copy of the score on file, dated March 1965, which reveals that "The Arab Revolt" matches the Prologue from *Seven Pillars of Wisdom* exactly, while "Fortune Favored the Bold Player" is a much shorter version of the sixth movement of *Seven Pillars*, including only the first forty-one of its nearly two hundred measures.* "The Fall of Babylon, Egypt" is a similarly shortened rendition of *Fall of Babylon*, abruptly cutting off long before the original's ending.[50]

So, what is the performer to make of all this? Which version is the authoritative *White Nile Suite*? Her surviving recital programs indicate Schuyler never performed this later version, even after its copyright date.[51] References to the suite in publications and program notes consistently describe it as being inspired by four cities on the banks of the Nile, often specifically listing Omdurman, Alexandria, Port Said, and Babylon as those cities.[52] To add even more confusion, as previously mentioned, "Nubian Legend" was copyrighted separately under the suite's original movement title *Legend of the Mahdi*, even though Schuyler continued to perform it separately as "Nubian Legend" after filing the copyright claim.[53]

Personally, I find the original version much more engaging and coherent. Musically, the shortened versions of both *Fortune Favored the Bold Player* and *Fall of Babylon* seem incomplete, with bizarre, abrupt endings. Narratively, the inclusion of movements from *Seven Pillars of Wisdom* makes little sense, given the extremely detailed plot of *Seven Pillars*, complete with themes named for characters, places, quotes, and concepts from T.E. Lawrence's memoir; the very title *Fortune Favored the Bold Player* is a direct quotation from Lawrence's book.[54]

Of course, the copyright issue raises more questions. Since she never recorded or published either version of *White Nile Suite*, why file the copyright claim at all? Schuyler may have wanted to publish some of her music and felt these were more marketable versions – shorter and easier to play, with the most physically challenging parts removed. She also could have been reacting to criticism of the repetitiveness and length of her compositions.[55] In a letter to her mother from April of that year, Schuyler expressed her fear that Stoll planned to use tapes of her pieces to steal her music; that para-

---

* This shortened version of *Fortune Favored the Bold Player* appears in Helen Walker-Hill's 1992 collection *Black Women Composers: A Century of Piano Music (1893-1990)*.

noia or suspicion could have contributed to the desire to copyright some of her works.[56] Regardless, the fact that she continued to perform the original set of movements after filing the copyright claim seems to reflect Schuyler's own preference for the first version of *White Nile Suite*. The original suite certainly provides a more cohesive narrative, with its focus on cities on the banks of the Nile River. Perhaps more importantly, as her first attempt at writing an entire work based on Arabic music traditions, Schuyler's original 1964 version of *White Nile Suite* remains a major watershed in her compositional output.

Chapter 6
Religious Devotion: Arranging *Uganda Martyrs*

When I became converted to Catholicism in 1958, I got the feeling that I must do something with my life to relate it to people and to humanity. And so, I thought that just sitting at my piano was not enough participation to make. But I found that writing and helping with the missions have not detracted from the music but made it deeper."
- Philippa Schuyler, undated interview[1]

Incredibly driven, Philippa Schuyler did not do anything halfway. She threw herself fully into every project and belief, and she spent countless hours practicing piano, learning new languages, studying, and generally working at a brutal pace, while concert tours planned by her mother included little time for rest or fun. Writing voluminous pages and able to lecture for hours on her thoughts about a wide range of topics such as African culture, Communism, the Catholic Church, and more, Schuyler declared strong opinions with confidence from an early age. Those who knew Schuyler tended to characterize her as stubborn and uncompromising to a fault, but that same tenacity helped build her careers in both music and journalism.

Throughout her childhood, her mother detailed Schuyler's rigorous education in secret scrapbooks which were only revealed to Schuyler as a teenager. Those scrapbooks describe strict schedules and physical punishments. In one example, after what her mother considered Schuyler's first lie, the four-year-old was required to practice the piano to earn her dinner. Both parents left messages for Schuyler, placed around the piano, that criticized her practicing, mentioning missed pitches and pieces which needed more rehearsal. The young Schuyler created an imaginary alternate persona named Rosewings; in contrast to the notes addressed to Schuyler, her parents' notes to Rosewings always praised her playing.[2] In her recital programs, her mother wrote critiques of each piece Schuyler performed, typically sparing with compliments.[3] Until she began attending half days at Manhattanville's Convent School in 1937, Schuyler was almost completely isolated in the environment created by her parents, never playing with children her own age.[4] Even so, as an adult, Schuyler appeared grateful for the work ethic ingrained in her as a child: "I am not sorry I was a child prodigy. There is so much to learn, and so little time in which to learn it. Childhood now is too often considered just the period for 'having fun'."[5]

In her autobiography, Schuyler mentions her intensive practice habits, describing eleven-hour days with little sleep or meal breaks. In one particularly extreme story from 1952, Schuyler learned Hungarian composer Franz Liszt's daunting piano concerto in three days, recalling, "I hardly ate, did not sleep at all. After seventy-two hours of work and no sleep, I played the concerto with the CMQ orchestra over nationwide television. It was a triumph. Directly afterwards, I dashed by taxi to the Club Atenas, where I gave a recital for a packed house."[6] She kept practice journals in which she filled every spare bit of paper with encoded records of the pieces rehearsed, time spent, interpretation issues, and errors to correct. In the margins, she jotted down motivational reminders that recall her mother's early comments:

Happiness is the enemy of achievement.
You must be prepared. You do not wish to lead the life of other people.
You must be strong and work.
There is never any excuse for not thinking. Keep on and on and on.
To have extraordinary results, you must make extraordinary efforts.[7]

When she decided to join the Catholic Church at twenty-seven, Schuyler committed to the idea with her characteristic single-mindedness. She wrote articles for Catholic publications and performed charity concerts to raise money for Catholic missions. Her constant travel in Africa now had a sacred purpose – to advance the cause of the Catholic Church there and help in their humanitarian efforts.[8] By 1963, Schuyler had visited approximately 150 African missions while giving fundraiser concerts and researching her book *Jungle Saints*.[9] She spoke and wrote about her faith continuously, even replying to love letters with lengthy treatises about the virtues of the Church.[10]

Raised in a secular household, Schuyler's route to her devout faith was not straightforward. The Schuylers believed in treating children as adults, so their young daughter was expected to select her own religion after thorough research.[11] At the same time, she would have been exposed to her mother's belief in numerology, astrology, tarot, dream interpretation, and seers, absorbing many of those ideas.[12] At various times, during her formative years, she studied and followed the tenets of Hinduism, Buddhism, and other world religions in the quest to develop her own faith.[13] Meanwhile, her attendance at Manhattanville's Convent School introduced her to Catholicism while providing some of her only experiences with other children her age. Faced with demanding parents and isolation at home, Schuyler seemed to find encouragement and emotional security with the nuns at the Convent School.[14]

According to her mother, Schuyler did not discuss the idea of conversion with her parents beforehand, although she continued to study the Catholic faith long after completing her studies at the Convent School.[15] Her personal practice notes from 1955 and 1956 include assignments to herself to read the Bible for an hour as penance for unspecified sins.[16] By 1958, Schuyler had decided to formally join the Catholic Church. On the same Uganda trip that introduced her to Kyagambiddwa and the music that would inspire so many of her compositions, Schuyler also met Monsignor Cornelius Drew. Curiously, she leaves the encounter out of the stories in her autobiography. A Catholic priest from Harlem, Monsignor Drew instructed Schuyler in the catechism during her time in Uganda, baptizing her later that fall in the United States.[17] In an article for Father Alfonso Zaratti's magazine, Schuyler detailed her newfound faith:

> I was in my twenties when I saw the Light after patient research, a long period of study, of self-doubt and painful uncertainty. The Light is so beautiful for one plunged in darkness! Perhaps only a few who are born Catholic are capable of appreciating the faith as do adult converts.[18]

In discussing her faith, Schuyler frequently mentioned a few specific motivations for her decision to join the Catholic Church. She appreciated its sense of history and the pageantry of the Mass, and, despite the Church's slow progression on gender issues, Schuyler believed Christianity treated women much better than Islam, likely based upon her experiences in countries like Sudan.[19] Schuyler also often praised the Church's stance on racism and integration, with a 1959 feature about the pianist specifically citing that reason for her conversion:

> Why? Because for one thing she had found from her personal experiences that Catholicism all along had been sympathetic with racial integration in America. Also because as a girl she was educated in a Catholic convent in NYC where she was born. The sisters there had always been kind to a coloured girl.[20]

Her published writings frequently circle back to the Church's views on race, and in *Jungle Saints*, she quotes South Africa's Catholic Bishops as stating in 1957 that "apartheid...is identified with white supremacy...It overrides justice. It transcends the teaching of Christ...One trembles at the blasphemy of thus attributing to God the offenses against charity and justice that are apartheid's necessary accompaniment."[21] In yet another article for a Catholic magazine, Schuyler indicates that one of the most important takeaways from her audience with Pope Paul VI was his being "completely free of racial prejudice," and she quotes him as asserting that "Africans are a great people and have a great future."[22]

With her stubbornness and drive, Schuyler was not content to simply practice her faith by attending Mass and participating in the sacraments. Two years after converting, she met Pope John XXIII in a semi-public audience, and, according to Schuyler, the pope asked her to dedicate her writing career to the Catholic Church in Africa. Schuyler took the request seriously, giving countless charity concerts for Catholic missions and writing articles for Catholic publications and secular newspapers.[23] Her radio interviews often discussed the Church's humanitarian efforts in Africa, as well as her own conversion experience.[24] Even conversations with potential suitors delved into Catholic topics; in response to a letter from Ernie Pereira in which he criticized Christianity as being for "simpletons," she replied, "My devotion to the great Catholic religion is complete...I am a Catholic intellectual – and I intend to devote most of my writing from now on to spreading the glory of the Church, and telling the saga of the nobility and heroism of its priests and nuns."[25]

Schuyler's devotion to her faith likely challenged her close relationship with her mother, who grew jealous of her daughter's time and attention to the Church, as well as, perhaps, the potential income lost. In an undated letter referencing Schuyler's charity performances in Africa, Josephine Schuyler wrote to her daughter:

Is it wise or fair to your talent to give it away? The church is full of mediocrities who could not make it outside. YOU ARE NOT A MEDIOCRITY, your place is NOT with them permanently...Oh, don't be angry with me for wanting to guard you from mistakes. I love you. Do these people love you as much as I? Could they ever do as much for you, without regard to profit? I have dedicated myself to you – do you know that? Now, things here need your presence. I love the Church but it, too, is a tyranny and devours the individual – as all institutions must.[26]

In attempting to salvage their relationship and pacify her mother, Schuyler seemed to avoid the topic of the Church in their later correspondences. She continued to discuss tarot cards and horoscopes with her mother, even attaching her name to Mrs. Schuyler's 1966 *Kingdom of Dreams*, a book that provides a guide for interpreting symbols and portents in one's dreams.[27] These continued references to tarot and horoscopes led Schuyler's biographer Talalay to hypothesize that she viewed the occult and reincarnation as compatible with Christianity, going so far as to think that Christ "had not simply been resurrected, he had been reincarnated."[28] Members of the clergy like Father Alfonso Zaratti unsurprisingly disagreed in their assessment of Schuyler's faith, asserting that she left behind ideas like reincarnation when she converted.[29] It is more likely Schuyler discussed her faith a bit differently with her mother than with representatives of the Church, as she tried to negotiate between the secular and sacred parts of her life. Some of her personal papers reflect attempts to reconcile the two, with particularly strange notes in which Schuyler combined horoscope symbols with the names of key figures in Christianity, including Jehovah, Christ, the Holy Spirit, the Virgin Mary, St. Jude, St. Anthony, and Satan.[30]

Despite expressing misgivings about her daughter's work for the Church, Josephine Schuyler rarely passed up an opportunity for good publicity. After receiving a copy of Kyagambiddwa's newly published *Uganda Martyrs African Oratorio* (1964), Mrs. Schuyler asked Kyagambiddwa if he would like her daughter to write a "classic piano version" of his *African Oratorio*. In a letter to Schuyler, she advised her daughter that such a composition would "give ultra respectability, and believe it or not, it would also be chic."[31] Between her devotion to the Church and respect for Kyagambiddwa, Schuyler was likely interested in arranging his oratorio regardless of how "chic" it might be. Schuyler quickly completed her transcription, with the first documented performance presented in Virginia in early 1965.³²

Kyagambiddwa's oratorio was remarkable for several reasons. The first published work by a Ugandan composer in the native Kiganda musical style, *Uganda Martyrs African Oratorio* marked one of the first examples of Catholic liturgical music written in an African vernacular language. The Second Vatican Council (1962-1964), which began two days after Uganda gained its independence, had recently decided to allow vernacular music to be performed in the mass. At that same council, Pope Paul VI not only announced the upcoming canonization of the Uganda Martyrs, but also that an African choir would sing at St. Peter's Basilica for the first time for the occasion. Bishop Joseph Kiwanuka asked Kyagambiddwa, as Uganda's leading composer, to write liturgical music in the Kiganda style for the canonization. Kyagambiddwa initially refused, as they planned for seminarians to write the text; he explained that the nature of the Luganda language meant that the words, pitches, and rhythms must be written together. After much debate, an agreement was reached, and Kyagambiddwa completed his oratorio, with twenty-two movements for the twenty-two martyrs.³³

Today, those twenty-two martyrs are well-known to Catholics in Africa, with many making a yearly pilgrimage to their shrine for the June 3 feast day of Charles Lwanga and his fellow martyrs. Their story began in the Buganda of the late nineteenth century, then ruled by King Mwanga. While his father King Mutesa had peacefully welcomed Catholic priests to Buganda in 1879, King Mwanga was more concerned than his father about the spread of Christianity in his nation. After taking the throne in 1884, King Mwanga ordered the killing of an Anglican Bishop upon arrival in Buganda the next year. Soon after, the king's chief page, Joseph Mukasa, criticized King Mwanga for the bishop's death. A recent Catholic convert, Mukasa was subsequently beheaded on November 15, 1885. Charles Lwanga then assumed the role of chief page and tried to protect the younger pages from the king. The next spring, King Mwanga discovered that one of the boys was studying Catholic catechism and ordered that all of them be interrogated to find the Christians. Fifteen Catholics were discovered, ranging in age from thirteen to twenty-five; all were sentenced to death, along with several Anglican Christians. The boys were forced to walk for two days to Namugongo, where they were burned at the stake. More killings followed, with the final Uganda martyr beheaded in January 1887.³⁴

The Church beatified the Uganda martyrs in June 1920, confirming them as blessed martyrs. Efforts to canonize the martyrs began soon afterward, with a tribunal convened to hear testimonies about miracles they performed. After a lengthy process, the Vatican's Congregation of Rites voted to declare the Uganda martyrs as saints, in a decision that the *New York Times* believed would "emphasize once more the church's opposition to racial discrimination."[35] The official canonization was proclaimed by Pope Paul VI in St. Peter's Basilica on October 18, 1964, with Kyagambiddwa leading an African choir in the performance of selections from his *Uganda Martyrs African Oratorio*. Ugandan drums accompanied the chorus, in the first use of African musical instruments in St. Peter's Basilica. In another notable milestone, his choir was the first mixed gender chorus to perform during mass at St. Peter's, as the Second Vatican Council had determined that women could actively participate in mass earlier that year.[36] The significance of the occasion was not lost on those in attendance; a member of the choir, David Kyeyune (Rev. Fr. Dr.), recalled years later:

> For the first time in St. Peters Basilica, drums and xylophones were sounded. To tell you most sincerely, I was lost in amazement. Hearing your own language (mother tongue) being sung at St. Peters yet originally we used to sing only in Latin, and only polyphonic music? As if that was not enough, even our own musical instruments that had originally been prohibited in the Catholic Church were now accompanying our own music. To me that was enough...It was wonderful and so marvelous.[37]

After the history making canonization of the Uganda martyrs, Schuyler's first documented performance of *Uganda Martyrs* was on January 15, 1965, as part of a lecture recital titled "Jungle Saints: The Influence of Christianity and Christian Missions on Africa."[38] The work appeared in a handful of Schuyler's recital programs from 1965 and 1966, typically as part of a lecture recital or themed program. Curiously, she always listed the composer as Kyagambiddwa, only crediting herself as the transcriber in the program notes.[39] Although that would seem to imply that her transcription follows Kyagambiddwa's oratorio exactly, Schuyler's version initially appears almost unrecognizable in comparison. Given her penchant for constantly revising her own compositions, Schuyler may have originally created a more straightforward transcription, at some point rewriting it to compose the surviving version. In the existing score, Schuyler pieces together short motives from different movements, out of their original order and often fragmented or

Example 6.1: *Uganda Martyrs*, mm. 1-13

transposed, rather than following Kyagambiddwa's oratorio chronologically (Appendix B). Her use of specific phrases seems only partially musically motivated, as their accompanying texts combine to create a narrative, although the words would be unknown to any audience hearing the piece.[40]

Schuyler's version begins with a dramatic introduction featuring chorale-like block chords, while the bass repeats a single dissonant harmony (Example 6.1). Her choice of voicing immediately sets her arrangement apart from the original oratorio, which only uses the typical single-line and call and response settings of traditional Kiganda music. In fact, Kyagambiddwa's oratorio is entirely without accompaniment, aside from optional African percussion instruments. Each movement either features a single voice singing alone, a chorus singing in unison, or a leader and chorus responding to one another. Searching Kyagambiddwa's oratorio for Schuyler's source reveals no exact matches to this opening melody, but the most similar phrase appears in Movement 14 (*Him Who Knows God Not*). Its text seems quite appropriate for beginning the piece: "Oh men that profess God, leap up! Hallelujah! I am leaping!" With a sudden change in key, the next phrase declares "We desire to be like you" from Movement 22 (*Oh Martyrs*), still in a chorale setting. Its ending D major chord is sustained with pedal into the next section.[41]

As the introduction's final chord slowly decays, four new motives enter in counterpoint, all altered from their appearances in Kyagambiddwa's version and once again diverging from the original's monophonic style. Initially, a much faster version of the melody from Movement 22 (*Oh Martyrs*) reappears in the treble. More of the phrase is included here, reading: "We desire to be like you in bravery here. We call and beseech for help." At the same time, the bass calls out "Oh Martyrs of Jesus," eventually transforming into the angel chorus singing "Yea!" from Movement 20 (*Congratulations to You*). At the same time, a melody higher on the keyboard declares "Hail to the celebrated youths," from Movement 3 (*Once Upon a Time*). Throughout the remainder of this section, Schuyler imitates the traditional style of the original oratorio, with a single melody repeated and developed over a percussion-like trill in the left hand.[42]

A return to the opening's chorale voicing functions as a bridge and more straightforwardly sets the same phrase from Movement 22. After this transition, Schuyler again recalls the oratorio's style, with a single melody accompanied by sustained or rolled chords that imitate African percussion instruments. At first, the melody draws on phrases that pray for strength, before focusing on the martyrs themselves by declaring, "They who died then, are being canonized now: they are Saints today." After further repetitions of those phrases, triumphant octaves in the bass again proclaim, "They are Saints today." As the left hand continues in octaves, its melody begins to recall Movement 20, in which God congratulates the martyrs. In the first phrase, God sings, "Open the gate, thou Porter, for the great ones to pass," while overlapping right-hand octaves reiterate, "They are Saints today." Momentum builds until the right hand, still in octaves, pounds out the movement's opening phrase, in which God sings, "Congratulations to you! On the battle you have fought; congratulations to you on your victory!" while an angel chorus echoes, "Congratulations to you!" As the section draws to a close, the treble melody recalls "Our Father who art in heaven" and "All you my many brethren," ending in a tremolo that repeats into the next section.[43]

As the tremolo continues, it transfers to the left hand, again imitating percussion rolls, and a new treble melody declares that "what I am narrating to you is a glorious story." That story, as retold by Schuyler, combines the words of Jesus from Movement 2 (*In the Name of the Father*) with short phrases from other movements and characters. First, a phrase from Movement 1, "It is all about the Saints," alternates with Jesus singing "Baptizing men for salvation. Preach unto creation this Gospel of peace." An altered version of "And of the Holy Ghost" follows, paired with "Pray for us sinners" from Movement 15 (*Holy Mary*). As this third section ends, the chorale-like bridge returns rather suddenly with the same melody, now concluding with repetitive patterns.[44]

When the fourth section begins, the left hand continues to reiterate its same motive for several phrases. Meanwhile, the melody again combines the words of Jesus with other phrases. At first, Jesus declares, "I am going to my Father's, where, later, you will see me again. May the (Holy) Spirit ever comfort and remind you," followed by another version of "And of the Holy Ghost," now partially inverted. Phrases from Movement 4 (*It was a great day*) and Movement 5 (*Fellow Believers!*) follow, in which the ensemble sings, "Oh, whom do we see! He is bringing a torch of Light," and "Fellow believers, be happy. If I am sacrificed for Jesus' sake, I will be very glad indeed." Repetitions of those phrases build until the leader interjects, "The Creator whom I love, to Whom I swear, and Who keeps me preoccupied. When I am sacrificed, the following is my will. I will send no post-mortem curse from the grave," as the chorus answers, "When I am sacrificed." After recalling the martyrs' sacrifice, Schuyler includes the only references to specific martyrs in the entire work – Joseph Mukasa and Matthias Kalemba. As the work reaches its finale, no other melodies from Kyagambiddwa's oratorio appear, as Schuyler builds momentum using virtuosic figuration and cross-rhythms. At its peak, the figuration transforms into the notes of the work's opening chord. The chorale-like introduction then returns in its entirety, concluding the work as it began, perhaps to symbolize the triumphant eternity of the saints it commemorates.[45]

Despite sharing similar goals and musical content, Schuyler ultimately transformed Kyagambiddwa's oratorio into something almost completely new, although some of the longer phrases might catch the ear of a discerning listener who is familiar with the original. Much more than a transcriber or even arranger, she pieced together seemingly disparate phrases and fragments into a cohesive work. *Uganda Martyrs* reveals the depth of Schuyler's faith through its detailed, thoroughly researched narrative, proving itself her most passionately religious composition.

Chapter 7
Strong Friends and Strong Enemies: *Seven Pillars of Wisdom*

> One can live life in safe mediocrity or one can make strong actions – which make as Lawrence said "strong friends and strong enemies."
> – Letter to Josephine Schuyler, undated[1]

As early as October 1964, Schuyler began developing a piece inspired by T.E. Lawrence's *Seven Pillars of Wisdom*. On October 28, she wrote to her mother: "I have been reading T.E. Lawrence's book 'The Seven Pillars of Wisdom'…It is a masterly work, and its descriptions of life in the Near East are superb. What a beautiful title that would make for a piece: 'The Seven Pillars of Wisdom.'"[2] In a letter the very next day, she continued to ruminate on the idea, describing the connection she felt with Lawrence:

> I am so enthralled by Lawrence's wonderful book – The Seven Pillars of Wisdom. Never have West and East been fused in so fascinating a volume. I feel a kinship with Lawrence – for he combined the intellectual with a life of action – he too felt placeless and torn in his own country because of his birth – and he too went forth to seek the unknown in foreign lands. Of course, had I been a man – maybe I could have done in Katanga something of what he did in Arabia. But I have known the terrors of the tropics too, the fevers and the blood. The feeling of disintegration under the boiling sun while one is devoured by insects and disease, disillusion and exaltations, world-weariness, and intensity of vital experience.[3]

Despite insisting she had no time to work on such a composition, Schuyler continued to plot out the possible movements, along with their corresponding quotations from Lawrence's book. While the order eventually changed, this early version is remarkably comparable to her final movement structure.

> Introduction: The Foundations of the Arab Revolt: The Clashing Jealousies[a]
> ~~Arab vs Turk and the Decay of the Ottoman Empire~~[b]
> "The Ottoman Empire was dying of overstrain and the attempt, with diminished resources, to hold on traditional terms the Empire bequeathed to it..."
> "The Arabs were a people of primary colors, or rather of black and white. They despised doubt, our modern crown of thorns. They knew only truth and untruth, belief and unbelief."
> I: ~~The Clashing Jealousies~~ The Decay of the Ottoman Empire
> II: ~~The Evil of My Tale~~ Fire and Reason
> III: BLOOD (Blood was always on our hands. We were licensed to it.)
> IV: The EVIL OF MY TALE[c]
> V: The Agony, The Terrors, and the Mistakes
> VI: Fortune Favored the Bold Player
> ~~VI: Fire and Reason~~
> VII: The Final Stroke: Red Victory
> Epilogue: Disillusion, Death, and the Eventual Liberty of the Arab Peoples
> "I had dreams of hustling into form, while I lived, the new Asia which time was inexorably bringing upon us..."[4]

Schuyler seems to have grown even more taken with the idea as she wrote. Later in the letter, she planned for the introduction (eventually the Prologue) to feature two contrasting themes representing the Ottomans and Arabs. In Part I, she intended to depict "the factionalism of the young Turks and the intriguing Arab movements and their varied leaders."[5] *The Evil of My Tale*, at that point planned to be Part II, would represent "the strange passions which torment the fighters for freedom as they grope painfully through the pitiless desert."[6] Part III (*Blood*) would show a "combat scene, gory and glorious, courageous and terrible."[7] In one significant difference

---

a *The Clashing Jealousies* was added later in different ink.
b Strikethroughs are from Schuyler's letter and reflect her evolving conception of the work's structure.
c *The Evil of My Tale* was added later in different ink.

from the final version, *The Agony, the Terrors and the Mistakes* originally was supposed to portray "marching to seize new strategic positions, achievements and setbacks."[8] *Fortune Favored the Bold Player* would show "Lawrence creating a brilliant, daring plan to push forward to victory," while *Fire and Reason* (then planned to be Part VI) would paint a musical portrait of Feisal.[9] As in the final draft, Part VII would illustrate the Arab Revolt's victory in Damascus and the end of the war. Finally, she described the epilogue as the "disillusionment of Lawrence when the Arabs are betrayed by the Allies at the peace table, his tragic death, and the final triumph when the idea that he had so many painful years ago takes shape and becomes a final reality..."[10] Before mailing the letter, she continued ruminating and made edits to her initial plan, as evidenced by the addition and crossing out of titles in different ink.[11]

Because David Lean's hugely popular film *Lawrence of Arabia* was released in 1962, it would be easy to label it as Schuyler's source of inspiration, particularly given her love of movies. Actually, she was derisive of the movie's lack of historical accuracy:

> This would not be like the film - which invented many incidents out of whole cloth – and gave no idea of the intellectuality and complexity of this remarkable man. This piece, in each section, would express a different facet of the personality and emotion of the Arab Revolt and the foreign adventures torn in his soul, lost in the limbo between degradation and glory with blood on his hands and a vivid ideal always in his soul.[12]

Lawrence's story inspired a compositional obsession unlike any of Schuyler's previous works. Nearly seventy minutes in length, *Seven Pillars of Wisdom* far eclipses her other music in scope, and throughout its prologue, seven movements, and extended epilogue, Schuyler uses encoded musical themes to explore challenging ideas about conflict, violence, and faith. With omissions and, at times, substantial edits scribbled into the margins of the score, it appears she worked on the piece even after it was ostensibly completed and premiered.[13]

While her acknowledgement of Lawrence's experiences in the desert and feeling "placeless and torn" in his home country provide some explanation for Schuyler's interest in the project, her reference to Katanga would have conveyed much more to her mother.[14] It could be tempting to skim past that line, but the allusion proves essential to fully understanding why Lawrence's story so intensely captured Schuyler's imagination. Considering Schuyler's own experiences in the Congo just a few years earlier helps explain her extreme affinity for Lawrence's memoir.

On June 7, 1960, Schuyler traveled to Elisabethville (now Lubumbashi), the capital of the Katanga province in the Belgian Congo (now the Democratic Republic of the Congo), in advance of the celebration of their independence from Belgium. She had been invited to perform at the June 30 inauguration of President Joseph Kasavabu and Prime Minister Patrice Lumumba in Léopoldville (now Kinshasa); considering the invitation an honor, Schuyler and her mother anticipated a grand event.[15] From its very beginning, the visit did not go according to plan, with a lone mattress on the floor of an unfurnished apartment being the best offer of lodging available. Her ride to the ceremony forgot to pick her up, so Schuyler was forced to find other transportation.[16] Upon arriving at the event venue, she discovered the concert stage was not set up exactly as expected. In *Who Killed the Congo?*, she describes the sight:

> But though many good grand pianos were available in Leo, they had forgotten to obtain one, and had had to drag out an ancient, battered upright at the last minute. They had put it in the middle of the swimming pool. They never gave any explanation for doing so, except that they had once seen this done in a movie. The pool was full of water. They had put a tiny wooden float under the piano but had forgotten to weight it down correctly, so that it bobbed perilously. Nor had they attached the piano to the float, so that it trembled and moved around constantly. They had also forgotten to turn off the noisy fountain at the back, so that it sprayed and jetted water toward the piano.[17]

Nevertheless, Schuyler soldiered on and played the full program, despite a noticeable lack of attention from the mostly intoxicated audience.[18]

During the remainder of her trip, parties and celebrations began to give way to chaos, with riots beginning July 2 in Orientale Province. Two days later, reports began coming in of mass rapes and violence in other areas, and by July 7, white refugees began streaming into Léopoldville. From there, over two thousand refugees escaped across the Congo River to French Brazzaville until that route was cut off, while others fled to neighboring countries. For the first few days, Schuyler remained in Léopoldville, collecting as many stories as possible and sending dispatches home.[19]

After leaving to perform in Ghana at a July 4 celebration of their independence from Britain, Schuyler continued to Brussels, where hundreds of refugees were arriving.[20] Their stories of extremely brutal rapes and beatings shocked the nation; Schuyler sent reports of their experiences back to the United States. Her dispatches from the Congo earned Schuyler a return trip, now as a United Press International (UPI) special correspondent, and in August, Schuyler arrived in the Congo, basing herself in Elisabethville.[21] Katanga province had seceded on July 11, led by Moïse Tshombe, and while the Republic of the Congo was aided by the Soviet Union, Katanga positioned itself as anti-Communist. With a better climate than the rest of the country and a variety of lucrative mines, including cobalt, copper, tin, uranium, and diamonds, Katanga contained a significant portion of the Congo's wealth.[22] Now the capital of the State of Katanga, Elisabethville housed numerous foreign journalists, with many of them complaining about the combination of Katangan propaganda and a lack of transportation outside the city. Somehow, Schuyler still managed to find her way into interesting stories, and by mid-August, she had flown to Bakwanga (now Mbuji-Mayi), about five hundred miles from Elisabethville. Reports indicated over sixty thousand refugees had fled from Luluabourg (now Kananga) to the diamond-mining town. On August 23, Lumumba sent his soldiers there, and Schuyler described "hideous corpses" in the street, as she reported on the carnage.[23]

By early December, Lumumba had been arrested and dismissed as prime minister, and the conditions of his imprisonment were deplorable enough that the United Nations tried unsuccessfully to intervene. For weeks, there was no official news of his fate, but in February 1961, the Katangan government announced Lumumba had been sent there for safekeeping and was killed during an escape attempt. Schuyler happened to be in the Congo at the time and received information that the reported story was likely false. She spent the next several weeks trying to track down the truth about Lumumba's death. In April, she reported her findings, which were so outlandish that one of her usual publishers declined to carry the story.[24] In *Who Killed the Congo?*, Schuyler presented alternate theories along with her own:

> According to this version, which the reader may best judge for himself, the Katanga authorities did not want to receive Lumumba at all...Lumumba was already dead when he arrived. He died from a

variety of causes en route to Elisabethville. Anxiety, terror, months of an upsetting and violently irregular life, the results of previous and present beatings combined to extinguish life through a combination of unhealed wounds, shock and heart failure.[25]

Schuyler went on to claim that Katangan authorities kept Lumumba's body in deep freeze while they decided what to do, making it difficult to determine an accurate time of death. According to Schuyler's biographer Talalay, a 1961 United Nations commission of inquiry published findings on Lumumba's death that confirmed much of Schuyler's story.[26] More recent scholarship presents a different account, alleging Lumumba and his associates had been loaded on a plane to Elisabethville in mid-January, but, soon after landing there, all three were shot and buried. Days later, their bodies were dug up and destroyed with sulphuric acid, although one of the perpetrators reportedly kept Lumumba's teeth.[27] Only the relatively recent declassification of Belgian documents in 2000 allowed the true story of Lumumba's murder to come to light.[28] Almost four decades prior, Schuyler published her 1962 account of the Congo conflict, including her own analysis of its roots and causes. Instantly controversial, *Who Killed the Congo?* was loved by conservatives and hated by liberals. Criticized for its partisan stance, shaky documentation, and for being too sympathetic to the Belgians, the book included numerous horror stories of the events and atrocities committed during the conflict.[29]

Two years after witnessing and reporting on a plethora of horrific violence and finding her opinions on it were not always well-received, Schuyler began reading Lawrence's memoir. The context of Schuyler's firsthand experience of the Congo conflict helps explain why a mixed-race American pianist would find so much kinship with a white British soldier and author. Beyond their shared personal qualities, Schuyler likely identified with Lawrence's tale of horrible acts in the pursuit of freedom, in which no one is truly a hero. It inspired her largest, most complex composition, filled with cryptographic messages and strong dissonances.

Once she began composing *Seven Pillars of Wisdom*, Schuyler worked quickly, despite her busy schedule, and most of *Seven Pillars* was completed by the end of 1964. In a home recording on Christmas Eve, she introduced and performed the following movements: *Fire and Reason*; *Foundations of the Arab Revolt*; *The Agonies, the Terrors, and the Mistakes*; *The Clashing Jealousies*; and *Fortune Favored the Bold Player*. These appear to have been preliminary versions, as the movement she called "Foundations of the Arab Revolt" would soon be titled *Decay of the Ottoman Empire*, while "The Clashing Jealousies" became the prologue (*Foundations of the Arab Revolt*). In introducing each movement, she read quotations from Lawrence's book which were eventually included as a typed sheet with her handwritten manuscript.[30]

In January 1965, Schuyler included *Fall of the Ottoman Empire* (Part I) in lecture recitals on "Jungle Saints: The Influence of Christianity and Christian Missions on Africa" and "The Influence of Christianity and Christian Missions on Africa."[31] She premiered the full work at New York University on February 6, 1965, although the program for that recital is missing.[32] The first surviving program containing the entire work is from its London premiere on April 8, 1965, at the American Embassy Theatre. By that point, the movements appear under their finalized, although shortened, titles:

> The Arab Revolt – The Decay of the Ottoman Empire – Fire and Reason – Blood – The Evil of My Tale – Agonies, Terrors and Mistakes (The Torture at Deraa) – Fortune Favored the Bold Player – Red Victory – Disillusion, and the death of Lawrence – The Final Liberty of the Afro-Asian Peoples[33]

At nearly seventy minutes in length, the full piece can be unwieldy to program, and Schuyler often included sets of movements rather than the entire work. She performed selections from *Seven Pillars of Wisdom* frequently in 1965, including at a fundraiser for the Mahatma Gandhi Memorial Fund and at the Gallery for Modern Art in New York. Typically, she shortened it to some combination of these movements: *Foundations of the Arab Revolt*; *The Decay of the Ottoman Empire*; *The Agonies, The Terrors, and the Mistakes*; *Fortune Favored the Bold Player*; and *The Final Liberty of the Afro-Asian Peoples*.[34]

After 1965, Schuyler largely replaced *Seven Pillars of Wisdom* with *Nile Fantasy*'s piano transcription in her recitals.[35] *Nile Fantasy* orchestrated movements of *Seven Pillars of Wisdom* and her *White Nile Suite*, so its piano transcription is a much-shortened version of those two works (see Chapter 8). Schuyler's final documented performance of *Seven Pillars of Wisdom* took place on February 2, 1966, at the hotel Le Benin, located in Lome, Togo.[36]

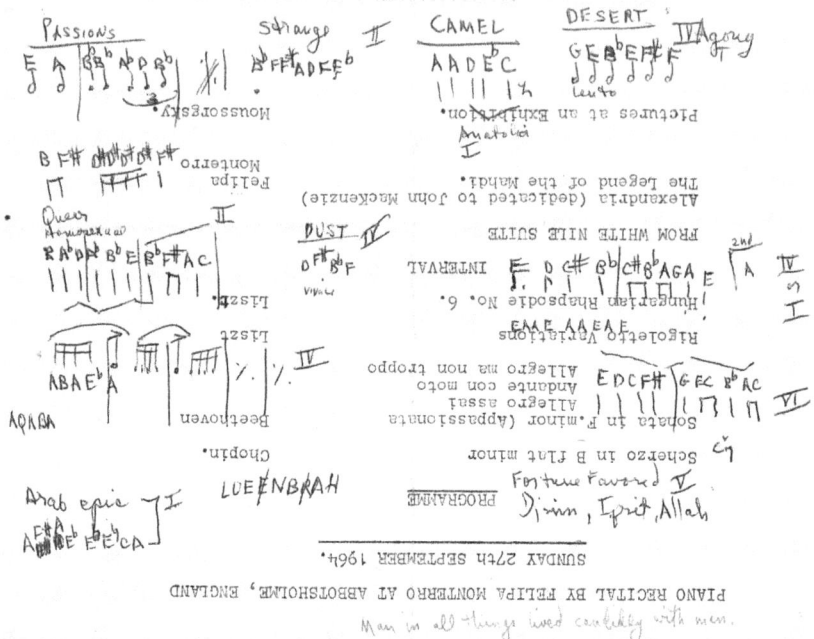

Figure 7.1: Notes on 1964 Concert Program

In researching *Seven Pillars of Wisdom*, I initially tried to track down a complete manuscript to use for performances. Although the catalog of Schuyler's papers lists a folder containing *Seven Pillars of Wisdom*, I quickly realized that its contents were incomplete. The fifth and sixth movements were entirely absent, the prologue was missing pages, the epilogue included pages that seemed to be out of place, and there was no ending. Archivists were able to help locate the missing movements, discovering they were simply cataloged as separate pieces. Schuyler worked on *Seven Pillars of Wisdom* at different times and in varying locations, so those two movements are in a separate spiral notebook.[37] Solving the mystery of the prologue and epilogue required sifting through several boxes of miscellaneous scores and papers, but they were eventually located. The prologue's missing pages were included in a folder labeled as "The Vistula at Night," while the ending for the epilogue was in a folder of miscellaneous sketches and notes.[38] From there, Schuyler's meticulous page and movement labels made it more straightforward to correctly assemble the complete work.

While searching for the prologue and epilogue's missing pages, I stum-

Letter	Musical pitch
A	A
B	E-flat
C	A
D	G
E	E or E-flat/D#
F	G
G	F
H	B
I	C
J	C
K	B
L	C
M	D-flat or D
N	D
O	G#/A-flat
P	E
Q	B
R	F#
S	B-flat
T	F
U	F#/G-flat
V	D
W	F#
X	B-flat
Y	C
Z	B-flat

Figure 7.2: Schuyler's Musical Alphabet

bled across some unexpected and uncatalogued notes related to *Seven Pillars of Wisdom*. As she traveled, Schuyler would scribble down ideas in the margins of whatever paper she had on hand, sometimes even repurposing old letters for new ones. Many of those notes involved horoscope readings and numerology, but others proved to be early sketches of musical themes from *Seven Pillars of Wisdom*. The backs and margins of a concert program, letter, business card, and a scrap of paper all contain a variety of labeled themes, either with note names only or basic rhythms.[39] The names of themes typically appear near the names of musical pitches, with the letters carefully printed above or below the pitch (Figure 7.1).[40] As I took my own notes on these themes, I started to notice a pattern - letters were consistently paired with the same note names. After comparing all her named musical themes, it became clear that Schuyler was using her own musical alphabet, shown in Figure 7.2. Likely beginning with J.C. Faber in the early eighteenth century, composers throughout history have encoded messages into their music, often including their own names or those of friends and colleagues. Schuyler's alphabet corresponds with neither the German alphabet popularized by Bach, nor the various French alphabets used by Ravel, Poulenc, Milhaud, and others.[41] Instead, Schuyler appears to have created her own version. As noted in Figure 7.2, she was not always fully consistent in which pitch represents each letter. Enharmonic pitches were used interchangeably at times, as in the case of E-flat and D-sharp. In other cases, a different musical pitch was used in earlier, discarded themes; in particular, D represents the letter M in the unused themes, while D-flat more consistently represents M in themes found in the final version of the work.

Along with those early sketches, I discovered a numbered list of musical themes related to *Seven Pillars of Wisdom*, buried in a box of miscellaneous papers. In one form or another, all but one theme from that list can be found in the final musical score, often somewhat altered. In the list, Schuyler carefully spells the titles of themes using her musical alphabet, but in writing the piece, she adapts them to better fit the surrounding music.[42] Only three themes appear in the score but not in that numbered list: "The Questor," "The beating of Lawrence," and "Aqaba." The first two are labeled in the music, while "Aqaba" can be found in Schuyler's early sketches.[43] Otherwise, there are fourteen themes in her handwritten notes that do not appear in the final score, and they seem to reflect a change in approach. Several of the titles of unused themes relate to T. E. Lawrence's rumored homosexuality, and no references to that topic appear in the final version.

The musical themes that appear in *Seven Pillars of Wisdom* can be categorized by topic: characters, places, events, quotations, and Islam. Fourteen untitled musical themes are also included in Schuyler's numbered list.*

Characters: T. E. Lawrence; Auda Abu Tai
Places: Ottoman Empire; Sublime Porte; Anatolia; Deraa; Mecca; Aqaba
Events: Arab Revolt; The beating of Lawrence
Quotations: Seven Pillars of Wisdom; Black and White; Truth and Untruth; The New Asia; Red Victory; Blood
Islam: Ar-Rum; Djinn and Ifrit; Al-Baqarah; Al-Taghabun; Inshallah; Allah; Al-Hashr; Those who drag forth; Al-Takwir; Al-Koran; Jehad; Saba; Al-Tahrim
Other: Tafta Hindi; Sudanese; The Questor[44]

While some themes directly connect to the plot of Lawrence's book, others reflect Schuyler's interpretation of its meaning. In particular, the inclusion of themes related to Islam indicate research far beyond simply reading Lawrence's memoir. Several themes are named for Surahs of the Qur'an, while "Djinn" and "Ifrit" are titled for figures from Islamic folklore.[45] While introductory quotations from Lawrence's book help clarify the plot, examining the appearances and modifications of these musical themes further illuminates the highly programmatic nature of this complex work.

Some Englishmen, of whom Kitchener was chief, believed that a rebellion of Arabs against Turks would enable England, while fighting

---

* All spellings and English transliterations are taken directly from Schuyler's list and do not necessarily match modern English transliterations of Arabic words.

Germany during the First World War, simultaneously to defeat Germany's ally Turkey. Their knowledge of the nature and country and power of the Arabic-speaking peoples made them think that the issue of such a rebellion would be happy, and indicated its character and method.

So they allowed it to begin, having obtained for it formal assurances of help from the British government. Yet, nonetheless, the rebellion of the Sherif of Mecca came to many as a surprise, and found the Allies unready. It aroused mixed feelings, and made strong friends and strong enemies, amidst whose <u>clashing jealousies</u> its affairs began to miscarry.[46]

In *Prologue: The Foundations of the Arab Revolt (The Clashing Jealousies)*, Schuyler begins by clearly and simply stating the most important musical themes that will recur throughout the rest of the piece. The book title (Example 7.1, page 102) and author (Example 7.2, page 102) are introduced, along with "Arab Revolt" (Example 7.3, page 102) and "Ottoman Empire" (Example 7.4, page 102), which reference the rebellion of the local Arab tribes against the Turkish Ottoman Empire. During World War I, Britain and France funded and encouraged the Arab Revolt in an effort to destabilize the Ottoman Empire, which was allied with Germany. In a deception that haunted Lawrence throughout the remainder of his life, Britain led the Arab tribes to believe they would be free to govern themselves afterward; in reality, Britain and France planned to control the Middle East after the war.[47] First presented here, the themes "Black and White" (Example 7.5, page 103) and "Truth and Untruth" (Example 7.6, page 103) also prove important in later movements. Rather than referencing characters or places, their titles come from Lawrence's introduction, in which he details his own views on the Arab tribes' temperament.[48]

After introducing and repeating these themes, the second half of the prologue fragments and transposes "T. E. Lawrence," but otherwise features new, untitled material. In the prologue's final measures, a dramatic crescendo into dissonant chords culminates in a large forearm tone cluster, sustained as the "Seven Pillars" theme is restated (Example 7.7, page 103). In this statement and its subsequent appearances, the "Wisdom" is always left out of this theme. This type of ending occurs in several movements, highlighting Schuyler's characteristic love of dissonance and perhaps also the dissonance

Example 7.1: *Prologue*, mm. 5-15

Example 7.2: *Prologue*, mm. 29-32

Example 7.3: *Prologue*, mm. 1-2

Example 7.4: *Prologue*, mm. 24-25

Example 7.5: *Prologue*, mm. 33-36

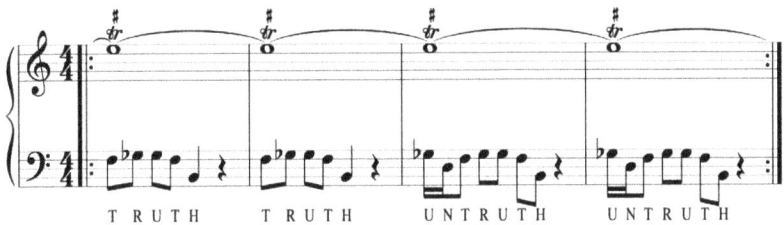

Example 7.6: *Prologue*, mm. 37-40

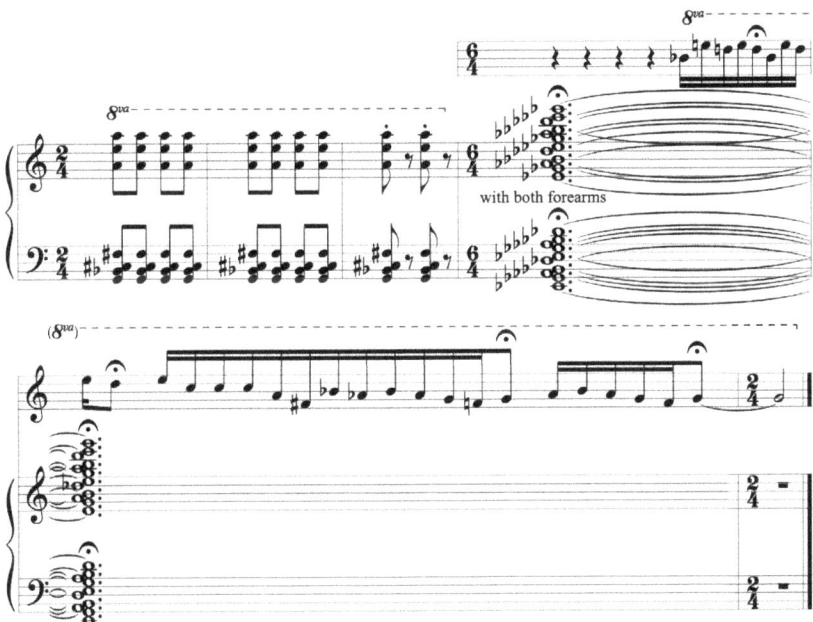

Example 7.7: *Prologue*, mm. 176-181

of Lawrence's story. The fourth and fifth movements, along with the first half of the epilogue, also end with a cluster harmony sustained beneath a mysterious tune, and Schuyler concludes Part II, Part III, and the finale of the epilogue with similarly thundering, dissonant chords, but without an accompanying melody.

> *The Ottoman Empire was dying of overstrain, and of the attempt, with diminished resources, to hold on traditional terms the empire bequeathed to it.*[49]

> *The Arabs were a people of primary colors, or rather of black and white. They despised doubt, our modern crown of thorns. They knew only truth and untruth, belief and unbelief.*[50]

Part I: The Decay of the Ottoman Empire then illustrates the declining state of the Turkish Ottoman Empire through related musical themes and an overall sense of stagnation. In a mysterious introduction, the movement opens with "Ar-Rum" (Example 7.8), followed by the untitled Theme #10 (Example 7.9). In Schuyler's early sketches, she labels "Ar-Rum" as "The Romans;" its title comes from the 30th Surah of the Qur'an.[51] That Surah's topics include monotheism and the defeat of the Byzantines by the Persians in 613 AD in Antioch, Turkey.[52]

After the sparse introduction sets the tone, a large section based on "Sublime Porte" (Example 7.10) follows. Sublime Porte was the center of the Ottoman Empire's government, and the theme's lethargic tempo and numerous repetitions portray the "decay" of the movement's title. After this extended, almost monotonous section, "Anatolia" (Example 7.11) appears, transitioning to the more spirited mood and tempo of the movement's second half. Lawrence writes that most of the Turkish foot soldiers were from the region of Anatolia.[53] In the slightly livelier second half, "Black and White," "Truth and Untruth," and "T.E. Lawrence" recur, now fragmented and combined in new ways. The movement closes with a return to its introduction's themes; Theme #10 is now marked *pianississimo* and concludes with a modified fragment of the "T. E. Lawrence" theme (Example 7.12, page 106).

> *I had believed the misfortunes of the Arab Revolt to be due to faulty leadership, or rather the lack of leadership, Arab and English. So I*

Example 7.8: *Part I*, mm. 1-4

Example 7.9: *Part I*, mm. 9-10

Example 7.10: *Part I*, mm. 13-16

Example 7.11: *Part I*, mm. 72-73

> *went down to Arabia to see and consider its great men. The first; the Sherif of Mecca, we knew to be aged: I found Abdulla too clever, Ali too clean, Zeid too cool. Then I rode up-country to Feisal, and found in him the leader with the necessary <u>fire</u>, and yet with <u>reason</u> to give effect to our science. His tribesmen seemed sufficient instrument, and his hills to provide natural advantage. So I returned pleased and confident to Egypt and told my superiors how Mecca was defended, not by the obstacle of Rabegh, but by the flank-threat of Feisal in Jebel Subh.*[54]

Subtitled "The momentous meeting between Lawrence and Emir Feisal

Example 7.12: *Part I*, mm. 171-178

Example 7.13: *Part II*, mm. 7-12

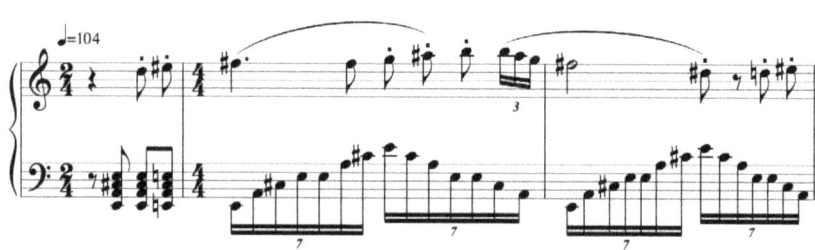

Example 7.14: *Part II*, mm. 26-28

Example 7.15: *Part II*, mm. 54-57

of Arabia, which lent new impetus to the Arab Revolt," *Part II: Fire and Reason* depicts Lawrence's alliance with Emir Feisal, whom Lawrence described as having the right balance of fire and reason to successfully lead the rebellion against the Ottoman Empire.[55] Here, Schuyler portrays the movement's topic through sharp musical contrasts, rather than titled themes. *Fire and Reason* opens and closes with bright, forceful A major triads, while the rest of the musical material alternates between the dissonant, rhythmic patterns of Theme #20 (Example 7.13), more lyrical settings of Theme #21 (Example 7.14), and the modal Theme #22 (Example 7.15).

When she first plotted out the movements, Schuyler planned to include Theme #21 in *Part IV: The Evil of My Tale*, with "masculine big chords." By her final draft, the theme was moved to Part II, and its accompaniment changed to the left-hand arpeggiations shown in Example 7.14.[56] Schuyler also labeled Theme #20 as "Fire and Reason" in that same sketch, but because its notes do not spell out the title, it remains unclear whether she meant that title for the theme itself or for the movement in which she planned to include it.

> <u>Blood</u> *was always on our hands: we were licensed to it. Wounding and killing seemed ephemeral pains – so very brief and sore was life with us. With the sorrow of living so great, the sorrow of punishment had to be pitiless. We lived for the day and died for it. When there was reason or desire to punish, we wrote our lesson immediately with gun or whip on the sullen flesh of the sufferer. The desert did not afford the refined slow penalties of courts and gaols. What now looks wanton or sadic, seemed in the field inevitable, or mere unimportant routine.*[57]

Part III: Blood portrays a specific event in Lawrence's book – the fight to seize the city of Aqaba. Geographically, Aqaba was extremely important to the Arab Revolt, and debates with the British and the Sherif of Mecca about how to take Aqaba occur throughout the early portions of Lawrence's book. Achieving that goal was a turning point in the revolt, providing access to southern Palestine and the supply line of the Hejaz Railway.[58] While the actual battle for Aqaba ended relatively quickly, the "blood" of the title may refer to a prior encounter, in which Lawrence and his fighters massacred hundreds of Turkish soldiers in Aba el Lissan.[59]

Constructed in three parts, *Blood* begins with a large section featuring an opening segment based on "Aqaba," "Saba," "Mecca" (Example 7.16),

Example 7.16: *Part III*, mm. 1-2

Example 7.17: *Part III*, mm. 37-44

Example 7.18: *Part III*, mm. 53-56

and Theme #22. "Mecca" refers to Islam's holiest city, the birthplace of the Prophet Muhammad; Emir Feisal was the son of the Sherif of Mecca.[60] The title of the 34th Surah of the Qur'an, "Saba" includes warnings and promises about the day of judgement.[61] This initial section's second half begins with a lyrical unlisted theme (Example 7.17) leading into dramatic repetitions of the descending triads of "Blood" (Example 7.18).[62]

The subsequent contrasting section draws most of its musical material from statements and fragments of "Al-Baqarah" and "Aqaba," although it ends with a short segment restating the "Ottoman Empire" and "Sudanese" themes, which were originally heard in the Prologue. An abbreviated but otherwise unaltered repetition of the opening section concludes the movement.

> Some of <u>the evil of my tale</u> may have been inherent in our circumstances. For years we lived anyhow with one another in the naked desert, under the indifferent heaven. By day the hot sun fermented us, and we were dizzied by the beating wind. At night we were stained by dew, and shamed into pettiness by the innumerable silences of the stars. We were a self-centered army without parade or gesture, devoted to freedom, the second of man's creeds, a purpose so ravenous that it devoured all our strength, a hope so transcendent that our earlier ambitions faded in its glare.
>
> As time went by our need to fight for the ideal increased to an unquestioning possession. We had sold ourselves into its slavery, manacled ourselves together in its chain-gang, bowed ourselves to serve its holiness with all our good and ill content. The mentality of ordinary human slaves is terrible, - they have lost the world - and we had surrendered, not body alone, but soul to the overmastering greed for victory. By our own act we were drained of morality, of volition, of responsibility, like dead leaves in the wind.[63]

The title of *Part IV: The Evil of My Tale* comes from the opening sentence in Lawrence's book, quoted above. Unlike the third movement, Part IV does not depict a specific event in the plot; Schuyler reflects instead on the meaning and implications of Lawrence's often violent story. Several themes related to Islam appear, with topics referencing angels, demons, and the day of judgement.

Musically, Part IV creates an appropriately ominous mood, beginning with the tonally ambiguous Theme #23 and extended repetitions and fragments of "New Asia" (Example 7.19, page 110). "New Asia" draws its name from Lawrence's epilogue, in which he writes of his unrealized dream of creating a "new Asia" in which the Arab tribes would govern themselves.[64] Altered and shortened versions of earlier material build to the dramatic en-

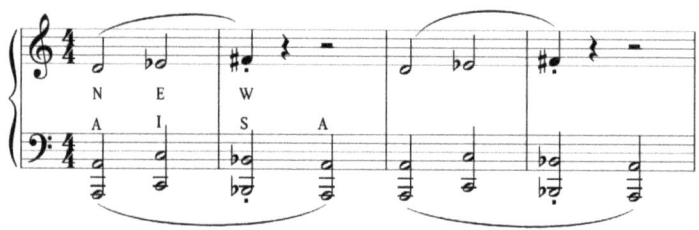

Example 7.19: *Part IV*, mm. 5-8

Example 7.20: *Part IV*, mm. 55-56

Example 7.21: *Part IV*, mm. 57-63

trance of "Tafta Hindi" (Example 7.20), which quotes a traditional Middle Eastern folk song and recurs throughout the remainder of *Seven Pillars*. In this movement, it serves as a bridge between sections.

"Djinn" and "Ifrit" (Example 7.21) follow immediately afterward, marked at a slower tempo. These two themes also include multiple full-measure rests, which create a sense of inertia. *Djinns* are angel-like beings made of smokeless fire, while *ifrit* are a type of demon or spirit of the dead. Slower, transposed versions of Themes #16 and #13 then lead to another statement of "Tafta Hindi," again serving to delineate sections and leading to a new, strange theme.

Marked in the score as "The Questor" (Example 7.22), this disjointed, *pianississimo* theme occurs only here. This unusual-sounding theme's title does not seem to connect to Lawrence's story or Islam in any way, but it could have been inspired by Schuyler's interest in tarot, as the individual

Example 7.22: *Part IV*, mm. 117-118

Example 7.23: *Part IV*, mm. 133-136

receiving a tarot reading is sometimes called "The Questor." Schuyler's obsession with astrology and tarot is well documented throughout her letters, audio recordings, and notes. Within the Schuyler Family Audio collection is a recording she made of a visit with a clairvoyant, and her papers are filled with notes on horoscopes and numerology.[65] Despite her conversion to Catholicism, she continued to consult psychics and tarot readers throughout her life. Letters with her mother often discuss their most recent horoscopes or readings, including her last letter written three days before her death.[66]

The "Questor" theme functions as a transition to the final section of the movement, which introduces "Those who drag forth" (Example 7.23) and closes with restatements of Theme #23 and "New Asia." "Those who drag forth" is an English translation of the title of the 79th Surah of the Qur'an (An-Naziat), which discusses angels reaping souls, continuing to generate an atmosphere of doom.[67] A brief codetta sustains tone clusters under a series of dissonant intervals, in another instance of Schuyler ending a movement with dissonant chords under a quiet melody (Example 7.24, page 112).

> *We no doubt enjoyed the rare moments of peace and forgetfulness, but I remember more <u>the agony, the terrors and the mistakes</u>. Our life is not summed up in what I have remembered (there are things not to be repeated in cold blood for very shame) but what I have written was in and of our life. Pray God that men reading this tale will not, for love of the glamour of strangeness, go out to prostitute themselves and their*

Example 7.24: *Part IV*, mm. 165-171

talents in serving another race (land).[68]

Deraa! Deraa was a city of cruelty and vice. It was in Deraa that the citadel of my integrity was irrevocably lost..."[69]

Part V: The Agonies, The Terrors, and The Mistakes is subtitled "The Torture at Deraa," making its connection to the plot obvious. This movement depicts a famous but possibly embellished or fictitious episode from Lawrence's book, in which the author is beaten and sexually assaulted by Turkish soldiers in Deraa.[70] When introducing her December 1964 recording, Schuyler remarked that this movement describes "torture which had a profound effect and significance on his soul."[71]

As one of the longest movements in *Seven Pillars*, Part V functions as both the centerpiece and turning point of the plot, much like the corresponding events in Lawrence's memoir. Regardless of what he really experienced in Deraa, Lawrence's demeanor and approach to the Arab Revolt changed markedly afterward. He began traveling with his own bodyguard of fifty to sixty warriors, and his brutality toward the Turkish troops increased significantly in later battles.[72] While most of Schuyler's quotations come from Lawrence's introduction, here she adapts the final sentence of the chapter depicting the events in Deraa.[73] The only new themes introduced relate explicitly to that incident – "Deraa" and "The beating of Lawrence," both of which occur later in the movement.

The opening theme is an altered version of Theme #17, which previ-

Example 7.25a: *Part I*, mm. 128-129 (Theme #17)

Example 7.25b: *Part V*, mm. 1-6 (Theme #17, altered)

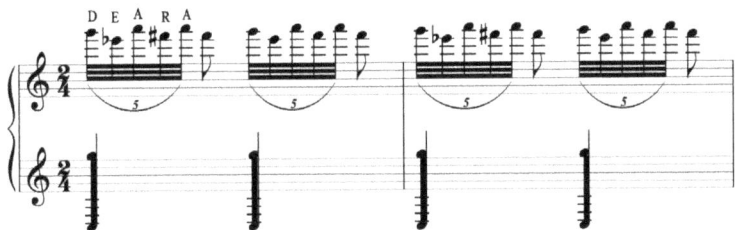

Example 7.26: *Part V*, mm. 46-47

ously appeared in Part I. As shown in Example 7.25, the original version's ornament is omitted, the measure of rest that followed is replaced with a descending seventh, the rhythms are augmented, and the tempo is slowed considerably. Part I's version of this theme is included in a spirited section which also features the themes "Black and White" and "Truth and Untruth." Here, Theme #17 enters alone, and the changes in rhythm and ornamentation create a dirge-like mood, reflecting the change in Lawrence. This theme recurs frequently throughout the movement, always followed by "Arab Revolt." In the first portion of Part V, repetitions of Theme #17 build to an extremely dissonant segment featuring "Deraa" in the right hand and forearm tone clusters in the left arm (Example 7.26). Earlier material then returns, growing in texture and dynamic until the "beating of Lawrence" theme (Example 7.27, page 114). The movement's second large section repeats that theme ninety times, interspersed with Part I's "Sublime Porte." After a section recalling other material from Part I, "Arab Revolt" leads to a new version of

Example 7.27: *Part V*, mm. 81-84

Example 7.28: *Part V*, mm. 241-245

Theme #10, now labeled with the expressive marking "with a feeling of utter humiliation." After three repetitions, a bass tone cluster sustained under a version of "Deraa" concludes the movement (Example 7.28).

> *Rebellion was the gravest step that political men could take, and the success or failure of the Arab Revolt was a gamble too hazardous for prophecy. Yet, for once, <u>fortune favored the bold player</u>.*[74]

Along with Part VII, *Part VI: Fortune Favored the Bold Player* portrays the Arab Revolt's success, and its title comes from the above quote from Lawrence's introduction.[75] As Schuyler reflects on the elements that contributed to their victory, she incorporates several themes from earlier movements, including "T.E. Lawrence," "Truth and Untruth," "Black and White," "New Asia," "Ottoman Empire," and "Arab Revolt." In fact, only three short new themes are introduced, all relating to Islam and always occurring together - "At-Takwir," "Al-Koran," and "Jehad." "Al-Koran" (alt. Qur'an) refers to the holy text of the Islamic faith, while "Jehad" (alt. jihad) translates literally as "struggle" and is often associated with battles. The title of the 81st Surah of the Qur'an, "At-Takwir" translates alternatively as "the overthrowing" or "the enfolding" and discusses the signs of the day of judgement.[76]

Despite Schuyler's use of numerous named themes, Part VI opens with

Example 7.29: *Part VI*, mm. 1-10

a new, untitled melody (Example 7.29) that returns in the first portion of the epilogue. It is the only theme reused in other movements but not included in Schuyler's list or sketches. This disjointed melody and a bass pattern based on Theme #18 are followed by recurrences of several earlier themes, particu-

Example 7.30: *Part VI*, mm. 44-49

Example 7.31: *Part VI*, mm. 93-98

Example 7.32: *Part VI*, mm. 168-173

larly "T.E. Lawrence" and "Truth and Untruth." As this first section ends, "Seven Pillars" returns (Example 7.30), now transposed and again occurring without its ending "Wisdom."

In the movement's second section, a melody comprised entirely of major triads is paired with "Ar-Rum" and then "The New Asia," leading to the first statements of "At-Takwir," "Al-Koran," and "Jehad" (Example 7.31). "Ottoman Empire" and "Arab Revolt" then transition to a bold recurrence of "Black and White," now in major triads with octave doublings (Example 7.32). A short codetta brings back Theme #18, concluding emphatically with repeated A major eleventh chords, *ad libitum*.

> *The Arab Revolt tossed up its stormy road from birth, through weakness, pain and doubt, to <u>Red Victory</u>!*[77]

Possibly intended to be paired with Part VI, *Part VII: The Final Stroke: Red Victory* depicts the Arab Revolt's eventual victory in Lawrence's story; its title references the quote above. It introduces new themes related to that topic, including one representing Auda Abu Tayeh, an important figure in the Arab Revolt. Auda Abu Tayeh initially joined Lawrence to take Aqaba but remained an essential part of the revolt until their victory in Damascus.[78] Other new themes include "Red Victory," "Al-Hashr," and "Inshallah." "Inshallah" translates as "If Allah wills it," and its inclusion here might refer to the idea of the revolt's unlikely success. "Al-Hashr" is the 59th Surah of the Qur'an; Schuyler translates its title as "the exile."[79] Here, this theme is paired with "Deraa." Near the end of Lawrence's book, he and his fighters returned to Deraa, which was now crucial for fully defeating the Turkish army. After finding a nearby village ransacked and filled with mutilated bodies, Lawrence and Auda Abu Tayeh ordered their men to take no prisoners; around four thousand Turkish troops were killed, many after the battle had ended.[80] Soon afterward, Lawrence entered Damascus to a celebration of their victory and began setting up a new government.[81]

One of the longest movements, Part VII begins with a section based on "Red Victory" (Example 7.33, page 118), "T. E. Lawrence," "Al-Hashr," "Deraa" (Example 7.34, page 118), "Auda Abu Tai" (Example 7.35, page 118), and "Inshallah" (Example 7.36, page 118). The contrasting middle section repeats several pages of the first movement with the left hand in octaves, recalling the beginning of the conflict as it reaches its close. To end the movement, a shortened version of the initial section returns with the "Red

Example 7.33: *Part VII*, mm. 3-4

Example 7.34: *Part VII*, mm. 32-37

Example 7.35: *Part VII*, mm. 38-40

Example 7.36: *Part VII*, mm. 43-50

Victory" theme.

> *I had dreamed of hustling into form, while I lived, the New Asia which time was inexorably bringing upon us.*[82]

> *The victory at Damascus was the just end to an adventure that had dared so much, but after the victory there came a slow time of disillu-*

sion, and then a night in which the fighting men found that all their hopes had failed them. Now at last, may there have come to them the white peace of the end, in the knowledge that they achieved a deathless thing, a lucent inspiration to the <u>children of the Arab race</u>![83]

Schuyler divides *Epilogue: Disillusion, Death, and the Final Liberty of the Afro-Asian Peoples* into three distinct sections, labeling their topics in the manuscript. The opening "Disillusion" continues seamlessly into "Death of Lawrence," while "Final Liberty" could function musically as its own movement; in fact, Schuyler sometimes performed "Final Liberty" without the rest of the epilogue. In the first two sections, only two new themes are introduced, both relating to Islam. Arabic for God, "Allah" could reference an incident near the end of Lawrence's book in which a mosque's call to prayer particularly affects him. He recounts:

The clamour hushed, as everyone seemed to obey the call to prayer on this their first night of perfect freedom. While my fancy, in the overwhelming pause, showed me my loneliness and lack of reason in their movement: since only for me, of all the hearers, was the event sorrowful and the phrase meaningless.[84]

The 64th Surah of the Qur'an, "Al-Taghabun" translates as "mutual disillusion," according to Schuyler, and most likely refers to Lawrence's disillusionment after the revolt ended.[85] Rather than ending his book with their victory, Lawrence describes finding an abandoned Turkish field hospital containing hundreds of appallingly sick men and rotting dead bodies.[86] The next day, Lawrence encounters a soldier who, upon hearing that Lawrence is in charge, slaps him and calls him a "bloody brute." Lawrence then writes that "in my heart I felt he was right, and that anyone who pushed through to success a rebellion of the weak against their masters must come out of it so stained in estimation that afterward nothing in the world would make him feel clean."[87] Lawrence's disillusion would have continued long afterward, as he was unsuccessful in assisting Feisal's negotiations with the Allies. The British and French ultimately controlled much of the Middle East, and a unified Arab nation was never founded. Britain was given Iraq and Palestine, while France governed Syria. According to Scott Anderson, "Everything T. E. Lawrence had fought for, schemed for, arguably betrayed his country for, turned to ashes in a single five-minute conversation between the prime ministers of Great Britain and

Example 7.37: *Epilogue*, mm. 1-2

Example 7.38: *Epilogue*, mm. 9-10

France."[88]

The epilogue immediately references the "mutual disillusion" of the title with Schuyler's similarly named theme (Example 7.37). "Allah" (Example 7.38) is introduced soon after, and earlier themes like "Al-Baqarah," "Red Victory," "Seven Pillars," and "T. E. Lawrence" recur in the "Disillusion" and "Death of Lawrence" sections of the epilogue. This portion of the epilogue ends dramatically, with accented, accelerating chords culminating in an imperfectly mirrored dissonant harmony (Example 7.39). Under this sustained dissonance, the "Seven Pillars" theme returns in the bass, now slower and again lacking the segment spelling "Wisdom." It seems in Schuyler's mind, wisdom was always absent in Lawrence's tale.

Labeled in the manuscript as the finale of the epilogue, "Final Liberty of the Afro-Asian Peoples" does not include any new themes from Schuyler's list. Instead, eighteen themes return, including "Tafta Hindi," "At-Takwir," "Al-Koran," "Jehad," and "T.E. Lawrence." In perhaps the most obviously major and tonal portion of the work, the finale begins and ends in the surprising key of G-flat major, which does not occur anywhere else in *Seven Pillars*. In fact, the first and last thirty measures are completely new. In the final measures, bright G-flat major chords are cut off by a harsh *fortissimo* harmony, ending the epilogue and the entire work with a shocking dissonance (Example 7.40). While the bulk of the movement depicts Lawrence's dream of freedom for the Arab tribes, the final chord shows its ultimate lack of success.

Example 7.39: *Epilogue*, mm. 99-108

Example 7.40: *Epilogue*, mm. 313-316

In combining Schuyler's Arabic inspired style with a complex, encoded narrative, *Seven Pillars of Wisdom* marks an important evolution in her compositional approach. After testing out her new style in *White Nile Suite*, she had become more confident as a composer, experimenting with a monumental structure that certainly tests an audience's attention span. Although it is impossible to know the direction her compositions may have taken after 1967, Schuyler's use of a musical alphabet, detailed program, and Arabic influences offer an indication of what could have become essential components of her mature compositional style.

Chapter 8
Professional Success and Personal Disillusionment in Cairo:
Nile Fantasy

> Who knows what's going to happen anywhere, from day to day, hour to hour, all is improvised, the result of momentary inspiration. There is no guide, no rule, except that one must trust nobody. There is no principle save that everybody is a traitor, even oneself. One swims between exaltation and malice, as between Scylla and Charibidis. And, as Pascal says, it is when one wants to be an angel that one becomes a beast. INSHALLAH!
> – Letter to Josephine Schuyler, January 22, 1965[1]

After a musically productive 1964, Schuyler's compositional output ground to a halt for much of 1965, due to a series of personal struggles. The previous June, her relationship with Maurice Raymond had ended quite badly. Schuyler had met Raymond in late 1963 in Rome when he rescued her from a mugger. She quickly fell in love, writing effusively to her mother about all his wonderful qualities. Raymond proposed surprisingly soon, and Schuyler seriously considered the offer, consulting the tarot cards and her mother. Less trusting than Schuyler, her mother had Raymond investigated and discovered he had a criminal record. Schuyler tried to end the relationship, but Raymond was able to convince her the inquiry's results were incorrect.

By February 13, 1964, Schuyler found herself on a train to Lyons to meet Raymond's mother. Even after discovering that he had an ex-wife and daughter, she remained convinced of their love, choosing March 29 as their wedding date, after consulting the tarot cards, of course. Raymond seemed to want a quick marriage without any background checks or waiting periods, even causing a scene at the French marriage bureau and insisting they marry in Scotland instead. When they encountered a three-week wait there as well,

Schuyler returned to the United States to prepare for concerts. Raymond wrote her increasingly bizarre letters, wanting to hurry and marry in Iceland or Mexico. When Schuyler's mother suggested that Raymond come to the United States instead, Raymond suddenly seemed to have multiple reasons why it was not possible, ultimately claiming he could not afford the plane ticket. Schuyler decided it might be wise to take a step back, and she stopped answering his letters and phone calls.[2]

Raymond gathered the belongings Schuyler had left in France and shipped them to her friends in Brussels, seeming to indicate the end of the relationship. However, in June, Raymond mailed the Schuylers some shockingly malicious letters and obscene postcards. The postcards included an explicit photo that appeared to be of Schuyler and text claiming she had an abortion. Even more upsettingly, he sent similar cards to friends of hers in Europe, Africa, and America, and even possibly the *New Yorker*. While it was easy to prove Schuyler had not been pregnant, the photos were more difficult to discredit, despite Schuyler's insistence they were fake. After trying futilely to convince the U.S. Postal Office to investigate, Schuyler's mother persuaded the Lyons police to launch an investigation, at which point Raymond promptly fled the country.[3]

Although she managed to pull herself together and complete *Seven Pillars of Wisdom* that winter, Schuyler delayed returning to Europe for several months after the ordeal with Raymond. When she did finally plan European concerts for March 1965, she encountered difficulty obtaining a labor permit. Schuyler's representative in Europe, Miss Jennings, had filed an application with the Incorporated Society of Musicians, but the permit was initially denied.[4] Schuyler's friend Dennis Gray Stoll spent the first two weeks of February attempting to gain support for an appeal, contacting well-known musicians and receiving letters from Aaron Copland, Yohanan Ramati, and others.[5] After a lot of worry, the appeal was ultimately approved, with Schuyler receiving the permit in time for her March trip.[6] Meanwhile, Stoll tried to convince Schuyler to wear "Nefertiti" jewelry and fashion for the performances there in order to play up her African connections; Schuyler was horrified by the idea.[7] Despite their disagreement on this issue, Schuyler's relationship with Stoll remained on good terms, and the London concerts were well-reviewed.[8]

Schuyler's troubles soon returned in April, however, when a French judge determined the Raymond photos were authentic. She struggled to focus at her April 8 performance of *Seven Pillars of Wisdom* at the U.S. Embassy in London, and Stoll noticed her change in demeanor. Schuyler confided in him the entire story, perhaps expecting rejection, but Stoll did not care and expressed deep feelings for her. Caught up in the moment, Schuyler told Stoll she loved him, and soon afterward, he asked his wife for a divorce.[9]

Days later, Schuyler left for Paris, with Stoll writing her an enthusiastic love letter not long after her departure. Addressed to "Sweetest One, My Love," the letter talks of his hope for a divorce and their impending nuptials. Stoll writes:

> As far as I'm concerned I married you there and then during that service while you took communion. Is this blasphemy? I hope not. I don't think God would think so. In my heart and my mind and my soul you are already my wife, I love you so much. I hope you feel the same way about me as a husband! The way you looked at me as your train began to move out of Victoria, I dare to think that perhaps you do. I hope you realise that you are the love of my life.[10]

Despite those sentiments, later letters from Stoll to Schuyler, and from Schuyler to her mother, indicate that Schuyler had not actually accepted a proposal from him at that point. As their correspondences continued, Stoll seemed to make many assumptions despite few replies from Schuyler.[11] Meanwhile, Schuyler reconnected with her longtime friend Georges Apedo-Amah during her Paris visit. Unexpectedly, Apedo-Amah also expressed his love for Schuyler, and they spent the night together. Although Schuyler would not realize it for some time, the night resulted in a pregnancy.[12]

Meanwhile, Stoll continued to pursue a divorce in hopes of marrying Schuyler, but, based on letters to her mother, Schuyler's lack of interest in marrying him caused her to avoid addressing the situation with Stoll. In a letter from April 15, two days after her visit with Apedo-Amah, Schuyler detailed all of Stoll's failings as a composer, conductor, and a man. Her handwriting grew messier and darker as she became increasingly upset, culminating in these frustrated lines about the difficulties associated with being a woman with a career at that time:

> How dreadful life is. I can't have a career without using asinine dopes like Dennis. If I marry him, he's going to shut me up in a box and I can just iron like Mme. Cosi or pick up baby clothes like Lineke. I can't be an independent personality unless I depart from

the conventional image of a respectable woman. How <u>confusing</u> it is. If ONLY I had money, my money. Karl Marx is right. Everything is economics.[13]

Schuyler, seeming to have resigned herself to pacifying Stoll, ended the letter by reassuring her mother that she would "put on some kind of an act, hold some kind of a carrot in front of his nose."[14] A few days later, she returned to England for a performance that Stoll had arranged at the Stroud Subscription Rooms.[15] Before the concert, Schuyler and the Stolls were in a car accident, injuring Schuyler and Stoll's wife. Schuyler's letter to her mother about the incident focused almost entirely on his wife Patricia, particularly on Stoll's lack of concern for her. She told her mother that Stoll had everything she could want in a husband – "high social position, money, contacts" – but that his attitude toward his wife made her question everything: "What makes me cool is seeing how he BLAMES Patsy for EVERYTHING. She's a Leo, her mother's from Texas. Will he someday be similarly insensitive to me?"[16]

Over the following weeks and months, Stoll grew increasingly desperate, pleading with Schuyler to write him back to express her feelings, and he continued to write her mother about their relationship as well.[17] Despite Schuyler's lack of reply, Stoll wrote in June that he was looking for an engagement ring and asked her preferences.[18] As time passed without a response that he considered sufficient, his letters grew a bit less flattering, with criticisms couched in compliments and references to how she could make it up to him when they next met. Before a June trip to Egypt, he wrote:

> You've got Egypt-mania. Well substitute 'Dennis' in your heart for that little word 'Egypt' and maybe if you're very, very good, and sometimes rather naughty in the right sort of way, he'll take you there. Why not put in a little practice on using the right sort of adjectives to your Beloved while he's in the land of the Arabian Nights? Surely your 'regards' should become rather warmer when I'm in that climate?[19]

The same letter managed to pay her work a back-handed compliment, expressing how he preferred her *White Nile Suite* to *Seven Pillars of Wisdom* and criticizing the latter for its length and many climaxes, even suggesting changes she might want to make. Stoll also brought up her idea for a piece based on *Carmilla* (her *Sonata diabolique*), questioning her reliance on narratives and program music. With an arguably passive-aggressive tone disguised as teasing, he wrote:

> Well, my diabolical witch girl, don't go spreading any plagues around New York. Do you realise you write that story as though you sympathised with Carmilla? If you're not careful your priest will start 'exorcising' you. They don't burn them at the stake nowadays.[20]

Throughout July, Stoll continued to write long letters that fluctuated between over-the-top expressions of love and frustration at not receiving the emotional response he wanted in return, complaining that Schuyler's letters "only come alive when you write about work."[21] At some point in August, however, the situation changed for Schuyler, as she realized she was four months pregnant by Georges Apedo-Amah. She flew to Holland and then Denmark by the end of the month, trying to find someone willing to perform an abortion, and her notebooks of sketches and ideas from that time are interspersed with notes on possible abortifacients and doctors.[22] In desperation, Schuyler and her mother apparently came up with a plan to quickly marry Stoll in Mexico, despite his divorce not being finalized. On September 3, Schuyler called Stoll, asking him to fly to Copenhagen to meet her, and, of course, he immediately dropped everything to do so. It is unclear exactly what happened during that visit, but no marriage resulted.[23] Afterward, Stoll wrote Schuyler's mother, blaming Schuyler and citing the "many psychological chips on her shoulder" for the meeting going poorly, revealingly calling her a "little jungle creature peering at me angrily through the undergrowth."[24] Schuyler described entirely different issues to her mother, including conflicting opinions on religion and politics, but she continued hoping for his Mexican divorce and their subsequent marriage.[25]

A few days later, Schuyler flew to New York and obtained the name of someone in California who could refer her to a doctor in Mexico willing to perform an abortion at five months. The next week, she flew to California and walked alone across the Mexican border to Tijuana. Someone met her there and drove her to a clinic where a two-stage operation was performed. Schuyler kept a detailed journal of the experience, describing the terrifying conditions and incredible pain; despite the ordeal, she also wrote that she dreaded leaving and facing her life again.[26]

The traumatic and life-changing experience, coupled with the loss of her primary motivation for marrying him, left Schuyler less inclined to maintain a personal relationship with Stoll. On October 29, she wrote him to end things, with Stoll responding by severing their professional relationship as well:

> Well, your missive of Oct. 29th has come, shattering in three machine-gunned sentences a big part of my personal future…Well, it's your decision. I am dismissed…I shall miss the friendship which you value so little that you can just cast it off in the course of a couple of lines. It's been nice to know you, if only in passing.[27]

He indicated he would fulfill his current professional commitments to her, including publicizing and conducting the premiere of her piano concerto *Nile Fantasy* in Cairo, but afterward, understandably, she would need to hire someone else to manage her British concerts.[28]

By *Nile Fantasy*'s December 10 premiere, in which Stoll conducted and Schuyler performed, tension between them reached its peak. Aside from a few terse exchanges in which Stoll took offense at Schuyler's "abusive" and "rude" tone, they seem to have communicated very little leading up to their arrival in Cairo.[29] Once there, Schuyler claimed in a letter to her mother that Stoll knelt before her to beg that she take him back, but Stoll's correspondences from around the same time give no indication of reconsidering their break.[30] Regardless, they spent weeks preparing for the premieres of his *Concerto Arabo* and her *Nile Fantasy*, rehearsing with the Cairo Symphony Orchestra. When talking about the premiere later, Schuyler praised its multiracial makeup, noting that in addition to Egyptian musicians, the orchestra included Czech, Bulgarian, Romanian, Yugoslavian, Lebanese, Greek, Italian, and Spanish musicians.[31] Privately, Schuyler grew frustrated with the rehearsal experience. Perhaps trying to justify her decision to end their relationship, Schuyler railed against Stoll in a letter to her mother about the premiere:

> He looked SO MUCH BETTER while Patsy was with him. His weaknesses are frightfully exposed without her. He looks like he's about to fall to pieces now. With her at a party before, when he wore his wonderful grin – they seemed a charming couple. But under that bright Egyptian sky, with him looking so peaked, petulant and pe-

culiar, grey and worn, decayed and overgrown – he was shockingly different. If only some of these egomaniac men would realize how infinitely their wives help their image. He has NO image without Patsy. Without her, he's just a bloated, garrulous, arrogant old fool. With her, he's passable. I wondered if he would collapse in Egypt![32]

She went on to criticize Stoll for only speaking English, which meant that Schuyler had to translate all his directions into French and Italian for the orchestra. She also rather cruelly disparaged him for sitting while conducting, which would have been due to his contracting polio as an adult.[33]

Despite all their drama and conflict, Stoll and Schuyler ultimately were quite successful in premiering their piano concertos in Cairo, although Schuyler's *Nile Fantasy* seems to have been better received, at least according to her.[34] The premiere was broadcast across the Middle East by Voice of America, and the premiere's recording still exists today in the Schuyler Family Audio collection.[35] The *Washington Afro-American* published a translation of Antoine Gennaoui's review from the *Egyptian Journal*, which described the reaction to the work as follows:

> This very interesting work revealed daring treatment of harmony put into effect with beautiful technical facility. The themes were brought out with expressive accentuation and melodic chromaticism. There was a leaning towards atonalism to which the audience, though not quite used to this type of thing, reacted receptively with restraint. There were, nevertheless, in this musical poem, moments where a dash of romanticism created passages of a transcendent beauty in contrast with unusual melodic effects.[36]

A review in the *West London Observer* focused more on Stoll's own concerto but mentioned that the author heard that Schuyler's concerto "also aroused great interest."[37] Surprisingly, Schuyler and Stoll continued to communicate after the premiere. By January, Stoll seemed to be recovering emotionally, with his letters becoming friendlier.[38] He wrote Schuyler multiple times in 1966, expressing his concern over the dangerous places she was traveling and stating his hope that they were still good friends, but they never saw one another in person again.[39]

In a 1966 lecture, Schuyler discussed the genesis of her piano concerto, explaining that she had been commissioned eight years earlier by the Egyptian government to compose an orchestral piece with "Afro-Arab" themes. Despite hearing Egyptian music on her travels and being supplied with tapes of it, she was initially unsure of how to begin. According to Schuyler, she needed the "spirit" and had not found it yet, but then, in 1964, the "spirit" suddenly came to her, resulting in the new "Afro-Arab" idiom she used in writing *White Nile Suite* and *Seven Pillars of Wisdom*.[40] Schuyler claimed the inspiration for *Nile Fantasy* developed slowly, when, in reality, she orchestrated, adapted, and combined parts of *White Nile Suite* and *Seven Pillars of Wisdom* to create the piano concerto. Some sections and even entire movements were incorporated nearly exactly as their original versions, while other portions were drastically reworked.[41]

Schuyler appears to have procrastinated composing *Nile Fantasy* until surprisingly close to its premiere, probably because of the challenges in her personal life. In a sketch from early fall, she designed a version with a prologue and four movements that would combine sections of *White Nile Suite* and *Seven Pillars of Wisdom*. In its margins, Schuyler scribbled a dosage for Ergotrate, which she might have been using as either an abortifacient or treatment for post-abortion hemorrhaging, indicating the sketch was likely written in September 1965. In this preliminary version, she planned for the prologue to primarily follow the prologue from *Seven Pillars*. The first movement would then correspond to part of *Port Said*, while the second movement would largely pull from *Alexandria*. She debated basing the third movement on *Legend of the Mahdi* or *Fortune Favored the Bold Player*, and she planned for the fourth movement to combine sections of *Red Victory*, *Blood*, *Fortune Favored the Bold Player*, and *Fall of Babylon*, with notes on how various phrases would be altered.[42] Her overall plan for the narrative reads:

> Enslavement
> The Stirrings of Revolt
> The Beginning of the New Era
> Meditation on the Past
> Fortune Favored the Bold Player (Red Victory)
> Triumph[43]

By the final version of *Nile Fantasy*, Schuyler had winnowed the material down to four movements, incorporating many of the ideas from her sketch. Programs from the concerto's 1966 performances listed it alternatively as *Le Nil* or *Nile Fantasy*, with the movements initially being labeled by their tempo markings rather than Schuyler's descriptive titles.[44] Later programs updated the movement titles to: *Oppression*; *The Will of Allah*; *Despair*; and *Victory*, while Schuyler labeled the movements in the score as: *The Rebellion*; *Inshallah*; *The Terror*; and *The Road to Victory*.[45] For clarity, the score's movement titles will be used here.

In her programs, Schuyler kept the narrative vague, simply stating that the concerto was based on folk music from the four countries – Uganda, Ethiopia, Sudan, and Egypt - through which the Nile River flowed.[46] In a 1966 lecture, however, she went into more detail, describing the concerto's four movements as representing the four stages of the "Arab surge toward independence," with *The Rebellion* depicting the initial rebellion against the Ottoman Empire. *Inshallah* portrays "the will of Allah," and *The Terror* relates how tyrants oppressed the people even more after the rebellion. In *The Road to Victory*, the concerto ends with the people's independence.[47]

Strangely, at some point Schuyler tried to rebrand the movements, although she does not appear to have changed their musical content. An undated publicity sheet for the concerto titled the work "Nile Fantasia: A Four Stanza Musical Poem Illustrating Recent African History," reiterating the program note's description of each movement representing a country through which the Nile flows. The explanation diverged significantly, however, in discussing the individual movements:

> Movement I...THE REBELLION...based on authentic themes of folk music inspired by Joseph Kyagambiddwa's 'Music at the Source of the Nile' while historically depicting the Rebellion against the KABAKA.
> Movement II...INSHALLAH...(fate)...based on Ethiopian folk music.
> Movement III...THE TERROR...The flight of the Christian Sudanese...based on Sudanese themes gathered during five trips to the Sudan.
> Movement IV...THE ROAD TO VICTORY...The Saga of the Aswan Dam, whose completion means a new era for Africa. Ancient Egyptian themes are used with modern instrumentation depicting the mingling of the past and the present to march into the future. The project has had international cooperation to pre-

serve the ancient temples while altering the age-old course of the Nile River.[48]

Assuming the musical content remained the same, the description of the first movement seems especially odd; based almost entirely on the prologue from *Seven Pillars of Wisdom*, the movement has little connection musically to Uganda or Kyagambiddwa's book. As discussed in Chapter 7, its themes spell out the names of people, places, and ideas from T.E. Lawrence's book. The other three movements potentially match their new descriptions better, but it remains unclear why Schuyler wanted to change the concerto's plot so drastically. It is possible she wanted to make it more marketable by connecting it to contemporary events like the 1960s construction of the Aswan Dam.

Regardless of the exact narrative Schuyler added, *Nile Fantasy* remains an oddity among her compositions because of the extent to which she reused previous works and her repurposing of those pieces' plots. Her original plan for the work did not describe a detailed story or characters. She alluded to the Ottoman Empire that featured so prominently in *Seven Pillars of Wisdom*, but otherwise avoided references to specific time periods, the identity of the oppressive tyrants, or which country was gaining independence. With a few important exceptions, her recycling of movements from *White Nile Suite* and *Seven Pillars of Wisdom* was very straightforward, piecing together orchestrated sections of each. Along the way, she added expressive, tempo, and dynamic markings. Where the original works had few expressive indications, *Nile Fantasy* includes instructions constantly, often making explicit aspects of interpretation that were previously only implied. Schuyler also rewrites some of the rhythms and key signatures to make the notation easier for a performer to read. Most of Schuyler's surviving manuscripts had not yet been prepared for publication, so they only included expressive markings and dynamics where Schuyler needed a reminder or thought it was especially important. In creating a *Nile Fantasy* score from which others would conduct and perform, Schuyler explained every detail, leaving much less room for the performer's own ideas.[49]

The Rebellion opens with a brief introduction for the entire orchestra and solo piano, based on the opening of *Fire and Reason*, from *Seven Pillars of Wisdom*. A piano cadenza follows, beginning with a tone cluster played with both forearms. The cadenza then reworks thirty measures from the middle of the *Prologue* from *Seven Pillars*, now written in duple but otherwise nearly identical. After a brief measure of rest, a transposed version of the "Seven Pillars" musical theme enters, with the rhythm altered to write out the original version's *rubato*. From that point on, *The Rebellion* simply orchestrates the entire *Prologue* from *Seven Pillars*. Schuyler seems to have taken the opportunity to write out every detail of how she performed the movement in *Seven Pillars*, updating how some rhythms were notated and adding in a few dramatic pauses. Aside from those small alterations, the remainder of the movement matches *Seven Pillars' Prologue* exactly.

With *Inshallah*, Schuyler combines material from *White Nile Suite*'s *Alexandria* and *Fall of Babylon*, much more significantly modified than the first movement's source material. Marked to begin *Andante lirico*, the second movement opens with melodies drawn from *Fall of Babylon*. Originally quick and lively, the phrases now proceed at a much slower tempo, indicated to be played expressively and freely, thus changing their original meaning and emotional effect. The melody begins in the piano but soon moves to other instruments, although the orchestration remains relatively sparse throughout the movement. As this opening section progresses, the phrases begin to be introduced in counterpoint, with their original order changed. After a long pause, several measures of figuration based on the movement's first measure lead into a statement of *Alexandria*'s primary theme, which was likely based on the First Delphic Hymn, as previously discussed in Chapter 5. Ninety measures of *Alexandria* follow, arranged almost entirely for woodwinds and piano. Just before reaching *Alexandria*'s ending phrase, melodies from *Fall of Babylon* begin to reappear, transposed and increasingly altered. When those melodies have become almost unrecognizable, the movement's opening theme returns, now low in the piano with ghostly *pianissimo* trills in the treble. As the piano holds its final chord, the woodwinds add their voices to the harmony one by one, sustained as the sound slowly dies away.

The most straightforward of the concerto's movements, *The Terror* corresponds exactly to *The Agonies, the Terrors, and the Mistakes* (from *Seven Pillars of Wisdom*), with only a few updates. Schuyler adds new expressive and tempo markings, explaining aspects of interpretation that she originally left to the performer. A few rhythms are altered, and repetitions are frequently left out, shortening the movement somewhat. Otherwise, *The Terror* is simply an orchestrated version of *The Agonies, the Terrors, and the Mistakes*. In preparing for the concerto's premiere, Stoll took issue with *The Terror*'s slow, deliberate tempo, which he felt was impossible for wind instruments to sustain.⁵⁰ However, it seems Schuyler won that argument, as both the score and the premiere's recording reflect her original tempo.⁵¹

In *The Road to Victory*, Schuyler creates more elaborate and fully developed combinations of material from both *White Nile Suite* and *Seven Pillars of Wisdom*. The movement's opening section is almost entirely new, with only brief instances of connections to previous works. Its orchestral introduction recalls the key of *Fire and Reason* but otherwise features new material. A version of a syncopated theme from *The Evil of My Tale* appears, followed by another new melody. Then, a recurring segment based on *Fall of Babylon*'s introduction enters, and this phrase returns to delineate sections throughout the movement. Here, it alternates with a melody using only the rhythm of *Fall of Babylon*'s primary theme.

The section which follows is more faithfully based on reused material, beginning with the primary theme's section of *Fall of Babylon*, with the omission of a few repetitions. That segment leads directly into the opening theme of *Fortune Favored the Bold Player*, with its sprightly, disjunct melody and repeating bass pattern. Another phrase from *Fall of Babylon* follows; it is interesting to note that Schuyler reverses the original order here, as this phrase preceded the previous portion in the original movement. Next, *Fortune Favored the Bold Player*'s disjointed theme returns, now in its later form. After a long pause, the recitative-like theme from the middle of *Blood* (from *Seven Pillars*) disrupts the movement's momentum. Unlike the original version, Schuyler now tries to write out the freeness of the rhythms, rather than leaving it up to the performer to interpret. The tempo then resumes, as the second phrase of *Fortune Favored the Bold Player* enters, with repeated measures omitted. This section culminates with an ominous version of the conclusion of that segment of *Fortune Favored the Bold Player*, with a significantly altered ending designed to better transition into the next portion of the movement.

The subsequent section of *The Road to Victory* begins much like the primary theme in *Fall of Babylon*, but soon diverges with a written-out version of the improvisatory section from that same movement. In a sudden shift, another short phrase based on *Fall of Babylon*'s introduction enters with a shockingly sudden forte and returns to that movement's tempo. The segment of *Fall of Babylon* that featured so prominently in *Inshallah* returns here, transposed, but at its original quick tempo, while repetitive descending figuration builds into the piano's cadenza. As expected, the cadenza highlights the pianist's skills with virtuosic gestures and returning motives, ending by recalling *Fall of Babylon*. As the orchestra reenters, a large section based on a later portion of *Fall of Babylon* begins. Some parts of this section are written enharmonically to be more easily read, a few trills are written out to better emphasize the melody notes, and the number of repeated measures is reduced, but, otherwise, this section proceeds quite similarly to its original version.

After a measure of rest, the movement's final section begins with a segment from the finale of *Seven Pillars of Wisdom*'s *Epilogue*, followed by the unused parts remaining from *Fortune Favored the Bold Player*. As the momentum starts to build, the last few measures of that segment are transposed and united with the treble pattern from the ending of *Fortune Favored*. The chordal melody from the finale of *Seven Pillars of Wisdom*'s *Epilogue* is then combined with the same treble pattern, until the remainder of the *Epilogue* continues almost exactly as in *Seven Pillars*. Only the ending rhythms differ, with chords now played twice as fast, making the two-octave leaps even more challenging to play. After triumphant major chords, Schuyler once again punctuates the movement with the same incredibly dissonant harmony that concluded *Seven Pillars of Wisdom*.

Despite its initial success, *Nile Fantasy* has rarely been performed in its original concerto form since its premiere. The expense and difficulty of arranging for an orchestral performance meant that Schuyler typically programmed the work as a piano transcription, often as an alternative to *White Nile Suite* and *Seven Pillars of Wisdom*.[52] That transcription is now lost, but it can be rather easily reconstructed by using the original versions of her recycled material as a model.

The orchestral version did receive one final performance posthumously at Schuyler's 1967 Town Hall memorial. Conducted by Leonard de Paur with Armenta Adams at the piano, the performance seems to have included only three of the movements, listed in the program as: "1. Inshallah or Fate... Contemplation and Submission; 2. Violence and Terror; 3. The Long Road to Peace."[53]

There have been no documented performances since, and the poorly aging recording of the Cairo premiere appears to be the only recorded copy in existence. The handwritten orchestral score, along with multiple copies of the individual instrument parts, remains archived in the Schuyler Family Papers, awaiting an ambitious conductor.

Chapter 9
Composing Africa's Independence

> What is the future of Africa? A big question mark, as far as I can see.
> – Letter to Josephine Schuyler, January 22, 1965[1]

For some time, Schuyler's *Nile Fantasy* has been considered her last surviving musical score completed before her death; however, a recent discovery in her archived papers challenges that assumption. Inspired by the story of African decolonization, this untitled composition narrates events which Schuyler witnessed and reported firsthand from Africa in the 1960s.[2] To understand how such a composition was overlooked thus far, it is important to consider the extent and content of Schuyler's archived papers.

With her mind constantly working, Schuyler churned out ideas for new pieces and article topics at a breakneck pace. Her mother apparently saved everything from letters and notebooks to music and stray scraps of paper. Today, Schuyler's archived papers fill approximately fifty boxes, with each containing multiple folders of material. While a catalog exists, it tends to be very general, and, in my own research, it quickly became clear a search through all the boxes was necessary to ensure nothing was overlooked.

My parents traveled with me from South Carolina for my last visit to the archive, and they helped sort through the remaining boxes I had not been able to fully examine during previous visits. We encountered a fascinating array of letters, poems, programs, contracts, musical scores, and other ephemera, all with sketches and musical fragments scattered in seemingly random folders. Multiple ideas appear to have gone unused, including folk songs from Madagascar and Ethiopia, themes spelling the names of Paul Wellensky and Sir Richard Francis Burton, and many more.[3] One particularly interesting sketch spelled out themes named for Schuyler herself, as well as her alternate persona Felipa Monterro, her mother, the seasons, and various men Schuyler knew; there was also a 1964 letter to her mother which pitched an idea for a piece about the Tomb of the Holy Sepulchre in Jerusalem.[4]

While looking through a notebook ostensibly containing the piano solo part for *Nile Fantasy*, my mother found an untitled and previously unknown piece, shown to be complete thanks to Schuyler's characteristic "FIN" at the ending bar line. The notebook begins with a sketch of the expected piano part for *Nile Fantasy*, although the movements are out of order, with part of Debussy's *Toccata* tucked amid them. This newly discovered work follows the sketch, with a list of named musical themes included. After a mostly blank page with the title "II: Uganda Martyrs," the remainder of the notebook is filled with Schuyler's handwritten copies of other composers' music she was practicing. Given its location, this untitled piece must have been written after or during the composition of *Nile Fantasy*, in late 1965 or 1966. It seems Schuyler never performed it, as its musical content rules out the possibility of this being her missing score *Rhapsodie togolaise*, which premiered in 1966. The page after it, labeled "II: Uganda Martyrs," implies this was the first movement in a planned multi-movement work that might have included her earlier *Uganda Martyrs*.[5]

Schuyler's list of musical themes included with the score help illuminate the work's topic while raising questions about the exact details of her narrative. The themes in the list's order are: Cannibal; Negritude; Osagyefo; Kenya; Tanganyika; Tanzania; Zimbabwe; Ruwenzori; Usumbura; Kwame Nkrumah; Oginga Odinga; Jomo Kenyatta; Moise Tshombe; Seretse Khama; Bechuanaland; and Kyagambiddwa. A comparison to Schuyler's musical alphabet used in *Seven Pillars of Wisdom* reveals that she spelled each name using that same alphabet, resulting in disjunct, dissonant themes.[6]

Most of Schuyler's themes relate directly to events occurring in Africa during decolonization in the 1960s. Ghana was the first African country to gain independence in March 1957. Instrumental in the fight for independence, Kwame Nkrumah first served as Ghana's prime minister, then as president in 1960. His supporters called him "Osagyefo," or "Redeemer," because of his work in gaining Ghana's independence and leading the new country while promoting African unity. Nkrumah worked tirelessly to create a united Africa, facilitating a series of conferences that led to the 1963 founding of the Organization of African Unity (OAU). His personal ambition, however, led other African countries to become suspicious of his motives, concerned that Nkrumah wanted to be sole leader of this future united Africa. He created a Bureau of African Affairs to investigate and subvert other African nations which were viewed as being too close to colonial powers; by

1960, over one hundred agents were working all over Africa.⁷ As Nkrumah became increasingly authoritarian, he was awarded the Lenin Peace Prize in 1962.⁸ Two years later, he decided to make Ghana a one-party state, holding a rigged election to guarantee the measure would be approved. Changes to the constitution allowed the president to serve for life and to dismiss Ghana's Supreme Court. Meanwhile, his economic policies proved disastrous for Ghana's economy, increasing the country's debts to $112 million short-term and $423 million medium-term debts (in U.S. dollars) by 1966. Around the time Schuyler was writing her composition, Nkrumah left Ghana for a state visit to China in early 1966, but, during his absence, the military carried out a coup and seized power.⁹ Nkrumah never returned to Ghana, dying of cancer in Guinea in 1972.¹⁰ Schuyler had met Nkrumah when she performed for Ghana's 1960 Independence Day celebration, and he subsequently wrote her a lengthy letter expressing offense over her characterizations of Patrice Lumumba and Moïse Tshombe, along with Ghana's politics, in her book *Who Killed the Congo?*.¹¹

Moïse Tshombe led Katanga's secession from the Congo mere weeks after its independence in 1960; Schuyler reported on the events and their aftermath.¹² After much bloodshed, the United Nations intervened in early 1963, using military action to end the secession. Tshombe was exiled to Spain while the Congo continued to destabilize. The following year, Tshombe was brought back from his exile and installed as Prime Minister through the intervention of Belgium and the United States, who considered him friendlier to the West.¹³

Tanganyika gained independence from Britain in December 1961, soon creating a one-party state led by Julius Nyerere. Tanganyika joined with Zanzibar in 1964 to form the United Republic of Tanganyika and Zanzibar, with its name changed to the United Republic of Tanzania the following year.¹⁴ A few months after Tanganyika's independence, Rwanda and Burundi separated and followed suit in 1962.¹⁵ Usumbura had been the capital of Ruanda-Urundi, but after the new nation of Burundi was established, Usumbura's name was changed to Bujumbura. Today, Bujumbura is the economic capital of Burundi, while Gitega serves as the political capital.

Unlike the other nations in Schuyler's list, Zimbabwe did not become independent until 1980. The Zimbabwe African People's Union (ZAPU) was founded as an opposition political party to Southern Rhodesia's white government in 1961, but after only three years, the party was banned. The organization moved its base of operations to Tanzania and later to Zambia, aided first by the People's Republic of China and then the Soviet Union. In 1967, ZAPU and its offshoots began guerrilla warfare which continued long after Schuyler's lifetime, until Zimbabwe's independence.[16]

Ruwenzori is a mountain range located on the border between Uganda and the Democratic Republic of the Congo. Sometimes referred to as the Mountains of the Moon, the Ruwenzori range was home to the kingdom of Toro, which Schuyler visited during her 1960 concert tour.[17] After Uganda became independent in 1962, the Rwenzururu Movement began to fight, first for equality for the Bakonzo and Baamba ethnic groups and later for the Rwenzururu kingdom to secede from Uganda. Based in the Ruwenzori mountains, the violence peaked in 1963 and 1964, but protests continued until the kingdom was given autonomy in a 1982 settlement. Afterward, not everyone involved accepted the terms of the settlement, and conflict persisted until the Ugandan government officially recognized the kingdom in 2008.[18]

Kenya gained independence in December 1963, with Jomo Kenyatta initially serving as prime minister after leading independence efforts. One year later, Kenya became a one-party state with Kenyatta as president. Oginga Odinga served as Kenyatta's vice president from 1964 to 1966, during which time he often disagreed with Kenyatta's policies. Odinga tended to lean toward Communist or Marxist ideas, and tension between the two men grew during Odinga's vice presidency, until he resigned in 1966 and created an opposing political party, the Kenya People's Union (KPU).[19]

Seretse Khama was the first president of Botswana, formerly Bechuanaland, which gained independence in September 1966. As the son of the chief of the Bamangwato people, Khama became *kgosi*, or king, at age 4, with his uncle serving as regent. While studying at Oxford, Khama met Ruth Williams in 1947, marrying her a year later. Their interracial marriage angered the tribal elders, who believed that as *kgosi*, Khama should have married one of their people. Upon returning to his home country, Khama and his wife were able to eventually repair relations with the tribal elders, with Ruth Williams Khama becoming well-liked by the populace. Neighboring South Africa, however, was extremely alarmed by the interracial couple ruling Bechuanaland. Under apartheid, interracial marriage was outlawed in South Africa, and the South African government began pressuring the United Kingdom to remove Khama from his role as *kgosi*. In 1951, Khama and his wife were exiled in what became a very controversial decision in Britain and Bechuanaland. Five years later, they were allowed to return home on the condition that Khama renounce his throne. He became involved in the push for independence, which was ultimately successful in 1966, with Khama serving as the country's first president.[20] The absence of the new nation's name Botswana in Schuyler's list suggests she completed this piece before independence occurred. Without her program notes or any further description, Schuyler's specific narrative remains opaque, but Khama's interracial marriage surely resonated personally with her.

Among Schuyler's list of themes, the only ones not obviously related to the fight for independence in Africa are "Negritude," "Cannibal," and "Kyagambiddwa." <u>Négritude</u> began as a literary movement among French-speaking African and Caribbean intellectuals in the 1930s, with one of its most important figures being poet Léopold Senghor, who was also Senegal's president from 1960 to 1980. Négritude aimed to develop a uniquely African identity based in valuing traditional African culture and arts as part of decolonization. Over time, it became not only an artistic movement but a cultural one, focused on combatting colonialism and racism.[21] The meaning of Schuyler's "Cannibal" theme, on the other hand, is a bit difficult to determine, but, while writing for ultraconservative publications, Schuyler tended to breathlessly tell stories of horrific violence in Africa. Often, she had observed the events herself, or had evidence, but she sometimes also repeated stories relayed to her, including accusations of cannibalism in the early years of the Angolan war for independence.[22] Of course, the meaning of "Kyagambiddwa" is more easily discerned since Joseph Kyagambiddwa composed the *Uganda Martyrs African Oratorio* which served as the basis for Schuyler's *Uganda Martyrs*.[23]

Less than half of the themes in Schuyler's list appear in this work, lending credence to the idea that she intended it to be the first movement in a multi-movement work. The piece's odd ending, very uncharacteristic for Schuyler, further supports that conclusion, as it seems something more should follow. Of the listed themes, only the following are used: Cannibal; Negritude; Tanganyika; Tanzania; Zimbabwe; Usumbura; and Kwame Nkrumah, most of which are based upon events earlier in the 1960s. The omission of Nkrumah's later moniker provides additional evidence that this was planned as the first movement in a larger composition telling a longer story. Sparse textures and simple repetitive accompaniment patterns highlight the musical themes, making them easier to recognize as Schuyler's narrative progresses.[24]

Interestingly, Schuyler's named themes only comprise a portion of the movement's melodies. Although Schuyler's "Kyagambiddwa" theme is ab-

Example 9.1: *Untitled*, mm. 1-2

Example 9.2: *Untitled*, mm. 43-44

Example 9.3: *Untitled*, mm. 47-49

sent, the remainder of the piece is based on segments of Kyagambiddwa's *Uganda Martyrs African Oratorio*, as shown in more detail in Appendix B. In fact, the opening section of the piece is entirely based on phrases from the oratorio. After a short yet very dissonant introduction (Example 9.1) that recurs at structurally important points later in the work, Schuyler begins by recalling phrases from the oratorio's opening movement that declare the texts "Our Father who art in heaven" and "All you my many brethren." A short phrase then repeats "We desire to be like you in bravery," after which Schuyler references heaven through melodies singing "Our Father who art in heaven" and "in the courtyard of that Father of ours." Unlike those in Schuyler's *Uganda Martyrs*, none of the phrases drawn from Kyagambiddwa's oratorio reference anything specific about the historical Uganda martyrs, implying that Schuyler is telling the story of a different group of martyrs.[25]

In the short section that follows, all the melodic material is based on four themes from Schuyler's list: "Cannibal" (Example 9.2), "Négritude"

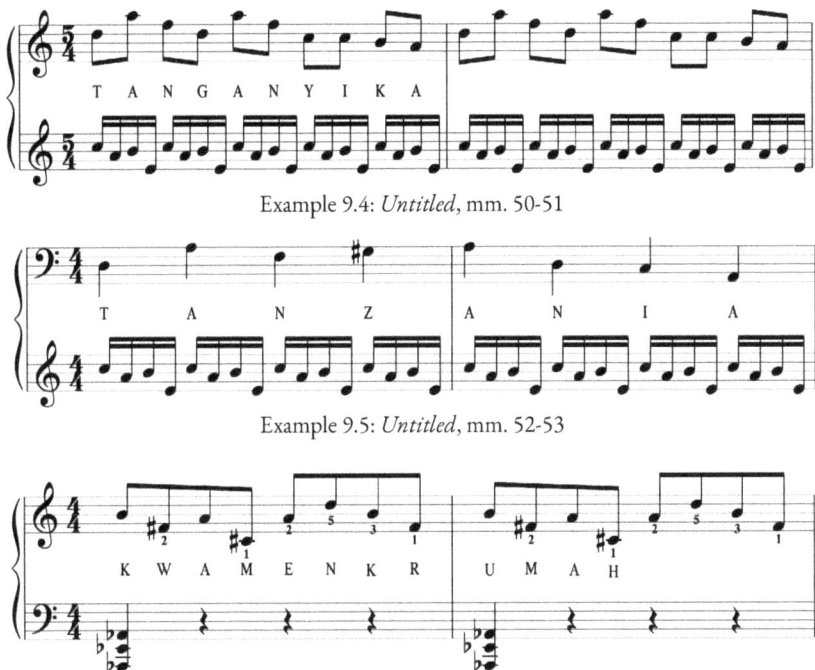

Example 9.4: *Untitled*, mm. 50-51

Example 9.5: *Untitled*, mm. 52-53

Example 9.6: *Untitled*, mm. 79-80

(Example 9.3), "Tanganyika" (Example 9.4), and "Tanzania" (Example 9.5). After those themes occur on their own, material from Kyagambiddwa's oratorio enters, slowly becoming intermingled with more of Schuyler's named themes. First, the brief introduction recurs, after which the melody sings the words of Jesus from Movement 2 while the introduction's bass harmony punctuates each downbeat. Their text reads: "In the name of the Father, and of the Son, and of the Holy Ghost; Go and teach all nations," "For I am departing, and saying goodbye, to return from whence I came," and "This Gospel of Peace." After several repetitions of these phrases, Schuyler's themes "Kwame Nkrumah" (Example 9.6), "Usumbura" (Example 9.7, page 142), and "Zimbabwe" (Example 9.8, page 142) enter, with the same simple accompaniment in the bass. As that pattern's rhythm grows faster, phrases from the oratorio appear in powerful treble chords, calling out the words: "Once upon a time;" "In the name of the Father, and of the Son;" and "Who are today great in heaven."[26]

Suddenly, the bass accompaniment disappears, as Schuyler's solitary theme "Négritude" repeats in a single line. An altered version of "Canni-

Example 9.7: *Untitled*, mm. 81-82

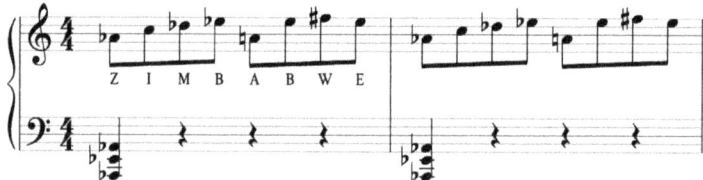

Example 9.8: *Untitled*, mm. 83-84

bal" returns, leading to more phrases drawn from Kyagambiddwa's oratorio, again focusing on the idea of heaven. A version of the introduction with thicker textures interrupts, until "And of the Holy Ghost" and "Go and teach all nations" reappear to end this section.

Without any pause, a new syncopated theme enters; interestingly, Schuyler draws not from Kyagambiddwa's oratorio or her own list, but instead recalls a short phrase from the middle of *The Evil of My Tale* (from *Seven Pillars of Wisdom*). That theme leads to new phrases from the oratorio, now celebrating the martyrs and repeating "Hallelujah, hallelujah, to the striplings resplendent with grace!" until an ominous version of "Cannibal" appears amid them.[27]

Transitioning into the work's last section, a simple chorale suddenly takes over with a phrase from the final movement of Kyagambiddwa's oratorio: "Now you are in heaven with God." "Tanganyika" and "Tanzania" briefly return, but the bulk of this section is devoted to a chorale setting of the entire twenty-second movement of the oratorio. Its text reads:

> Oh Martyrs of Jesus sitting by Him
> Our Brothers; pray for us.
> Celebrated and blessed heroes,
> Now you are in heaven with God. Pray for us.
> Oh Brothers! We pray you for strength: pray for us.
> We desire to be like you in bravery here. Pray for us.[28]

Rather than ending at that point, Schuyler brings back the introduction, now without its original dissonance, as the bass's A-flat and E-flat are transformed into A-natural and E-natural. Finally, "Négritude" repeats three times, alone and quietly trailing off in a mysteriously open-ended conclusion.

Based on her named musical themes, Schuyler was clearly trying to tell a story about African nations fighting for and gaining independence in the 1960s, but who did she believe were the martyrs in this scenario? Because Schuyler did not leave behind additional notes on this piece, any definitive answers may be lost to history. Her own views on Communism and Africa could often seem contradictory, with her published writings tending to be stridently anti-Communist, and her personal letters at times reinforcing those beliefs. However, the most extreme anti-Communist sentiments more often appear in her mother's letters to her.[29] Schuyler's own personal views seem to have been more nuanced, evolving as she gained life experience. While she complained to her mother when various love interests expressed sentiments she viewed as "red,"[30] she also began to see the benefits of socialized medicine, writing in 1964:

> They have quasi-socialized medicine in France now - so if I marry Maurice - and I ever get sick it will all be paid for by the state. Now I approve highly of that. Medicine should be socialized - for it's a public service. The result of socialized medicine is a healthy populace like you have in Denmark and Sweden.[31]

She seemed to passionately support the cause of nations trying to gain independence in Africa, speaking often on the topic in interviews and lectures.[32] At the same time, she did not hesitate to report on the violence and atrocities committed in areas like the Congo and Angola even when it was perpetuated by the side seeking freedom. Schuyler also worried about the influence of Communism in Africa, which she believed was growing because of racism in the United States. In a 1966 interview, she explained her views on the topic:

> How do we win supporters in Africa and Asia? By showing them friendship. Why did Dr. Kwame Nkrumah of Ghana go Communist? He encountered nothing but racial prejudice while he was a

student in the United States.[33]

While it is possible the martyrs in this piece were the people she felt were taken advantage of by their leaders' Communist beliefs, it seems more likely Schuyler intended the martyrs to represent those who died during the 1960s fights for independence. Her juxtaposition of the themes for "Cannibal" and "Négritude" calls to mind the contradiction between her support of the cause of independence and her opposition to the related violence, particularly against civilians.

As seen in *Seven Pillars of Wisdom*, the topic of horrible acts committed in the pursuit of freedom preoccupied Schuyler in the final years of her life. This work appears to be the first movement of a composition intended to not only tell the story of the fight for a free Africa, but also to honor those who died in the process.

Epilogue

> Every story must have a trick ending - a sudden surprise.
> – Schuyler's 1955 practice notes[1]

Schuyler followed up the triumphant Cairo performance of *Nile Fantasy* with a particularly dangerous African tour in early 1966, during which she premiered her *Rhapsodie togolaise* in Togo.[2] It was her last completed composition to have been performed publicly, but, unfortunately, its score is now lost.

By summer, her attention turned to a series of concerts in Asia during which the U.S. Ambassador to South Vietnam, Henry Cabot Lodge, invited her to visit Vietnam. While it remains unclear if a performance was initially planned, an August letter from Schuyler's mother mentions having sent two programs to Ambassador Lodge's cultural attaché, so "they must know that you can play if they want you to. But of course, they are running a war so maybe this won't make much impression. But try to play for the soldiers."[3] A few days later, Schuyler confirmed that she had arranged a concert at the Saigon Conservatory, to follow a tour of the Philippines.[4] Arriving in Vietnam on September 2, she quickly became fascinated by the situation there. After only ten days, Schuyler had already traveled all over Saigon, investigating as much as possible; her fluency in French, along with her Catholic faith and the ability to disguise herself as Vietnamese, proved extremely helpful.[5] She wrote her mother:

> Greetings from Saigon. I was here throughout all the pre-election and election violence. I visited 8 of the voting places on election day, and watched the people vote...I have been everywhere – orphanages, military hospitals, asylums, to see doctors, social workers, military leaders. What an involved situation. Corruption plus idealism plus brutality plus deceit plus incompetence, plus everything else con-

fusing...I run around here in Vietnam digging up hidden facts like a little pig digging up roots.[6]

The next evening, she visited African American soldiers in the Viet Cong area, and then she spent a day touring Long-Xuyen Province by jeep, canoe, and pedi-cart with "seats small enough to accommodate fairies."[7] In a letter home, she excitedly wrote, "My luck, she is running very good!...Boy, have I found out lots here! Especially the things I wasn't supposed to!"[8]

Meanwhile, she found that the American military was not particularly receptive to her presence. She told her mother about a "CIA lady" who was watching her and trying to keep her "under wraps," while an official from the Joint United States Public Affairs Office (JUSPAO) asked her "Why don't you stay in BED?"[9] Given her association with the ultraconservative *Manchester Union Leader* and support for the war, Schuyler may have been surprised by just how unwelcome she was there. Her shock is evident in the postscript to a letter home, in which she wrote:

> PS: These white Americans have not been sufficiently nice to me out here for me to feel any obligation to be otherwise than objective in my reporting of the war. One man in JUSPAO even tried to keep me from having a Press Card...This war is not being handled right, and a lot of effort is being dissipated in foolish prejudice and corruption.[10]

Although she still believed the war to be a necessary fight against Communism, she quickly grew disgusted by the level of corruption and ineptitude she encountered. In a letter that was unlikely to comfort her mother, she described the sound of constant but ineffective shelling: "The different sides are firing at each other with Tweedledee accuracy. I don't think they have the least idea whom they are going to hit half the time."[11] Tucked in amongst those letters to her mother, a short poem in Schuyler's handwriting goes even further:

> The American soldiers in Vietnam are
> great big clumsy white buffaloes
> plowing through the field of Asian culture
> like a marching four-letter word.[12]

Despite encountering much opposition and discrimination, Schuyler managed to arrange interviews of President Nguyen van Thieu and Foreign Minister Tran van Do in September. Around the same time, she bought fatigues on the black market so that she could go to Da Nang to "view ACTION."[13] She remained in Vietnam several weeks, leaving occasionally for concerts elsewhere and only returning home to the United States at the end of October for a concert in Pittsburgh.[14]

Schuyler could not quite leave behind an unfinished story, however, and, despite her mother's objections, she returned to Vietnam the following March, spending much of her time in Hue.[15] One of her only documented performances on that trip was a recital at the Hue MACV Compound Chapel.[16] Investigative reporting and humanitarian work consumed most of her time, although she reported to her mother that she continued practicing piano for hours each day.[17] As her frustration with the U.S. military grew, her letters home began to be filled with references to "THE BASTARDS," always in all caps.[18] Her reassurances to her mother never mentioned help or safety from American soldiers; rather, she breezily claimed there was no need to worry because "Vietnamese of all outlooks adore me!"[19]

Schuyler became involved in evacuating people from Hue to Da Nang, estimating that by April's end, she had helped seventy nuns, priests, and Catholic school students escape.[20] She explained the lengthy and circuitous process to her mother as follows:

> This means I had to get military travel orders for each one and wait and beg and go and persuade and call and wait and call and wait and sit in the heat and etc. Living under martial law is about the same whether it is Fascist or Communist...1) No road travel because the VC blow up the road every day. 2) No USAID airplane travel for Vietnamese because Mr. Kelly who runs OCO is a hard-boiled son of a bitch. 3) Air Vietnam booked weeks in advance. So nothing is left but to sneak in people on the USA military airplanes through the help of American Air Force personnel whom I personally convince with my charm to do it.[21]

Around the same time, Schuyler began serving as corporate secretary for the new Amerasian Foundation, which intended to help the illegitimate children of American soldiers and their Vietnamese mothers. She seems to have become even more disillusioned with the war, writing of her work with the foundation, "What the hell – if Americans are going to claim they are 'saving' Vietnam, let them save the women and children too."[22]

Amid her humanitarian efforts, Schuyler made time to perform on Da Nang television in a broadcast from a tv station on Monkey Mountain; the April 15 performance included her own composition *Normandie* and Gershwin's *Rhapsody in Blue*.[23] Otherwise, April proved to be an especially difficult month for Schuyler personally, as she was injured by a bike, all her clothes and jewelry were stolen, and she was growing increasingly frustrated with the racism she witnessed daily from American GIs.[24] Her final letters to her mother lambast segregation and the treatment she and others constantly experienced from the white American soldiers. In her last letter home, she wrote:

> Half my encounters with THE WHITE AMERICAN are abortive, negative, or unpleasant. They are the worst advertisement for America's supposed democracy I ever saw....You can't find a common meeting ground with these white Americans – for THEY HAVE NO CULTURE. But they have a phony synthetic quality – like the synthetic foods they eat, and the phony TV shows they look at.[25]

Like so many times before, Schuyler sought guidance from an astrologer who said her troubles would soon ease, ending what she called the Month of the Dragon, which Schuyler described as a "three-month malefic period."[26] Downplaying her mother's concern for her safety, Schuyler delayed her planned return home to help evacuate children from a hot zone in Hue province.[27] On Saturday, May 6, she wrote to her mother that she "could hardly wait to emerge from [her] Dragon Month" that Tuesday, with reassurances she would be home in time for a May 20 concert. Schuyler had an opportunity to meet the Prime Minister and asked her mother to please give her "a few days grace."[28]

Tragically, the respite for which she yearned was not to be, and on Wednesday, the helicopter carrying Schuyler crashed seventy-five yards from shore, killing her and a child sitting in her lap, along with one serviceman.[29] Her obituary ran on the front page of *The New York Times*,[30] and a memorial service was held in Harlem the next week, followed two days later by a requiem mass at St. Patrick's Cathedral attended by approximately two thousand people. Catholic schoolchildren, members of Harlem's Haryou-Act drum corps, and representatives of the U.S. military joined the funeral procession down Fifth Avenue, while six U.S. sailors carried her coffin.[31]

During the weeks and months following Schuyler's death, her parents set up the Philippa Schuyler Memorial Foundation and organized memorials. Two years later, her mother Josephine committed suicide, and her father George passed away eight years after that, in 1977.[32] Over time, the memory of Schuyler's life began to fade, with her unpublished writings and compositions languishing in storage. Over five decades after her death, Schuyler's legacy remains unfinished, but hopefully is now a bit more complete.

Notes

PROLOGUE

1. Philippa Duke Schuyler (hereafter cited PS), edited by Tara Betts, *Adventures in Black and White*, (New York: 2Leaf Press, 2018), 283.

2. Helen Walker-Hill, *From Spirituals to Symphonies: African American Women Composers and Their Music*, (Urbana: University of Illinois Press, 2007); Nathan Holder, illustrated by Charity Russell, *Where Are All the Black Female Composers? The Ultimate Fun Facts Guide*, (Holders Hill Publishing, 2020).

3. Rae Linda Brown, edited by Guthrie Ramsey, Jr., *The Heart of a Woman: The Life and Music of Florence B. Price*, (Urbana: University of Illinois Press, 2020); Alejandro L. Madrid, *Tania León's Stride: A Polyrhythmic Life*, (Urbana: University of Illinois Press, 2022).

4. Michael Andor Brodeur, "A Pioneering Black Composer Gets Her Due, 110 years After Her Debut," *The Washington Post*, October 20, 2022.

5. Caroline A. Streeter, "High (Mulatto) Hopes: The Rise and Fall of Philippa Schuyler," in *Tragic No More: Mixed-Race Women and the Nexus of Sex and Celebrity*, (Amherst: University of Massachusetts Press, 2012); Catherine Keyser, "Genius in the Raw: The Schuyler Family and the Modern Mulatta," in *Artificial Color: Modern Food and Racial Fictions*, (Oxford: Oxford University Press, 2019).

6. PS, *Adventures in Black and White*, viii.

CHAPTER 1

1. PS to Andre Gascht, n.d., box 22, folder 1, Schuyler Family Papers (hereafter cited SFP), Schomburg Center for Research in Black Culture: Manuscripts, Archives and Rare Books Division, New York, NY.

2. Kathryn Talalay, *Composition in Black and White: The Tragic Saga of Harlem's Biracial Prodigy*, (Oxford: Oxford University Press, 1995), 55-59; Ann Hulbert, *Off the Charts: The Hidden Lives and Lessons of American Child Prodigies*, (New York: Vintage Books, 2019), 127-131. A detailed discussion of Josephine Schuyler's documentation of Schuyler's childhood can be found in: Camille S. Owens, "'Fine Discords': Anarranging the Archives of Philippa Schuyler," *American Quarterly* 73, no. 2 (June 2021): 205-231.

3. Talalay, *Composition in Black and White*, 85-91.

4. Hulbert, 138-140.

5. "Super-Girl: Philippa Schuyler is a Musical Genius but Bobby-soxer at Heart," *Ebony* I, no. 5 (March 1946): 21-25; "Society World," *Jet*, December 2, 1954, 41; "Travelogue," *Jet*, October 27, 1955, 41; "People Are," *Jet*, March 19, 1959, 44; "People Are," *Jet*, February 25, 1960, 42.

6. Assorted letters to PS, boxes 22-24, SFP.

7. Talalay, *Composition in Black and White*, 201-212, 261, 267-274.

8. PS to Father Lyons, n.d., box 22, folder 1, SFP.

9. PS to Josephine Schuyler (hereafter cited JS), March 25, 1967, box 73, folder 5, SFP.

10. "Children's Notebook - Philippa Schuyler, 1941-1942," New York Philharmonic Shelby White & Leon Levy Digital Archives.

11. PS, handwritten manuscripts for *Cockroach Ballet* and *Death of the Nightingale*, box 25, folder 3 and box 29, folder 10, SFP.

12. PS, handwritten manuscripts, box 25, folders 1-4, SFP.

13. "Children's Notebook - Philippa Schuyler, 1938-1939," New York Philharmonic Shelby White & Leon Levy Digital Archives.

14. PS, scrapbook for Young People's Concerts, 20th Season, n.d., box 28, SFP.

15. PS, *Adventures in Black and White*, viii.

16. "On the Cover: Young Artist Abroad," *Musical Courier* CLIII, no. 1 (January 1956): 2.

17. PS, handwritten manuscripts, box 25, folder 10, SFP.

18. PS, handwritten manuscripts, boxes 25 and 29, SFP.

19. Audio recording 464367, Schuyler Family Audio (hereafter cited SFA), Schomburg Center for Research in Black Culture: Moving Image and Recorded Sound Division, New York, NY.

20. Audio recordings 378061, 378068, 378079, 378438, 378439, 378443, 378445, 378446, 464341, 464343, 464344, 464346, 464350, 378075, 464357, 378081, 464361, 464363, 464365, SFA.

21. Assorted musical scores, boxes 35-42, SFP.

22. PS, *Adventures in Black and White*, 299.

23. Luix Overbea, "Visiting Concert Pianist Focuses Many Talents," 1966, clipping, box 57, folder 6, SFP.

24. Assorted letters from PS to JS, 1963, box 73, folder 1; September 15, 1966, box 73, folder 4; April 16 and May 6, 1967, box 73, folder 5, SFP.

25. Talalay, *Composition in Black and White*, 194, 222-223.

26. PS, personal astrology notes, possibly April 15, 1960, box 21, folder 8, SFP.

27. Assorted letters, "Schuyler, Philippa," Folders 1-4, Record Group 18: Alumni Collection, Manhattanville College Library Special Collections, Purchase, NY.

28. PS to JS, May 10, 1963, box 73, folder 1; JS to PS, n.d., box 22, folder 3; PS to Ernie Pereira, n.d., box 22, folder 1, SFP.

29. PS, *Jungle Saints: Africa's Heroic Catholic Missionaries*, (Rome: Casa Editrice Herder, 1963).

30. Ernie Pereira, "Nothing Could Stop Philippa," *Hong Kong Sunday Tiger Standard*, January 11, 1959, 1, 7.

31. PS to JS, January 22, 1965, box 73, folder 3, SFP.

32. PS, handwritten list of musical themes for *Seven Pillars of Wisdom*, n.d., box 30, folder 3, SFP.

33. PS, *Adventures in Black and White*, 37-48.

34. PS, additional English lyrics for "Erzulie Malad'oh," box 64, folder 6, SFP.

35. Assorted letters from PS to JS, boxes 72-73, SFP.

36. PS, tarot notes, n.d., box 64, folder 8, SFP.

37. PS, astrological notes, box 21, folder 1, 6, and 8; box 24, folder 11; box 30, folder 3; box 31; box 37, SFP.

38. PS, facsimile of practice notes with astrological symbols, box 13, series 14 [13:4], file 35.4, Helen Walker-Hill Collection, Center for Black Music Research, Chicago, Illinois.

39. PS to JS, October 22, 1964, box 73, folder 2, SFP.

40. PS, astrology notes, box 21, folder 8, SFP.

41. PS, handwritten notes, box 31, folder 1, SFP.

42. PS, astrology notes, box 21, folder 8, SFP.

43. PS, handwritten sketches, box 30, folder 3, SFP.

44. PS, handwritten manuscripts, box 25, folders, 5, 6, and 8; box 29, folder 1; box 30, folder 3, SFP.

45. PS, assorted notes and sketches, box 25, folder 4; box 26, folders 1 and 2; box 27, notebook 1; box 30, folder 3; box 31, SFP.

CHAPTER 2

1. Phyllis Rose, "Prodigy and Prejudice," *The New York Times*, Dec. 10, 1995; "The Shirley Temple of America's Negroes," *Look*, November 7, 1939.

2. Joseph Mitchell, "Evening with a Gifted Child," *The New Yorker*, August 31, 1940.

3. Talalay, *Composition in Black and White*, 105-108.

4. Programs for 1950s recitals, box 54, folders 5-7, and box 56, folders 1-6, SFP.

5. Programs for recitals, 1960-1967, box 55, folders 1-4, and box 56, folders 7-11, SFP.

6. "Children's Notebook - Philippa Schuyler, 1939-1940," New York Philharmonic Shelby White & Leon Levy Digital Archives.

7. "Children's Notebook - Philippa Schuyler, 1941-1942," New York Philharmonic Shelby White & Leon Levy Digital Archives.

8. PS, handwritten manuscript for *Cockroach Ballet*, box 29, folder 10, SFP; PS, *Nine Little Pieces*, (New York: Mrs. George Schuyler, 1938), box 25, folder 2, SFP.

9. PS, handwritten manuscript for *Christmas Eve*, box 25, folder 3, SFP.

10. PS, handwritten manuscripts for *Fairies Dance*, box 25, folder 3 and 4, SFP.

11. PS, handwritten manuscript for *The Jolly Pig*, box 25, folder 3, SFP.

12. Program for recital at Manhattanville College of the Sacred Heart, December 8, 1938, "Schuyler, Philippa," Manhattanville College Library Special Collections.

13. PS, handwritten manuscript for *Cockroach Ballet*, box 29, folder 10, SFP.

14. PS, handwritten manuscript for *Suite from the Arabian Nights*, box 29, folder 10, SFP; Program for recital at Manhattanville College of the Sacred Heart, December 8, 1938, "Schuyler, Philippa," Manhattanville College Library Special Collections.

15. PS, handwritten manuscript for *Suite from the Arabian Nights*, box 29, folder 10, SFP.

16. PS, handwritten manuscript for *Dance of the Forty Thieves*, box 25, folder 3, SFP.

17. Arnetta Jones to New York University, n.d., box 23, folder 1, SFP.

18. Talalay, *Composition in Black and White*, 85.

19. Ibid., 91.

20. Helen Walker-Hill, unpublished biographical essay, box 13, series 14 [13:4], file 35.2, Helen Walker-Hill Collection, Center for Black Music Research, Chicago, Illinois.

21. Program for recital at First Presbyterian Church, Elmira, NY, May 7, 1946, box 54, folder 3, SFP; Program for recital at English Theater, Indianapolis, IN, May 4, 1947, box 54, folder 4, SFP; PS, *Adventures in Black and White*, 12-13.

22. PS, *Adventures in Black and White*, 12-13.

23. "Manhattan Nocturne," n.d., box 64, folder 6, SFP.

24. Talalay, *Composition in Black and White*, 101-102.

25. Program for recital at Queen's College, Georgetown, Guyana, May 9, 1964, box 56, folder 9, SFP.

26. PS, untitled handwritten manuscript, box 29, folder 12, SFP.

27. "Original Girl," *Time* Magazine, March 25, 1946.

28. Programs, box 54, folders 3-7; box 55, folder 1; box 56, folders 1-8, SFP.

29. Talalay, *Composition in Black and White*, 122-124.

30. PS, *Adventures in Black and White*, 39-40.

31. Ibid., 41-42.

32. Benjamin Hebblethwaite, with editorial assistance of Bartley, et al., *Vodou songs in Haitian Creole and English*, (Philadelphia: Temple University Press, 2012), 55.

33. Werner A. Jaegerhuber, *Complaintes Haitiennes*, 2nd edition, (Port au Prince: 1950).

34. Lauren Michelle Brandon Lindsey, "Werner Jaegerhuber's 'Messe Folklorique Haitienne': A conductor's guide," DMA Dissertation, University of Southern Mississippi, 2012.

35. PS, *Adventures in Black and White*, 41.

36. Jaegerhuber, *Complaintes Haitiennes*, box 40, SFP.

37. Program for recital at Waco Hall, Waco, TX, March 26, 1951, box 54, folder 5, SFP; Program for recital at The Agricultural and Technical College, Greensboro, NC, April 1, 1951, box 54, folder 5, SFP; Program for recital at Armstrong Technical High School, Washington, D.C., April 27, 1951, box 54, folder 5, SFP.

38. Programs, box 54, folder 7 and box 56, folder 5-7, SFP; PS, *Adventures in Black and White*, 42.

39. Programs, box 54, folder 7 and box 56, folder 5-7, SFP.

40. Jaegerhuber, *Complaintes Haitiennes*, "Erzulie Malade."

41. Hebblethwaite, 233-234.

42. PS, combined recordings, box 26, cassette 17, Helen Walker-Hill Collection, American Music Research Center, University of Colorado at Boulder, Boulder, CO.

43. Jaegerhuber, *Complaintes Haitiennes*, "Invocation a Dambala."

44. Hebblethwaite, 70.

45. Paul Johnson, unpublished transcription of Philippa Schuyler's *Damballa*; Jaegerhuber, *Complaintes Haitiennes*, "M'agué Ta Royo."

46. Programs from recitals, July 1, 1958, to March 26, 1959, box 54, folder 7 and box 56, folders 5-6, SFP.

47. PS, handwritten manuscript for *Voodoo Festival*, box 25, folder 10, SFP.

48. Jaegerhuber, *Complaintes Haitiennes*, "Gros Loa Moin".

49. Hebblethwaite, 19, 291.

50. Jaegerhuber, *Complaintes Haitiennes*, "Erzulie Oh! Erzulie Sa!".

51. Hebblethwaite, 233.

52. Ibid., 70.

53. Program for concert with Honolulu Symphony, Honolulu, HI, August 29, 1958, box 54, folder 7, SFP.

54. Inscription from John M. Kelly, Jr. to PS, August 31, 1958, box 38, SFP.

55. "His Save Our Surf Gave Waves a Break: John M. Kelly Jr 1919-2007," *Honolulu Star-Bulletin*, October 5, 2007.

56. John M. Kelly, Jr., Foreword to *Folk Songs Hawaii Sings: A Collection of Songs from Polynesia and Asia for Piano and Voice*, (Tokyo, Japan: Charles E. Tuttle Company, Inc., 1962), Kindle edition.

57. John M. Kelly, Jr. to JS, November 21, 1958, box 75, folder 6, SFP.

58. Program for recital at Palama Settlement, Honolulu, HI, December 13, 1958, box 56, folder 5, SFP.

59. PS, *Adventures in Black and White*, 258.

60. PS, handwritten manuscript for *New Moon*, box 25, folder 10, SFP.

61. Kelly, "New Moon Over Kangting: Kang-ting Siting Yueh."

62. PS, combined recordings, box 26, cassette 17, Helen Walker-Hill Collection, American Music Research Center.

63. PS, *Adventures in Black and White*, 255-257.

64. Kelly, "Hills of Arirang: Arirang."

65. Program for recital at John Hancock Hall, Boston, MA, October 25, 1959, box 54, folder 7, SFP; PS, liner notes for *Pianologue*, Circe Records, 1965, box 28, SFP.

66. Richard Mason, *The World of Suzie Wong*, reprint (Cleveland: World Pub. Co, 1957; New York: Penguin Books, 2012).

67. Kelly, "Honorable Koto: On-koto."

68. Programs for recital at Carnegie Hall, New York, May 17, 1959, box 54, folder 7 and box 56, folder 6, SFP.

69. PS, handwritten manuscript for *Wanchai Road*, box 25, folder 10, SFP.

70. PS, *Adventures in Black and White*, 266.

71. Letters from Ernie Pereira to PS, box 23, folder 9, SFP; Letters from PS to Ernie Pereira, box 22, folder 1, SFP.

72. PS, liner notes for *Pianologue*, box 28, SFP.

73. Kelly, "Blue Flower: Lan Hua-hua."

74. Programs, December 11, 1958, to May 17, 1959, box 54, folder 7 and box 56, folder 6, SFP; Kelly, "Blue Flower: Lan Hua-hua."

75. PS, *Around the World Suite*, January 27, 1960, Music Division, Library of Congress, Washington, D.C.

76. PS, handwritten manuscript for *Khanghai*, box 25, folder 10, SFP.

77. Assorted letters from PS to JS, 1953-1956, box 72, folders 11-14, SFP; PS to JS, January 5, 1958, box 72, folder 15, SFP; PS to JS, August 4, 1959, box 72, folder 16, SFP.

78. PS, tape labeled "Lecture on Romantic Love," SFA.

79. Talalay, *Composition in Black and White*, 223-230.

80. PS, tape labeled "Lecture on Romantic Love," SFA.

81. Ibid.

82. PS, handwritten manuscript for *Carnival in Languedoc*, box 29, folder 9, SFP; PS, handwritten manuscripts for *The King of France* and *The Poet's Love*, box 25, folder 10, SFP.

83. Program for recital at Westminster Theatre, London, March 21, 1965, box 56, folder 10, SFP; Program for recitals, 1965-1967, box 56, folders 10-11, SFP.

84. Program for recital at Westminster Theatre, London, March 21, 1965, box 56, folder 10, SFP.

85. PS, combined recordings, box 26, cassette 17, Helen Walker-Hill Collection, American Music Research Center.

86. PS, combined recordings, box 26, cassette 17, Helen Walker-Hill Collection, American Music Research Center.

87. Dennis Gray Stoll (hereafter cited DGS) to PS, August 14, 1965, box 24, folder 3, SFP.

88. PS, liner notes for *Pianologue*, box 28, SFP.

89. "Chanson LXXXVII", In *Le Manuscrit de Bayeux: Texte et Musique d'un Requeil de Chansons*, (New York: Columbia University Press, 1921), 108.

90. PS, liner notes for *Pianologue*, box 28, SFP.

91. Handwritten manuscript for *The King of France*, box 25, folder 10, SFP.

92. Handwritten preface and manuscript for *Carnival in Languedoc*, box 29, folder 9, SFP.

93. Joseph Canteloube, *Anthologie des chants populaires français, groupés et présentés par pays ou provinces*, (Paris: Durand, 1951), 64.

94. Ibid., 243, 141.

95. Program for recital at National Theatre, Nairobi, February 28, 1962, box 56, folder 9, SFP.

96. Ludovic Cassan and Vincent Gambau, *Vieilles chansons de la terre d'Aude: 32 chansons en langue d'Oc*, (France: Syndicat national des Institutrices et Instituteurs, 1948). Given the evidence, this collection is likely Schuyler's source. I have been unable to confirm, however, as the book is extremely rare, not circulating at any libraries worldwide, and unavailable to be scanned.

97. PS, sketch of *Carnival in Languedoc*, box 30, folder 3, SFP.

98. Programs for recitals at Omega Psi Phi Fraternity, Boston, MA, November 7, 1954; Lincoln University, Jefferson City, MO, December 3, 1954; Huston-Tillotson College, Austin, TX, December 7, 1954; and Texas Southern University, Houston, TX, December 19, 1954, box 54, folder 5, SFP; Programs for recitals at Benefit for Adam Clayton Powell Community Center, October 12, 1962; Lincoln Center, New York, NY, October 14, 1962; Miles College Chapel, Birmingham, AL, April 1, 1962; Texas Southern University, Houston, TX, April 3, 1962; Central High School Auditorium, Galveston, TX, April 5, 1962; and Second Baptist Church, Los Angeles, CA, April 10, 1962, box 55, folder 2, SFP; Program for recital at Charlotte Amalie High School Auditorium, St. Thomas, Virgin Islands, February 21, 1957, Series VII, Box 1, Philippa Duke Schuyler – Concert Tours file, Alton Augustus Adams Collection, Center for Black Music Research, Chicago, Illinois; Program for recital at Wayne State University, De-

troit, Michigan, November 19, 1963, The Blockson Clipping File, Charles L. Blockson Afro-American Collection, Temple University Libraries, Philadelphia, Pennsylvania.

99. Annotated scores by others, boxes 35-42, SFP.

100. Hand-copied scores throughout box 25, folder 5; box 27; box 30, folder 3; box 31; box 34, folder 2, SFP.

101. Programs for recitals, 1961-1967, box 55, folders 1-4 and box 56, folders 8-11, SFP.

102. Program for recital at Cinema Palacio, Beiro, Mozambique, July 13, 1962, box 56, folder 9, SFP; Program for recital at Queens College, May 9 and 10, 1964, box 56, folder 9, SFP; Program for recital at Philharmonic Hall, Lincoln Center, New York, NY, October 14, 1962, box 55, folder 2, SFP.

103. Handwritten sketches labeled "Argentina," box 29, folder 10, SFP; Kathryn Talalay, "Philippa Duke Schuyler, Pianist/Composer/Writer," *The Black Perspective in Music* 10, no. 1 (Spring 1982): 64.

104. Julian Aguirre, *Aires Nacionales Argentinos*, 3rd Edition, (Buenos Aires: G. Ricordi & Co, 1930), 6-9.

105. Susana Salgado, "Aguirre, Julián," in *Grove Music Online*, published online, 2001.

106. PS, liner notes for *Pianologue*, box 28, SFP.

107. Alberto Ginastera, *Canción al árbol del olvido: para canto y piano*, (Buenos Aires: Ricordi Americana, 1955); Programs for recitals at Bethune-Cookman College Auditorium, Daytona Beach, FL, January 24, 1955, and Grambling Auditorium, Grambling, LA, April 12, 1956, box 54, folder 6, SFP.

108. PS, liner notes for *Pianologue*, box 28, SFP.

109. PS, handwritten manuscript for *Patagonian Triste*, box 25, folder 10, SFP.

110. PS, *Who Killed the Congo?*, (New York: The Devin-Adair Company, 1962); PS, *Jungle Saints: Africa's Heroic Catholic Missionaries*.

111. PS, "The Music of Modern Africa," *Music Journal* 18 (October 1960): 18, 60-63; PS, handwritten manuscripts for *African Suite* and *African Rhapsody*, box 29, folder 4, SFP.

112. Program for recital at Ursuline Convent Hall, Barbados, October 7, 1960, box 56, folder 7, SFP.

113. Program for recital at Town Hall, New York, NY, September 13, 1964, box 55, folder 3, SFP; Program for recital at St. Francis deSales High School, Powhatan, VA, January 15, 1965, box 55, folder 3, SFP.

114. PS, handwritten manuscript for *Uganda Martyrs*, box 25, folder 6, SFP; Joseph Kyagambiddwa, *Uganda Martyrs African Oratorio*, (Rome: Casimiri-Capra, 1964).

115. PS, handwritten manuscript for *White Nile Suite*, box 29, folder 1, SFP; PS, handwritten manuscript for *Seven Pillars of Wisdom*, box 25, folders 5-6, 8 and box 31, folder 1, SFP; PS, handwritten manuscript for *Nile Fantasy*, box 34, folders 1-7, SFP.

116. Talalay, "Philippa Duke Schuyler, Pianist/Composer/Writer," 67.

117. PS, *Around the World Suite*, January 27, 1960, Music Division, Library of Congress, Washington, D.C.

118. Program for recital at John Hancock Hall, Boston, MA, October 25, 1959, box 54, folder 7, SFP.

119. Program for recital at Queen's College, Georgetown, Guyana, May 9, 1964, box 56, folder 9, SFP; Program for recital at National Theatre, Nairobi, February 28, 1962, box 56, folder 9, SFP; Program for recital at Sacramento High School, Sacramento, CA, April 14, 1962, box 55, folder 2, SFP.

120. PS, liner notes for *Pianologue*, box 28, SFP.

121. Library of Congress, Copyright Office, "Catalog of Copyright Entries, Third Series, Volume 14, Part 5, Number 1: Music, January-June, 1960," Washington, D.C.: Copyright Office, Library of Congress: For sale by the Supt. Of Docs., U.S. G.P.O., 1961.

122. PS, *Adventures in Black and White*, 39.

123. PS, handwritten sketch for *Sonata diabolique*, box 30, folder 3, SFP; PS, handwritten pages from *Sonata diabolique*, box 27, notebook 2, SFP.

124. Joris-Karl Huysmans, translated by Terry Hale, *La-Bas (The Damned)*, (London: Penguin Classics, 2001), vii-xxxi.

125. Joseph Sheridan Le Fanu, edited by Kathleen Costello-Sullivan, *Carmilla*, Critical Edition, (Syracuse: Syracuse University Press, 2013).

126. John Dickinson Carr, *The Burning Court*, (London: Tandem Books, 1969).

127. PS, handwritten sketch for *Sonata diabolique*, box 30, folder 3, SFP.

128. DGS to PS, June 25, 1965, box 24, folder 2, SFP.

129. DGS to PS, August 17, 1965, box 24, folder 3, SFP.

130. Program for recital at Le Benin, Togo, February 2, 1966, box 56, folder 11, SFP.

CHAPTER 3

1. PS, "The Music of Modern Africa," *Music Journal* 18 (October 1960): 63.

2. PS, *Adventures in Black and White*, 275.

3. Ibid., 155-252, 275-280.

4. PS, *Jungle Saints*, 15, 233; Talalay, *Composition in Black and White*, 223.

5. PS, *Adventures in Black and White*, 205.

6. Ibid., 195, 213, 248-249

7. Ibid., 246.

8. Ibid., 233-234, 242-244.

9. PS, *Adventures in Black and White*, 199, 241, 246.

10. Ibid., 251.

11. PS, notebooks, box 21, folder 5 and box 58, folder 7, SFP.

12. PS, "The Music of Modern Africa." For a more current introduction to African musical styles, see: Kofi Agawu, *The African Imagination in Music*, (Oxford: Oxford University Press, 2016).

13. PS, recordings labeled 378061, 387445, 378446, 464344, 464357, 464365, SFA.

14. PS, *Jungle Saints*, 54, 57, 64, 68, 97, 140, 153-154, 185.

15. Recordings labeled 378440, 378438, 378439, 378443, 464341, 464346, 464350, 378081, 464361, 464363, SFA.

16. PS, *Adventures in Black and White*, 172-175.

17. Ibid., 176.

18. Ibid., 176.

19. PS, "The Music of Modern Africa," 60.

20. Ibid. 60-61.

21. PS, *Adventures in Black and White*, 161-164.

22. Ibid., 162.

23. Ibid., 168-169.

24. PS, "The Music of Modern Africa," 18.

25. Ibid., 18, 60.

26. Program for recital at Westminster Theatre, London, March 21, 1965, box 56, folder 10, SFP.

27. PS, handwritten score for *White Nile Suite*, box 29, folder 1, SFP; PS, handwritten list of musical themes for *Seven Pillars of Wisdom*, box 30, folder 3, SFP.

28. PS, *Adventures in Black and White*, 179-180.

29. Peter Cooke, "Kyagambiddwa, Joseph," in *Grove Music Online*, published online, 2001.

30. Joseph Kyagambiddwa, *African Music from the Source of the Nile*, (New York: Frederick A. Praeger, 1955).

31. PS, *Adventures in Black and White*, 180-181.

32. Ibid., 181.

33. Ibid., 181.

34. Ibid., 182-184.

35. PS, "The Music of Modern Africa," 61-62.

36. Kyagambiddwa, *African Music from the Source of the Nile*, 18-23.

37. PS, "The Music of Modern Africa," 62.

38. Ibid., 62.

39. Ibid., 62.

40. PS, tape labeled PS 26, 1966, SFA.

41. PS, "The Music of Modern Africa," 18

42. PS, *Adventures in Black and White*, 277.

43. PS, "The Music of Modern Africa," 18.

44. PS, PS 26, 1966, SFA.

45. PS, "The Music of Modern Africa," 18.

46. PS, *Adventures in Black and White*, 221-229, 277-281.

47. PS, "The Music of Modern Africa," 62.

48. PS, *Adventures in Black and White*, 279-280.

49. PS, PS 26, 1966, SFA.

50. Ibid.

51. Hugh Tracey, "Obituary: Ba Joseph Kiwele – Mrs. E.M. Dougall," *African Music: Journal of the International Library of African Music* 2(4) (May 1961): 102.

52. PS, PS 26, 1966, SFA.

53. PS, tape labeled 378067 SC Audio TC-386, SFA.

54. Talalay, *Composition in Black and White*, 191.

55. PS, "The Music of Modern Africa," 61.

56. PS, PS 26, 1966, SFA.

57. Guy Arnold, *Africa: A Modern History*, (London: Atlantic Books, 2005), xiii-xiv, xviii-xix, 333-334.

58. PS, *Jungle Saints*, 120.

59. Programs for recitals, October 7, 1960, to May 9, 1964, box 55, folder 1-2 and box 56, folders 7-9, SFP.

60. Kyagambiddwa, *African Music from the Source of the Nile*, 39, 51-52.

61. PS to JS, February 12, 1959, box 72, folder 16, SFP; John Kelly, Jr. to JS, November 21, 1958, box 75, folder 6, SFP.

62. Program from Texas Southern University, April 3, 1962, box 55, folder 2, SFP; Program from Zoa House, Tel Aviv, Israel, date unknown but prior to May 5, 1962, box 56, folder 9, SFP.

63. Program for recital presented by Delta Sigma Theta, Sacramento High School Auditorium, April 14, 1962, box 55, folder 2, SFP.

64. Program for recital at Ursuline Convent Hall, Barbados, October 7, 1960, box 56, folder 7, SFP.

65. PS, liner notes for *Pianologue*, box 28, SFP.

66. PS, handwritten manuscript for *African Suite*, box 29, folder 4, SFP.

67. Waito shepherd, "Shepherd's Flute Song," recorded and edited by Lin Lerner and Chad Wollner, *Folk Music and Ceremonies of Ethiopia*, Folkways Records, 1974.

68. PS, handwritten manuscript for *African Suite*, box 29, folder 4, SFP.

69. Kyagambiddwa, *African Music from the Source of the Nile*, 39.

70. Ibid., 51-52.

71. PS, *Adventures in Black and White*, 184.

72. Program for recital at Texas Southern University, Houston, TX, April 3, 1962, box 55, folder 2, SFP; Program for recital at Sacramento High School, Sacramento, CA, April 14, 1962, box 55, folder 2, SFP.

73. "Danse de la Pleine Lune," recorded by Marcel Thonnon and Anne Thonnon-Noury, *Musiques et Danses du Congo Kivu-Uele*, Arion, 1998.

CHAPTER 4

1. PS, *Jungle Saints*, 17.

2. Program for recital at Town Hall, New York, NY, September 13, 1964, box 55, folder 3, SFP.

3. Advertisement for Town Hall Concert, September 13, 1964, box 55, folder 3, SFP.

4. Raymond Ericson, "Philippa Duke Schuyler Plays Works for Piano Inspired by her African Tours," *The New York Times*, September 14, 1964, 42.

5. PS, recordings labelled SCM 79-27 and 464357, SFA; PS, *White Nile Suite*, March 10, 1965, Music Division, Library of Congress, Washington, D.C.

6. A. Nicolaides, "Early Portuguese Imperialism: Using the Jesuits in the Mutapa Empire of Zimbabwe," *International Journal of Peace and Development Studies* Vol. 2(4) (April 2011): 132-133. For a general introduction to African history of this time period, see: Christopher Ehret, *The Civilizations of Africa: A History to 1800*, 2nd edition, (Charlottesville: University of Virginia Press, 2016).

7. Nicolaides, 133-134.

8. Ibid., 134.

9. Gai Roufe, "The Reasons for a Murder: Local Cultural Conceptualizations of the Martyrdom of Gonçalo da Silveira in 1561," *Cahiers d'Études africaines* LV (3) (2015): 467-487; Nicolaides, 135-137; An abbreviated version of this story appears in Schuyler's *Jungle Saints*, 104.

10. PS, *Jungle Saints*, 105.

11. PS, *African Rhapsody* or *Chisamharu the Nogomo*, February 2, 1965, Music Division, Library of Congress, Washington, D.C.

12. PS, *Jungle Saints*, 26-28.

13. Ibid., 104- 105.

14. PS, handwritten manuscript for *Chisamharu the Nogomo*, box 29, folder 4, SFP.

15. PS, lecture recital on the music of Portuguese Africa, tape labeled 378067 SC Audio TC-386, SFA.

16. Jeanne E. Robinson, Administrative Assistant to the National Council of the Churches of Christ in the USA's Africa Committee to PS, December 14, 1964, box 43, folder 4, SFP.

17. Howard Markel, "Dr. Albert Schweitzer, a Renowned Medical Missionary with a Complicated History," *PBS NewsHour*, January 14, 2016.

18. Erwin R. Jacobi, "Schweitzer, Albert," in *Grove Music Online*, published online, 2001.

19. "Albert Schweitzer, 90, Dies at His Hospital," *The New York Times*, September 6, 1965, 1, 16.

20. "Philippa Schuyler: American Pianist Played for Monarchs and Desert Saint," *Musical Courier* CLIX, no. 6 (May 1959): 12.

21. PS to JS, February 7, 1959, box 72, folder 16, SFP.

22. Ibid.

23. PS, *Adventures in Black and White*, 233.

24. Ibid., 233.

25. PS to JS, February 7, 1959, box 72, folder 16, SFP.

26. PS, *Adventures in Black and White*, 234.

27. Ibid., 235.

28. Ibid., 235.

29. Ibid., 235.

30. Ibid., 236-237.

31. Ibid., 237.

32. Ibid., 238.

33. Ibid., 238.

34. DGS to PS, December 18, 1964, box 24, folder 1, SFP.

35. Howard Klein, "Musical Tribute Paid Schweitzer: Concert's Proceeds Given to His African Mission," *The New York Times*, January 15, 1965, 22.

36. Program from recital at St. Francis deSales High School, Powhatan, Virginia, January 15, 1965, box 55, folder 3, SFP.

37. PS to Albert Schweitzer, box 22, folder 1, SFP.

38. Programs for recitals, January 15, 1965, to August 31, 1966, box 55, folders 3-4 and box 56, folders 10-11, SFP.

39. PS, recording labeled 464370, SFA.

40. Program for recital in Lome, Togo, January 6, 1966, box 56, folder 11, SFP.

41. PS, tape labeled SCM 79-27, December 24, 1964, SFA.

42. Program for recital at Town Hall, New York, NY, September 13, 1964, box 55, folder 3, SFP.

43. Program for recital at St. Francis deSales High School, Powhatan, VA, January 15, 1965, box 55, folder 3, SFP.

44. PS, *Jungle Saints*, 17.

45. Nicolaides, 132.

46. PS, handwritten manuscript for *Chisamharu the Nogomo*, box 29, folder 4, SFP.

47. Nicolaides, 132.

48. PS, *African Rhapsody* or *Chisamharu the Nogomo*, February 2, 1965, Music Division, Library of Congress, Washington, D.C.

49. Examples of *timbila* musical style can be heard in *Music from Mozambique, Volume 2: Chopi Timbila, Two Orchestral Performances*, Folkways Records, 1982, and *Music from Mozambique, Volume 3*, Folkways Records, 1983.

50. PS, recording labeled 464370, SFA.

51. PS, *Adventures in Black and White*, 184.

52. Kyagambiddwa, *African Music from the Source of the Nile*, 41.

53. Ibid., 41.

54. Programs for recitals, January 15, 1965, to August 31, 1966, box 55, folders 3-4 and box 56, folders 10-11, SFP.

CHAPTER 5

1. PS to JS, n.d., likely November 1964, box 72, folder 19, SFP.

2. Program for recital at Town Hall, New York, NY, September 13, 1964, box 55, folder 3, SFP.

3. Talalay, *Composition in Black and White*, 240; DGS to PS, November 10, 1964, box 24, folder 1, SFP; DGS to Leopold Stokowski, November 12, 1964, box 24, folder 1, SFP. Although neither letter specifies when and where Stoll heard *White Nile Suite*, its first public performance in London did not occur until March 1965, so the October 1964 cocktail party where Stoll and Schuyler met would have been the only opportunity. Talalay's biography states that Schuyler performed "three of her own African compositions" (p. 240) but does not specify which works.

4. Talalay, *Composition in Black and White*, 240.

5. DGS to PS, November 10, 1964, box 24, folder 1, SFP.

6. Lux Overbea, "Visiting Concert Pianist Focuses Many Talents," 1966, clipping, box 57, folder 6, SFP.

7. PS to JS, November 4, 1964, box 73, folder 2, SFP.

8. DGS to PS, November 10, 14, and 25, 1964, box 24, folder 1, SFP.

9. PS to JS, November 4, 1964, box 73, folder 2, SFP.

10. Ibid.

11. PS to JS, n.d., April 15 or 16, 1965, box 73, folder 3, SFP. Although the letter is not dated, references to Good Friday and 1965 events help establish an approximate date.

12. Program from recital at Westminster Theatre, March 21, 1965, box 56, folder 10, SFP. For a more current and in-depth examination of Arabic music, see: Johnny Farraj and Sami Abu Shumays, *Inside Arabic Music: Arabic Maqam Performance and Theory in the 20th Century*, (Oxford: Oxford University Press, 2019).

13. PS, handwritten manuscript for *White Nile Suite*, box 29, folder 1, SFP.

14. Program for recital at Town Hall, New York, September 13, 1964, box 55, folder 3, SFP.

15. Alan Moorehead, *The White Nile*, (London: Hamish Hamilton, 1960; London: Penguin Books, 1963), 13-19. The book describes searches for the source of the Nile and would have been available to Schuyler at the time of *White Nile Suite*'s composition.

16. Gabriel R. Warburg, "The Search for Sources of the White Nile and Egyptian-Sudanese Relations," *Middle Eastern Studies* 43, No. 3 (May 2007): 479, 483-484.

17. Program for recital at Town Hall, New York, NY, September 13, 1964, box 55, folder 3, SFP.

18. DGS, untitled review of *White Nile Suite*'s London premiere in "The Journal Reviews," *Music Journal* 23, no. 3 (March 1965): 75.

19. Program for recital at Hue MACV Chapel, Hue, Vietnam, March 22, 1967, box 56, folder 11, SFP.

20. PS, tape labeled SCM 79-27, December 24, 1964; PS, recording labeled 464357, SFA.

21. Library of Congress, Copyright Office, "Catalog of Copyright Entries, Third Series, Volume 18, Part 5, Number 2: Music, July-December, 1964," Washington, D.C.: Copyright Office, Library of Congress: For sale by the Supt. of Docs., U.S. G.P.O., 1967.

22. "Philippa Schuyler's African Music Hailed at Town Hall," *The Pittsburgh Courier*, September 26, 1964, clipping, box 57, folder 5, SFP.

23. Program for recital at St. Louis University, August 13, 1966, box 56, folder 11, SFP.

24. PS, handwritten manuscript for *Umdurman*, box 29, folder 2, SFP.

25. PS, *Adventures in Black and White*, 169.

26. Neil Faulkner, *Empire and Jihad: The Anglo-Arab Wars of 1870-1920*, (New Haven: Yale University Press, 2021), 182, 218-219, 256-258, 290-291, 331-333.

27. Program for recital at Town Hall, New York, September 13, 1964, box 55, folder 3, SFP.

28. Program for lecture recital at St. Francis deSales High School, Powhatan, VA, January 15, 1965, box 55, folder 3, SFP.

29. PS, handwritten manuscript for *White Nile Suite*, box 29, folder 1, SFP.

30. PS, tape labeled SCM 79-27, December 24, 1964; PS, recording labeled 464357, SFA.

31. Program for lecture recital at St. Francis deSales High School, Powhatan, VA, January 15, 1965, box 55, folder 3, SFP.

32. Justin Pollard and Howard Reid, *The Rise and Fall of Alexandria: Birthplace of the Modern World*, (New York: Penguin Books, 2006), Kindle edition, "Chapter 1: Flour and Sand," "Chronology."

33. Ibid., "Chapter 11: The Last Pharaoh."

34. Peter Sheehan, *Babylon of Egypt: The Archaeology of Old Cairo and the Origins of the City*, revised edition, (Cairo: The American University in Cairo Press, 2010), xviii.

35. Pollard and Reid, "Chapter 19: The Shipwreck of Time," "Chronology."

36. Program for recital at Town Hall, New York, NY, September 13, 1964, box 55, folder 3, SFP; PS, tape labeled SCM 79-27, December 24, 1964, SFA.

37. Warren Anderson, revised by Thomas J. Mathiesen, "Hymn: I. Ancient Greek," in *Grove Music Online*, published online, 2001, updated 2013.

38. Curt Sachs, *The Rise of Music in the Ancient World: East and West*, (New York: W.W. Norton & Company, 1943), 240-242, 245.

39. PS, tape labeled SCM 79-27, December 24, 1964; PS, recording labeled 464357, SFA; PS, handwritten manuscript for *Nile Fantasy*, movement 2, box 34, folder 3, SFP.

40. PS, tape labeled SCM 79-27, side 2, December 24, 1964, SFA.

41. Lucia Carminati, "An Unhappy Happy Port: Fin-de-siècle Port Said and Its Connections and Disconnections of Water and Iron," *International Journal of Middle East Studies* 54 (2022): 731-732.

42. Michael H. Coles, "Suez, 1956 – A Successful Naval Operation Compromised by Inept Political Leadership," *Naval War College Review* 59, No. 4 (Autumn 2006): 107-109, 113.

43. PS, handwritten manuscript for *White Nile Suite*, box 29, folder 1, SFP.

44. PS, recording of lecture recital on Portuguese Africa labeled 378067, SFA.

45. Program for recital at Town Hall, New York, NY, September 13, 1964, box 55, folder 3, SFP.

46. Petra M. Sijpesteijn, "The Arab Conquest of Egypt and the Beginning of Muslim Rule," in *Egypt in the Byzantine World, 300-700*, edited by Roger S. Bagnall, (Cambridge: Cambridge University Press, 2007), 437.

47. Sheehan, xx, 79.

48. Sijpesteijn, 451-455.

49. Copyright form for *White Nile Suite*, box 43, folder 11, SFP.

50. PS, *White Nile Suite*, March 10, 1965, Music Division, Library of Congress, Washington, D.C.

51. Programs for recitals, March 21, 1965, to March 22, 1967, box 55, folders 3-4 and box 56, folders 10-11, SFP.

52. Alfonso Zaratti, *Circle of Love*, (Italy: Casamari Abbey Publishing Co., 1969), 560; Stoll, "The Journal Reviews," 75; Programs for recitals, March 21, 1965, to March 22, 1967, box 55, folders 3-4 and box 56, folders 10-11, SFP.

53. Library of Congress, Copyright Office, "Catalog of Copyright Entries, Third Series, Volume 18, Part 5, Number 2: Music, July-December, 1964," Washington, D.C.: Copyright Office, Library of Congress: For sale by the Supt. of Docs., U.S. G.P.O., 1967; Programs for recitals at Lome, Togo, January 6, 1966; Saint Louis Hall, Baguio City, Philippines, August 13, 1966; and Naga City, Philippines, August 16, 1966, box 56, folder 11, SFP; Programs for recitals at North Carolina College at Durham, Durham, NC, March 2, 1966, and Olivet Baptist Church, Chicago, IL, March 25, 1966, box 55, folder 4, SFP.

54. T.E. Lawrence, *Seven Pillars of Wisdom*, (Hertfordshire: Wordsworth Editions Limited, 1997), 37.

55. Ericson, "Philippa Duke Schuyler Plays Works for Piano Inspired by her African Tours," 42.

56. PS to JS, n.d., April 15 or 16, 1965, box 73, folder 3, SFP.

CHAPTER 6

1. PS, Interview with *Conversation at Large*, Charlotte, North Carolina, n.d., tape labeled PS #18, SFA.

2. Talalay, *Composition in Black and White*, 58-59.

3. Programs for recitals at Pilgrim Baptist Church, October 23, 1938, and Manhattanville College of the Sacred Heart, December 8, 1938, box 54, folder 1, SFP.

4. Talalay, *Composition in Black and White*, 60-61.

5. PS, *Adventures in Black and White*, 283.

6. Ibid., 23.

7. PS, handwritten practice journal stapled into scale book, 1955-1956, box 71, SFP.

8. Talalay, *Composition in Black and White*, 213-214.

9. PS, *Jungle Saints*, 15.

10. PS to Ernie Pereira, n.d., box 22, folder 1, SFP.

11. Pereira, "Nothing Could Stop Philippa," 7.

12. Talalay, *Composition in Black and White*, 212.

13. Zaratti, 532-534.

14. Talalay, *Composition in Black and White*, 213.

15. Zaratti, 534.

16. PS, handwritten practice journal stapled into scale book, 1955-1956, box 71, SFP.

17. Zaratti, 536-538.

18. Ibid., 536.

19. Ibid., 532, 534.

20. Pereira, "Nothing Could Stop Philippa," 7.

21. PS, *Jungle Saints*, 122.

22. Zaratti, 544.

23. Ibid., 540.

24. PS, recordings labeled 464344 and 464356, SFA.

25. PS to Ernie Pereira, n.d., box 22, folder 1, SFP.

26. JS to PS, n.d., box 22, folder 3, SFP.

27. JS and PS, *Kingdom of Dreams*, (New York: Robert Speller & Sons, 1966).

28. Talalay, *Composition in Black and White*, 212.

29. Zaratti, 534.

30. PS, handwritten notes on business card, box 24, folder 11, SFP.

31. JS to PS, October 9, box 22, folder 3, SFP. Although the year is not included, references to the publication of *African Oratorio* place this letter in 1964.

32. Program for recital at St. Francis deSales High School, Powhatan, Virginia, January 15, 1965, box 55, folder 3, SFP.

33. Nicholas Ssempijja, "Globalizing Catholicism Through Musical Performance: Kampala Archdioc-

esan Post-Primary Schools Music Festivals," Ph.D. dissertation, (University of Bergen, 2011): 113-116.

34. James Martin, S.J., "The Story of the Ugandan Martyrs," *America: The Jesuit Review*, June 3, 2011; "St. Charles Lwanga and Companions, Martyrs of Uganda," Catholic News Agency, undated description of the Feast Day of the Martyrs of Uganda; An abbreviated but corresponding version of this story appears in Schuyler's *Jungle Saints*, 57-58. For a more in-depth and detailed account available to Schuyler at the time of the composition of *Uganda Martyrs*, see: John F. Faupel, *African Holocaust: The Story of the Uganda Martyrs*, (New York: P.J. Kenedy, 1962; Muriwai Books, 2018, Kindle edition).

35. "Vatican to Canonize 22 Negro Martyrs," *The New York Times*, July 8, 1964, 1.

36. Ssempija, 116, 118-119.

37. Ibid., 118.

38. Program for recital at St. Francis deSales High School, Powhatan, Virginia, January 15, 1965, box 55, folder 3, SFP.

39. Programs for recitals at Blessed Sacrament College, January 24, 1965; L'Atelier, Brussels, Belgium, April 6, 1965; and The Gallery of Modern Art, New York, NY, June 13, 1965, box 55, folder 3, SFP; Programs for recitals at Saint Louis Hall, Baguio City, Philippines, August 13, 1966, and Thomas Jefferson Library Auditorium, Manila, Philippines, August 20, 1966, box 56, folder 11, SFP.

40. PS, handwritten manuscript for *Uganda Martyrs*, box 25, folder 6, SFP; Kyagambiddwa, *Uganda Martyrs African Oratorio*.

41. Kyagambiddwa, English translations for *Uganda Martyrs African Oratorio*, 9-31.

42. Ibid., 9-31.

43. Ibid., 9-31.

44. Ibid., 9-31.

45. Ibid., 9-31.

CHAPTER 7

1. PS to JS, n.d., possibly 1966, box 73, folder 4, SFP.

2. PS to JS, October 28, 1964, box 73, folder 2, SFP.

3. PS to JS, October 29, 1964, box 73, folder 2, SFP.

4. Ibid.

5. Ibid.

6. Ibid.

7. Ibid.

8. Ibid.

9. Ibid.

10. Ibid.

11. Ibid.

12. PS to JS, October 29, 1964, box 73, folder 2, SFP.

13. PS, handwritten manuscript for *Seven Pillars of Wisdom*, box 25, folders 5-6, 8, and box 31, folder 1, SFP.

14. PS to JS, October 29, 1964, box 73, folder 2, SFP.

15. Talalay, *Composition in Black and White*, 201-202.

16. PS, *Who Killed the Congo?*, 6-10.

17. Ibid., 6-7.

18. Ibid., 8-9.

19. Talalay, *Composition in Black and White*, 202-203.

20. Program for recital at University College, Accra, Ghana, July 4, 1960, box 56, folder 7, SFP.

21. Talalay, *Composition in Black and White*, 203-205.

22. Christopher Othen, *Katanga 1960-63: Mercenaries, Spies and the African Nation that Waged War on the World*, (Gloucestershire: The History Press, 2015), Kindle edition, "Chapter 4: Emperor Msiri's Ghost," "Chapter 9: The Rhodesian Connection."

23. Talalay, *Composition in Black and White*, 206.

24. Ibid., 206-207.

25. PS, *Who Killed the Congo?*, 245-246.

26. Talalay, *Composition in Black and White*, 207.

27. Othen, "Chapter 6: Assignment – Léopoldville."

28. Arnold, 24-26.

29. Talalay, *Composition in Black and White*, 210-211; John H. Clarke, "New Books on Africa," *Freedomways: A Quarterly Review of the Negro Freedom Movement* 2, no. 3 (Summer 1962): 334-335.

30. PS, tape labeled SCM 79-27, SFA.

31. Program for recitals at St. Francis DeSales High School, Powhatan, VA, January 15, 1965, and Blessed Sacrament College Auditorium, January 24, 1965, box 55, folder 3, SFP; Program for recital at L'Atelier, Brussels, Belgium, April 6, 1965, box 55, folder 3, SFP.

32. Program for recital at Stroud Subscription Rooms, Stroud Festival, April 21, 1965, box 56, folder 10, SFP.

33. Program for recital at American Embassy Theatre, London, April 8, 1965, box 55, folder 3 and box 56, folder 10, SFP. Only the version in box 55, folder 3 contains the movement titles.

34. Programs for recitals at India House, London, May 3, 1965, box 56, folder 10, SFP; and The Gallery of Modern Art, New York, NY, June 13, 1965, box 55, folder 3, SFP.

35. Programs for recitals, January 7, 1966, to October 30, 1966, box 55, folder 4 and box 56, folder 11, SFP.

36. Program for recital at Le Benin, Lome Togo, February 2, 1966, box 56, folder 11, SFP.

37. PS, handwritten manuscripts for *The Agonies, The Terrors and the Mistakes* and *Fortune Favored the Bold Player*, box 25, folder 6, SFP.

38. PS, pages from handwritten manuscript for prologue to *Seven Pillars of Wisdom*, box 25, folder 5, SFP; PS, pages from handwritten manuscript for epilogue to *Seven Pillars of Wisdom*, box 31, folder 1, SFP.

39. PS, handwritten notes on recital program, September 27, 1964, box 30, folder 3, SFP; PS, handwritten notes on letter from Pat and Rick Haynes, September 1964, box 30, folder 3, SFP; PS, handwritten notes on Henri Cuypers business card, box 30, folder 3, SFP; PS, handwritten notes on loose paper with

1960s horoscope charts, box 30, folder 3, SFP.

40. PS, handwritten notes on recital program, September 27, 1964, box 30, folder 3, SFP.

41. Eric Sams, "Cryptography, musical," in *Grove Music Online*, published online, 2001.

42. PS, handwritten list of musical themes, box 30, folder 3, SFP.

43. PS, handwritten notes on recital program, September 27, 1964, SFP.

44. PS, handwritten list of musical themes, box 30, folder 3, SFP.

45. PS, handwritten list of musical themes, box 30, folder 3, SFP.

46. Lawrence, *Seven Pillars of Wisdom*, 9.

47. Scott Anderson, *Lawrence in Arabia: War, Deceit, Imperial Folly, and the Making of the Modern Middle East* (New York: Anchor Books, 2013), 162-164, 321-322.

48. Lawrence, 20.

49. Ibid., 37.

50. Ibid., 37.

51. PS, handwritten notes, box 30, folder 3, SFP.

52. Seyyed Hossein Nasr, Editor-in-Chief, *The Study Quran: A New Translation and Commentary*, (New York: HarperOne, 2015), 984-998.

53. Lawrence, 38.

54. Ibid., 47.

55. Ibid., 47.

56. PS, handwritten notes, box 30, folder 3, SFP.

57. Lawrence, 13.

58. Anderson, 261.

59. Ibid., 335-338.

60. Lawrence, 47.

61. Nasr, 1042-1054.

62. Lawrence, 13.

63. Ibid., 11.

64. Ibid., 657.

65. PS, recording labeled 378074, SFA; PS, astrology notes, box 21, folder 8, SFP.

66. PS to JS, May 6, 1967, box 73, folder 5, SFP.

67. Nasr, 1468-1473.

68. Lawrence, 13.

69. Ibid., 438 (adapted).

70. Ibid., 432-438.

71. PS, tape labeled SCM 79-27, December 24, 1964, SFA.

72. Anderson, 401-402.

73. Lawrence, 438.

74. Ibid., 37.

75. Ibid., 37.

76. PS, handwritten list of musical themes, box 30, folder 3, SFP; Nasr, 1479-1483.

77. Lawrence, 37.

78. Anderson, 288-291, 461, 470.

79. Nasr, 1349-1357; PS, handwritten list of musical themes, box 30, folder 3, SFP.

80. Anderson, 468-471.

81. Ibid., 474-475.

82. Lawrence, 657.

83. Ibid., 37 (adapted).

84. Ibid., 650.

85. Nasr, 1378-1382.

86. Lawrence, 650-654.

87. Ibid., 655.

88. Anderson, 485.

CHAPTER 8

1. PS to JS, January 22, 1965, box 73, folder 3, SFP.

2. Talalay, *Composition in Black and White*, 231-237.

3. Ibid., 237-238.

4. Ibid., 242.

5. DGS to Miss S. Forth, Ministry of Labour, January 27, 1965, box 22, folder 1, SFP; DGS to PS, February 6 and 18, 1965, box 22, folder 1, SFP.

6. DGS to PS, February 12, 1965, box 24, folder 1, SFP.

7. DGS to PS, February 18 and 26, 1965, box 24, folder 1, SFP.

8. "Arab Influence on European Music," *Time & Tide: The British News Magazine* 46, No. 13, April 7, 1965, clipping, box 57, folder 5, SFP; "The Iran Society," *Diplomatic Bulletin*, April 1, 1965, clipping, box 57, folder 5, SFP; Talalay, *Composition in Black and White*, 245.

9. Ibid., 245.

10. DGS to PS, April 7, 1965, likely misdated, box 24, folder 2, SFP.

11. DGS to PS, May 4 and 29, June 4, 7, and 18, 1965, box 24, folder 2, SFP; PS to JS, April 15 and 21, 1965, box 73, folder 3, SFP.

12. Talalay, *Composition in Black and White*, 245-246, 251.

13. PS to JS, n.d., likely April 15 or 16, 1965, box 73, folder 3, SFP. The letter lacks a date, but references to Good Friday and 1965 events help establish an approximate date.

14. Ibid.

15. Program for recital at Stroud Subscription Rooms, Stroud, UK, April 21, 1965, box 56, folder 10, SFP.

16. PS to JS, April 21, 1965, box 73, folder 3, SFP.

17. DGS to PS, May 16, 26, 27, and 29, 1965, box 24, folder 2, SFP; DGS to JS, May 5, 21, 25, 27, 29, and June 3, 1965, box 74, folder 8, SFP.

18. DGS to PS, June 11, 1965, box 24, folder 2, SFP.

19. DGS to PS, June 25, 1965, box 24, folder 2, SFP.

20. DGS to PS, June 21, 1965, box 24, folder 2, SFP.

21. DGS to PS, July 27, 1965, box 24, folder 2, SFP.

22. Talalay, *Composition in Black and White*, 251-252; PS, notebooks, box 21, folder 5, SFP; PS, assorted notes, box 25, folder 2, SFP.

23. Talalay, *Composition in Black and White*, 252-253.

24. DGS to JS, September 8, 1965, box 74, folder 8, SFP.

25. PS to JS, September 5 and 6, 1965, box 73, folder 3, SFP.

26. Talalay, *Composition in Black and White*, 255-264; PS, handwritten journal, 1965, box 21, folder 4, SFP.

27. DGS to PS, November 2, 1965, box 24, folder 3, SFP.

28. Ibid.

29. DGS to PS, November 6, 1965, box 24, folder 3, SFP.

30. PS to JS, December 3, 1965, box 73, folder 3, SFP.

31. PS to JS, December 3, 1965, box 73, folder 3, SFP.

32. PS to JS, December 26, 1965, box 73, folder 3, SFP.

33. Ibid.

34. PS to JS, December 17, 1965, box 73, folder 3, SFP.

35. PS to JS, December 17, 1965, box 73, folder 3, SFP; PS, recordings labeled 378062 and 378063, *Nile Fantasy*, reels 1 and 2, SFA.

36. "Philippa Schuyler Triumphs in Cairo," *The Washington Afro-American*, January 4, 1966, clipping, box 57, folder 6, SFP.

37. "Success in Cairo", *West London Observer*, January 6, 1966, clipping, box 57, folder 6, SFP.

38. DGS to PS, January 2, 1966, box 24, folder 3, SFP.

39. DGS to PS, March 4 and September 20, 1966, box 24, folder 3, SFP.

40. PS, recording labeled PS 26, 1966, SFA.

41. PS, handwritten manuscript for *Nile Fantasy*, box 34, folder 3, SFP.

42. PS, sketch on loose paper, n.d., box 25, folder 2, SFP.

43. Ibid.

44. Program from recital at Lome, Togo, January 7, 1966, box 56, folder 11, SFP.

45. Programs for recitals at North Carolina College at Durham, Durham, NC, March 2, 1966; Olivet Baptist Church, Chicago, IL, March 25, 1966; and Winston-Salem State College, Winston-Salem, NC,

June 27, 1966, box 55, folder 4, SFP; PS, handwritten manuscript for *Nile Fantasy*, box 34, folder 3, SFP.

46. Program for recital at North Carolina College at Durham, Durham, NC, March 2, 1966, box 55, folder 4, SFP.

47. PS, recording labeled PS 26, 1966, SFA.

48. Typed publicity sheet for *Nile Fantasy*, n.d., box 6, Philippa Schuyler Collection, Special Collections Research Center, Syracuse University Libraries, Syracuse, NY.

49. PS, handwritten manuscript for Nile Fantasy, box 34, folder 3, SFP.

50. DGS to PS, October 15, 1965, box 24, folder 3, SFP.

51. PS, handwritten manuscript for *Nile Fantasy*, box 34, folder 3, SFP; PS, recordings labeled 378062 and 378063, *Nile Fantasy*, reels 1 and 2, SFA.

52. Programs for recitals March 2, 1966, to October 30, 1966, box 55, folder 4 and box 56, folder 11, SFP.

53. Program for Philippa Schuyler Memorial, Town Hall, New York, September 24, 1967, box 55, folder 4, SFP.

CHAPTER 9

1. PS to JS, January 22, 1965, box 73, folder 3, SFP.

2. PS, handwritten manuscript and list of musical themes, box 34, folder 2, SFP.

3. PS, handwritten notes, box 27, notebook 5, SFP; PS, handwritten notes, box 27, notebook 6, SFP.

4. PS, handwritten sketch, box 31, SFP; PS to JS, October 1, 1964, box 73, folder 2, SFP.

5. PS, handwritten manuscript and list of musical themes, box 34, folder 2, SFP.

6. Ibid.

7. Arnold, 46, 95, 106, 110, 119.

8. Alden Whitman, "Nkrumah, 62, Dead; Ghana's Ex-Leader," *The New York Times*, April 28, 1972, 1, 44. For an example of American media coverage of Nkrumah during Schuyler's lifetime: Lloyd Garrison, "Portrait of Nkrumah as Dictator," *The New York Times*, May 3, 1964: 15.

9. Arnold, 120, 220-224.

10. Whitman, "Nkrumah, 62, Dead; Ghana's Ex-Leader," 1, 44.

11. Talalay, *Composition in Black and White*, 210-211.

12. Ibid., 205-208.

13. Arnold, 82-85.

14. Ibid., 68, 131-132, 258, 273-274.

15. Ibid., 68, 281-282.

16. Ibid., 288, 520-523.

17. PS, *Adventures in Black and White*, 277.

18. Arthur Syahuka-Muhindo and Kristof Titeca, "The Rwenzururu Movement and the Struggle for the Rwenzururu Kingdom in Uganda," Discussion Paper, Institute of Development Policy and Management, (University of Antwerp, 2016): 6-11, 19-20.

19. Arnold, 265-269.

20. Willie Henderson, "Seretse Khama: A Personal Appreciation," *African Affairs* 89, No. 354 (January 1990): 27-38.

21. Souleymane Bachir Diagne, "Négritude," *The Stanford Encyclopedia of Philosophy* (Spring 2023 Edition), edited by Edward N. Zalta & Uri Nodelman; Arnold, 57-58.

22. Felipa Monterro, "Terror in Angola," *American Opinion*, April 1963, box 65, folder 3, SFP.

23. Kyagambiddwa, *Uganda Martyrs African Oratorio*.

24. PS, handwritten manuscript and list of musical themes, box 34, folder 2, SFP.

25. Kyagambiddwa, English translations for *Uganda Martyrs African Oratorio*, 9-31.

26. Ibid.

27. Ibid.

28. Ibid.

29. JS to PS, July 29, 1966, August 1, 1966, "Sunday 12," 1966 or 1967, and February 8, 1967, box 22, folder 3, SFP.

30. PS to JS, March 8, 1964, box 73, folder 2, SFP; PS to JS, September 6, 1965, box 73, folder 3, SFP.

31. PS to JS, February 29, 1964, box 73, folder 2, SFP.

32. Chester Davis, "Miss Schuyler is Driven to Prove She Can Be Truly Superior," *Winston-Salem Journal*, July 5, 1966, 12. The article mentions Schuyler's efforts to build bridges between leaders of newly independent African nations and U.S. politicians and journalists.

33. Luix Overbea, "Visiting Concert Pianist Focuses Many Talents," 1966, clipping, box 57, folder 6, SFP.

EPILOGUE

1. PS, practice notes, 1955, box 71, SFP.

2. Talalay, *Composition in Black and White*, 261; Program for recital at Le Benin, Lome, Togo, February 2, 1966, box 56, folder 11, SFP.

3. JS to PS, August 1, 1966, box 22, folder 3, SFP.

4. PS to JS, August 6, 1966, box 73, folder 4, SFP.

5. Talalay, *Composition in Black and White*, 265-266.

6. PS to JS, September 12, 1966, box 73, folder 4, SFP.

7. PS to JS, September 13, 1966, box 73, folder 4, SFP.

8. Ibid.

9. Ibid.

10. PS to JS, September 15, 1966, box 73, folder 4, SFP.

11. PS to JS, September 13, 1966, box 73, folder 4, SFP.

12. PS, poem attached to letter from PS to JS, September 7, 1966, box 73, folder 4, SFP.

13. PS to JS, September 15, 1966, box 73, folder 4, SFP.

14. Program for recital at Mount Mercy College, Pittsburgh, PA, October 30, 1966, box 55, folder 4, SFP.

15. Talalay, *Composition in Black and White*, 270.

16. Program for recital at Hue MACV Chapel, Hue, Vietnam, March 22, 1967, box 56, folder 11, SFP.

17. PS to JS, March 25, 1967, box 73, folder 5, SFP.

18. PS to JS, April 29, 1967, box 73, folder 5, SFP.

19. PS to JS, April 16, 1967, box 73, folder 5, SFP.

20. PS to JS, April 29, 1967, box 73, folder 5, SFP.

21. Ibid.

22. Ibid.

23. PS to JS, April 16, 1967, box 73, folder 5, SFP.

24. Talalay, *Composition in Black and White*, 271, 273-274.

25. PS to JS, May 6, 1967, box 73, folder 5, SFP.

26. Ibid.

27. Talalay, *Composition in Black and White*, 6.

28. PS to JS, May 6, 1967, box 73, folder 5, SFP.

29. Talalay, *Composition in Black and White*, 3.

30. "Philippa Schuyler, Pianist, Dies in Crash of a Copter in Vietnam," *The New York Times*, May 10, 1967, 1, 15.

31. "2,000 at St. Patrick's Attend Requiem for Philippa Schuyler," *The New York Times*, May 19, 1967, 39.

32. Talalay, *Composition in Black and White*, 276-279.

Appendix A

List of Compositions

Date of Composition	Composition Title	First Documented Performance	Archive Location
Undated, by 1937[a]	B Merry Go Round (incomplete)		SFP (b. 25, f. 4)
Undated, by 1937	Convent Gardens		SFP (b. 25, f. 3)
Undated, by 1937	The Doll's Lesson		SFP (b. 25, f. 3)
Undated, by 1937	Fairies Dance		SFP (b. 25, f.3 and f. 4)
Undated, by 1937	Pansy Bells		SFP (b. 25, f. 3)
Undated, by 1937	Pumpkin Dance		SFP (b. 25, f. 3 and f. 4)
Undated, by 1937	Pussy Willows		SFP (b. 25, f. 3)
Undated, by 1937	Teddy Bear		SFP (b. 25, f. 3)
Undated, by 1937	Tragedy		SFP (b. 25, f. 3)
Age 4	The Butterfly	YMCA, Harlem, NYC, 1937, "Philippa's First Recital Alone"[1]	SFP (b. 25, f. 3)
Age 4	Dance of the Vegetables Alt: The Vegetable Dance	YMCA, Harlem, NYC, 1937[2]	SFP (b. 25, f. 3)
Age 4	The Goldfish	YMCA, Harlem, NYC, 1937[3]	SFP (b. 25, f. 3)
Age 4	The Wolf	YMCA, Harlem, NYC, 1937[4]	*Three, Five, Eight and Nine Little Pieces*[b] SFP (b. 25, f. 3)
Age 4 (9/4/35)	Rolling Home		SFP (b. 25, f. 3 and f. 4)

Age 4 (1/20/36)	Nigerian Dance	YMCA, Harlem, NYC, 1937	SFP (b. 25, f. 3 and f. 4)
Age 4 (1936)	Up the Airy Mountain		SFP (b. 25, f. 4)
Age 5	The Doll's Party[c]	YMCA, Harlem, NYC, 1937[6]	Lost manuscript
Age 5	Wild Fruits (alt: The Wild Fruit)	YMCA, Harlem, NYC, 1937[7]	SFP (b. 25, f. 3 and f. 4)
Age 5	Suite of the Seasons[d] I. Autumn Rain II. Christmas Eve III. Spring (alt: Spring Improvisation) Alternate version:[e] I. Winter II. Summer III. Christmas Eve IV. Spring Improvisation	Clyde Barrie Recital featuring Philippa Duke Schuyler, Fuld Hall, Newark, N.J., June 12, 1937[8]	Autumn Rain: *Three, Five, Eight, and Nine Little Pieces* Alt. version: SFP (b. 25, f. 3)
Age 6	Cockroach Ballet	YMCA, Harlem, NYC, 1937[9]	SFP (b. 29, f. 10)
Age 6	Death of the Nightingale	YMCA, Harlem, NYC, 1937[10]	SFP (b. 25, f. 3)

a. Versions of these first pieces found in box 25, folder 4 appear to have been transcribed or copied by Josephine Schuyler, as there are handwritten notes from JS to PS. The rest were likely transcribed by Schuyler's piano teacher Arnetta Jones before summer 1937.
b. All four collections were published by Josephine Schuyler as "Mrs. George Schuyler" in 1938. The contents of the collections overlap significantly.
c. It is possible this was the same piece as *The Doll's Lesson*.
d. This version is found in a program from a recital at Manhattanville College of the Sacred Heart on December 8, 1938.
e. This version is found in box 25, folder 3, labeled in someone else's hand. Alternate movement titles are also used in some programs from 1937 to 1939.

Age	Title	Venue/Date	Source
Age 6	The Jolly Pig	The Proto Club of the YWCA, Ann Street YWCA, Hartford, Ct., May 22, 1938[11]	*Three, Five, Eight and Nine Little Pieces* SFP (b. 25, f. 3)
Age 6	Suite from the Arabian Nights I. Sandstorm II. The Caravan III. Streets of Damascus IV. Camel Race	Manhattanville College of the Sacred Heart, Purchase, N.Y., December 8, 1938[12]	SFP (b. 29, f. 10)
Age 6	Dance of the Forty Thieves (added to *Suite from the Arabian Nights*)	Auditorium of Public School 136, New York, N.Y., February 12, 1939[13]	SFP (b. 25, f. 3)
Undated, in own hand[f]	All American Newsreel		SFP (b. 25, f. 3)
Undated, in own hand	Andante con moto		SFP (b. 25, f. 3)
Undated, in own hand	A Sentimental Story		SFP (b. 25, f. 3)
Age 7	Panda had a Party	New Lincoln Auditorium, Trenton, N.J., June 16, 1940[14]	SFP (Carnegie Hall Concert Notes, 1939-40, box 28)
Age 7	Pinocchio	New Lincoln Auditorium, Trenton, N.J., June 16, 1940[15]	Lost manuscript
Age 7	The Priest's Song	Auditorium at Public School 136, New York, N.Y., February 12, 1939[16]	SFP (Children's Notebook, 1938-1939, box 28)
Age 7 or 9[g]	Twilight and Morning	Irvine Auditorium, Philadelphia, Pa., December 27, 1941[17]	Lost manuscript

Age	Title	Venue/Date	Source
Age 7	World's Fair (Alt: Impressions of the World's Fair)	New Lincoln Auditorium, Trenton, N.J., June 16, 1940[18]	SFP (b. 25, f. 3)
Age 7	At the Circus	Arnetta Jones Studio Recital, Imperial Elks Hall, New York, N.Y., June 4, 1939[19]	*Five, Eight, and Nine Little Pieces* SFP (Carnegie Hall Concert Notes 1939-40, box 28) SFP (b. 25, f. 3)
by 1938	Farewell		*Five, Eight, and Nine Little Pieces* SFP (b. 25, f. 3)
by 1938	Morning Miniature		*Eight and Nine Little Pieces*
by 1938	Postscript		*Eight and Nine Little Pieces*
Age 8	A Christmas Story	Edward Waters College, Jacksonville, Fla., March 15, 1942[20]	SFP (b. 25, f. 9)
Age 8	The Little Frog	New Lincoln Auditorium, Trenton, N.J., June 16, 1940[21]	Lost manuscript
Age 8	Men at Work (The WPA on a Construction Job)	New Lincoln Auditorium, Trenton, N.J., June 16, 1940[22]	*Eight and Nine Little Pieces*
Age 8	Shadows	The Irvine Auditorium, Philadelphia, Pa., December 27, 1941[23]	Lost manuscript

f. Childhood works in Schuyler's own handwriting were likely composed after 1937.
g. The age of composition listed in different programs is inconsistent, varying from age 7 in programs dated 1950, to age 9 in those dated 1942.

Age 8	Sombrero	Edward Waters College, Jacksonville, Fla., March 15, 1942[24]	Lost manuscript
Age 8	Spanish Harlem	New Lincoln Auditorium, Trenton, N.J., June 16, 1940[25]	Lost manuscript
Age 9	Circus Act[h]	Edward Waters College, Jacksonville, Fla., March 15, 1942[26]	Lost manuscript
Age 9	Hallowe'en Night[i]	Saint Paul Women's Council, April 7, 1942[27]	Lost manuscript
Age 9	Minuet	Edward Waters College, Jacksonville, Fla., March 15, 1942[28]	Lost manuscript
Age 9	Old Witches Dance	Edward Waters College, Jacksonville, Fla., March 15, 1942[29]	Lost manuscript
Age 9	Song of the Machine (in a Defense Factory)	The Irvine Auditorium, Philadelphia, Pa., December 27, 1941[30]	*Nine Little Pieces*
by 1941	The Mystery Story	Manhattanville College of the Sacred Heart, Purchase, N.Y., May 19, 1941[31]	Lost manuscript
by 1941	South American Caprice	Manhattanville College of the Sacred Heart, Purchase, N.Y., May 19, 1941[32]	Lost manuscript
by 1941	The Toy-Maker's Ball	Manhattanville College of the Sacred Heart, Purchase, N.Y., May 19, 1941[33]	Lost manuscript
1941	Leaves in the Wind		SFP (b. 25, f. 9)
1942	The Waves	South High School Auditorium, February 7, 1943[34]	SFP (b. 25, f. 9)

1943-1945	Manhattan Nocturne (piano transcription)[j]	First Presbyterian Church, Elmira, N.Y., May 7, 1946[35]	SFP (b. 25, f. 3)
1944-1946	Rumpelstiltsken (piano transcription)	Asbury Methodist Church, Washington, D.C., May 9, 1948[36]	Published 1955[37]
Unknown; likely 1940s	Untitled in 7 Movements		SFP (b. 25, f. 1)
Age 14	Legends of Sleepy Hollow (piano transcription)[k]	Theatre Massillon Coicou, Port-au-Prince, Haiti, March 5, 1950[38]	Lost piano transcription
Age 15	Maelstrom (from the suite "Afternoon at the Library")	Asbury Methodist Church, Washington, D.C., May 9, 1948[39]	Lost manuscript
Age 16	Au Revoir to a Young Man	Theatre Massillon Coicou, Port-au-Prince, Haiti, March 5, 1950[40]	Lost manuscript
Premiered 1950	Rhapsody of Youth[l]	Waco Hall, Waco, Tex., March 26, 1951[l,41]	
by 1958	Arirang	Ewha Womans University, South Korea, December 7, 1958[42]	Lost manuscript Audio: *Pianologue* Transcribed from audio

h. Given the difference in the listed age of composition, this is likely a different piece than "At the Circus," despite the similar title and missing score.
i. This potentially could be the same as a movement from "Untitled in 7 movements" labeled "Hallowe'en" in the score.
j. Multiple handwritten versions exist; all appear to either be incomplete or a shorthand Schuyler used. None are exact matches to each other.
k. Most programs list the movements as *Rip van Winkle* and *The Headless Horseman*, although one includes *The Wild Horse* instead. Orchestral versions of *Rip van Winkle* and *The Headless Horseman* were originally part of her *Fairy Tale Symphony*, which also included the orchestral version of *Rumpelstiltsken*.
l. This was likely a piano transcription of the work, which was described as a one-movement piano concerto. It premiered December 1950 in Haiti, at President Paul Magloire's inauguration, but the program is missing.

by 1958	The God of the Sea retitled: Damballa[m]	Manhattan College of the Sacred Heart, Purchase, N.Y., July 1, 1958[43]	Lost manuscript Audio: *Pianologue*[n] Transcribed from audio
by 1958	The Goddess of Love	People's Community Church, Detroit, Mich., November 6, 1958[44]	Lost manuscript
by 1958	On-Koto retitled: Wanchai Road[o]	Ewha Womans University, South Korea, December 7, 1958[45]	Retitled, possibly revised SFP (b. 25, f. 10)[p]
by 1958	Voodoo Festival alt. title: Festival in Port-au-Prince	Manhattan College of the Sacred Heart, Purchase, N.Y., July 1, 1958[46]	SFP (b. 25, f. 10)
by 1958	Sakura	Marines Memorial Theatre, San Francisco, Calif., December 11, 1958[47]	Lost manuscript Audio: *Pianologue* Transcribed from audio
by 1958	Love Song from North Shenshi retitled: Khanghai[q]	Marines Memorial Theatre, San Francisco, Calif., December 11, 1958[48]	Retitled, possibly revised SFP (b. 25, f. 10)
by 1959	Patagonian Triste	John Hancock Hall, Boston, Mass., October 25, 1959[49]	SFP (b. 25, f. 10)
by 1959	New Moon	John Hancock Hall, Boston, Mass., October 25, 1959[50]	SFP (b. 25, f. 10)

by 1959[r]	African Suite
	alt. title: Negro Suite
	alt. title: Suite Africaine
	Movement titles:
	  I. Sanga
	  II. Tweyanze
	  III. Fumitta Embogo
		John Hancock Hall, Boston, Mass., October 25, 1959[s1]	SFP (b. 29, f. 4)[s]

Copyright 1960	Around the World Suite Patagonian Triste Voodoo Festival Khanghai Wanchai Road Sanga Tweyanze Fumitta Embogo The Poet's Love The King of France	Never performed with this title and order	Library of Congress, Music Division[t]

m. First performance as *Damballa* (often spelled *Dambala*) at Emerson Hall, Ewha Womans University, South Korea, December 7, 1958.
n. Titled *Damballa* in the liner notes.
o. First performance as *Wanchai Road* at Carnegie Hall on May 17, 1959. Two versions of the program can be found in SFP, one with each title.
p. *Wanchai Road* version.
q. First performance as *Khanghai* at John Hancock Hall, Boston, MA, on October 25, 1959.
r. Talalay dates this as being composed by 1958, but the manuscript is undated, and the full suite first appeared in surviving programs in 1960. *Tweyanze* and *Sanga* were programmed on a concert alone on October 25, 1959.
s. Folder 4 contains both the originals and transcriptions edited by Michael Parker, as per communication on May 6, 2022, from Dr. Kathryn Talalay.
t. Not included in the online catalog; housed in an off-site facility.

by 1960	Suite de Normandie du Moyen-Age
	Revised version:
	  Normandie
	Movements:
	  I. The King of France (Le Roi de France)
	  II. The Poet's Love (L'amour d'un Poete)
	  III. Flowers of Death (Fleurs de Mort)
		Norfolk Division of Virginia State College, Norfolk, Va., February 12, 1960[52]	SFP (b. 25, f. 10)
			
			III. Flowers of Death - lost
			Revised version - lost

by 1961[u]	Carnival in Languedoc Alt. title: Medley of Languedoc Folk-Themes[v]	The Agricultural and Technical College of North Carolina, Greensboro, N.C., July 6, 1961[53]	SFP (b. 29, f. 9)
Premiered 1964	Chisamharu the Nogomo Retitled: African Rhapsody[w]	Town Hall, New York, N.Y, September 13, 1964 (premiere)[54]	SFP (b. 29, f. 4)[x]

Premiered 1964	White Nile Suite I. Legend of the Mahdi (Omdurman) and his Dancing Dervishes - Alt: Legend of the Mahdi - Alt: Nubian Legend - Alt: Omdurman II. Alexandria III. The Water-Front at Port Said on a Hot Night - Alt: Port Said IV. The Fall of Babylon - Alt: Egyptian Babylon	Town Hall, New York, N.Y., September 13, 1964 (premiere)[55]	SFP (b. 29, f. 1)[y]
by 1965	Uganda Martyrs	St. Francis deSales High School, Powhatan, Va., January 15, 1965[56]	SFP (b. 25, f. 6)

u. Talalay dates this as premiering in 1955, but any recording or program from that premiere is now missing. The handwriting and compositional style strongly resemble Schuyler's other 1960s works, particularly those with named musical themes.

v. All documented performances used this alternate title. The title *Carnival in Languedoc* only appears in the manuscript score.

w. First documented performance as *African Rhapsody* on January 15, 1965, at St. Francis deSales High School, Powhatan, VA. Some program notes indicate its premiere under that title occurred at a reception for Togo officials in New York, for the closing of the 19th United Nations Assembly.

x. The SFP catalog incorrectly lists this folder as containing only *African Suite*.

y. Folder 1 contains both the originals and transcriptions edited by Michael Parker, as per communication on May 6, 2022, from Dr. Kathryn Talalay. Folder 2 contains an alternate version of the first movement titled *Omdurman*.

| Premiered 1965 | Seven Pillars of Wisdom
- Prologue: The Foundations of the Arab Revolt (The Clashing Jealousies)
- Part I: The Decay of the Ottoman Empire
- Part II: Fire and Reason
- Part III: Blood
- Part IV: The Evil of my Tale
- Part V: The Agonies, the Terrors, and the Mistakes (Torture at Deraa)
- Part VI: Fortune Favored the Bold Player
- Part VII: The Final Stroke: Red Victory
- Epilogue: Disillusion, Death, and the Final Liberty of the Afro-Asian Peoples | New York University, New York, N.Y., February 6, 1965[57] | SFP

Prologue (p. 2-3 only); Epilogue-Finale (incomplete version), b. 25, f. 5.

Parts V and VI, b. 25, f. 6.

Introductory quotes, Prologue (missing p. 2-3), Parts I-IV, Part VII, Epilogue (first half),
Epilogue-Finale (p. 0 only), b. 25, f. 8.

Epilogue-Finale (p. 1, 4, 5 of complete version), b. 31, f. 1 |
| Premiered 1965 | Nile Fantasy
Alt. title: Le Nil | Theatre de i'Opera, Cairo, Egypt, December 10, 1965[58] | Piano concerto: SFP (b. 34)

Piano transcription: Lost[z] |

ca. 1965	Sonata diabolique (incomplete; 3 pages)	N/A	SFP Sketch: b. 30, f. 3 Incomplete score: b. 27, notebook 2
Premiered 1966	Rhapsodie Togolaise	Le Benin, Lome, Togo, February 2, 1966[59]	Lost manuscript
ca. 1966	Untitled, on themes related to African independence	N/A	SFP (b. 34, f. 2)
Unknown, likely not by Schuyler	Vistula at Night (incomplete; 2 pages)[aa]	N/A	SFP (b. 25, f. 5)

z. The SFP catalog lists an incomplete piano solo transcription in box 34, folder 3. The folder actually contains the orchestral score. No folders in box 34 or elsewhere in the archive include a solo piano transcription.

aa. Although the SFP catalog lists this as Schuyler's composition, it is likely by another composer. The score's shorthand strongly resembles other instances in which Schuyler copied out a composer's music by hand while studying it. Matching it to a source has proven difficult, but clues point to one possibility. In a 1964 concert, Schuyler programmed Yohanan Ramati's *Memories of Poland. Vistula at Night* may be her solo piano arrangement of a movement from Ramati's *Quintet in c minor, op. 2: Memories of Warsaw.* While a list of that work's movements has proven difficult to locate, it certainly could have included a movement about Poland's Vistula River, and the other contents of the notebook containing *Vistula at Night* date from 1964.

Notes for list

1. Program for "Philippa's First Recital Alone" at YMCA, Harlem, New York, NY, 1937, box 54, folder 1, SFP.
2. Ibid.
3. Ibid.
4. Ibid.
5. Ibid.
6. Ibid.
7. Ibid.
8. Program for recital with Clyde Barrie, Fuld Hall, Newark, NJ, June 12, 1937, box 54, folder 1, SFP.
9. Program for "Philippa's First Recital Alone" at YMCA, Harlem, New York, NY, 1937, box 54, folder 1, SFP.
10. Ibid.
11. Program for recital at the Proto Club of the YWCA, Ann St YWCA, Hartford, CT, May 22, 1938, box 54, folder 1, SFP.
12. Program for recital at Manhattanville College of the Sacred Heart, Purchase, NY, December 8, 1938, box 54, folder 1, SFP.
13. Program for recital at Public School 136, New York, NY, February 12, 1939, box 54, folder 1, SFP.
14. Program for recital at the New Lincoln Auditorium, Trenton, NJ, June 16, 1940, box 54, folder 2, SFP.
15. Ibid.
16. Program for recital at Public School 136, New York, NY, February 12, 1939, box 54, folder 1, SFP.
17. Program for recital at the Irvine Auditorium, Philadelphia, PA, December 27, 1941, box 54, folder 2, SFP.
18. Program for recital at the New Lincoln Auditorium, Trenton, NJ, June 16, 1940, box 54, folder 2, SFP.
19. Program for Arnetta Jones Studio Recital, Imperial Elks Hall, New York, NY, June 4, 1939, box 54, folder 1, SFP.
20. Program for recital at Edward Waters College, Jacksonville, FL, March 15, 1942, box 54, folder 2, SFP.
21. Ibid.
22. Ibid.
23. Program for recital at the Irvine Auditorium, Philadelphia, PA, December 27, 1941, box 54, folder 2, SFP.
24. Program for recital at Edward Waters College, Jacksonville, FL, March 15, 1942, box 54, folder 2, SFP.
25. Ibid.
26. Ibid.
27. Program for recital at Saint Paul Women's Council, April 7, 1942, box 54, folder 2, SFP.
28. Program for recital at Edward Waters College, Jacksonville, FL, March 15, 1942, box 54,

folder 2, SFP.
29. Ibid.
30. Program for recital at the Irvine Auditorium, Philadelphia, PA, December 27, 1941, box 54, folder 2, SFP.
31. Program for recital at Manhattanville College of the Sacred Heart, Purchase, NY, May 19, 1941, "Schuyler, Philippa," Folders 1-4, Record Group 18: Alumni Collection, Manhattanville College Library Special Collections, Purchase, NY.
32. Ibid.
33. Ibid.
34. Program for recital at South High School Auditorium, February 7, 1943, box 54, folder 2, SFP.
35. Recital with William Warfield, First Presbyterian Church, Elmira, NY, May 7, 1946, box 54, folder 3, SFP. The orchestral version premiered at the Young People's Concerts, Carnegie Hall, New York, NY, on April 7, 1945.
36. Program for recital at Asbury Methodist Church, Washington, D.C., May 9, 1948, box 54, folder 4, SFP. The orchestral version was premiered by the American Youth Orchestra under Dean Dixon at Hunter College Assembly Hall, New York, NY, on April 6, 1946.
37. PS, Rumpelstiltsken para piano, (Buenos Aires: Ricordi Americana S.A., 1955).
38. Program for recital at Exposition Internationale du Bicentenaire de Port-au-Prince, Theatre Massillon Coicou, Port-au-Prince, Haiti, March 5, 1950, box 56, folder 1, SFP.
39. Program for recital at Asbury Methodist Church, Washington, D.C., May 9, 1948, box 54, folder 4, SFP.
40. Program for recital at Exposition Internationale du Bicentenaire de Port-au-Prince, Theatre Massillon Coicou, Port-au-Prince, Haiti, March 5, 1950, box 56, folder 1, SFP.
41. Program for recital at Waco Hall, Waco, TX, March 26, 1951, box 54, folder 5, SFP.
42. Program for recital at Emerson Hall, Ewha Womans University, South Korea, December 7, 1958, box 56, folder 5, SFP.
43. Program for lecture recital at Manhattanville College of the Sacred Heart, Purchase, NY, July 1, 1958, box 54, folder 7, SFP.
44. Program for recital at Peoples Community Church, Detroit, MI, November 6, 1958, box 54, folder 7, SFP.
45. Program for recital at Emerson Hall, Ewha Womans University, South Korea, December 7, 1958, box 56, folder 5, SFP.
46. Program for lecture recital at Manhattanville College of the Sacred Heart, Purchase, NY, July 1, 1958, box 54, folder 7, SFP.
47. Program for recital at Marines Memorial Theatre, San Francisco, CA, December 11, 1958, box 54, folder 7, SFP.
48. Ibid.
49. Program for recital at John Hancock Hall, Boston, MA, October 25, 1959, box 54, folder 7, SFP.
50. Ibid.
51. Ibid.
52. Program for recital at Norfolk Division of Virginia State College, Norfolk, VA, February 12, 1960, box 55, folder 1, SFP.
53. Program for recital at the Agricultural and Technical College of North Carolina, Greensboro, NC, July 6, 1961, box 55, folder 1, SFP.

54. Program for recital at Town Hall, New York, NY, September 13, 1964, box 55, folder 3, SFP.
55. Ibid.
56. Program for recital at St. Francis deSales High School, Powhatan, VA, January 15, 1965, box 55, folder 3, SFP.
57. Program notes for recital at Stroud Subscription Rooms, Stroud, UK, April 21, 1965, box 56, folder 10, SFP. Although the premiere's program is lost, the notes for this recital list the premiere's date and location.
58. Program for concert at Theatre de l'Opera, Cairo, Egypt, December 10, 1965, box 56, folder 10, SFP.
59. Program for recital at Le Benin, Lome, Togo, February 2, 1966, box 56, folder 11, SFP.

Appendix B

Source texts in
Uganda Martyrs
and *Untitled*

Uganda Martyrs

Measures	Movement in Oratorio	Text
1-13	#14, mm. 15-16, transposed	"Oh men that profess God, leap up! Hallelujah! I am leaping"
14-28	#22, mm. 14	"We desire to be like you"
29-30, RH	#22, mm. 14-15	1. "We desire to be like you in bravery here." 2. "We call and beseech for help."
29-30, LH	#22, m. 1	"Oh Martyrs of Jesus"
31-32, RH	#3, mm. 8-9, transposed	"Hail to the celebrated youths"
31-32, LH	#20, mm. 29-32	Angels: "Yea!"
33-34	Figuration	N/A
35-36	#22, mm. 14-15	1. "We desire to be like you in bravery here." 2. "We call and beseech for help."
37-38	#3, mm. 8-9, transposed	"Hail to the celebrated youths"
39-40	#22, mm. 14-15	1. "We desire to be like you in bravery here." 2. "We call and beseech for help."
41-42	#3, mm. 8-9, transposed	"Hail to the celebrated youths"
43-44	---	Based on motive from 41-42
45-52	---	---
53-63	#22, mm. 14-15	1. "We desire to be like you in bravery here." 2. "We call and beseech for help."
64-67	#22, mm. 11-13	1. "We pray to you for strength; pray for us." 2. "We pray for thy succor; pray for us."
68, b. 1-2	#21, m. 55	"And who judges even the heavens"
68, b. 3-4	#21, m. 58	"They who died then, are being canonized now; they are Saints today"
69, b. 1-2	#21, m. 55	"And who judges even the heavens"
69, b. 3-4	#21, m. 58	"They who died then, are being canonized now; they are Saints today"
70-73	#22, mm. 11-13	1. "We pray to you for strength; pray for us." 2. "We pray for thy succor; pray for us."
74-77	#21, m. 19	"They are Saints today"
78-79, LH	#20, mm. 61-62	God: "Open the gate, thou Porter, for the great ones to pass."
78-81, RH	#21, m. 19	"They are Saints today"

Measures	Movement in Oratorio	Text
82	---	---
83-86	#20, m. 1-4	God: "Congratulations to you! On the battle you have fought; congratulations to you on your victory!"
87-88	#20, m. 5, transposed	Angels: "Congratulations to you!"
89-90	#1, m. 1, transposed	"Our Father who art in heaven"
91-92	#1, m. 5, transposed	"All you my many brethren"
93	---	---
94	#1, m. 11, soprano	"What I am narrating to you is a glorious story"
95	---	---
96-99	#1, m. 34, soprano	"It is all about the saints"
100-107	#2, mm. 6-8	Jesus: "Baptizing men for salvation. Preach unto creation this Gospel of peace."
108-111	#1, m. 34, soprano	"It is all about the saints"
112-119	#2, mm. 6-8	Jesus: "Baptizing men for salvation. Preach unto creation this Gospel of peace."
120	#2, m. 2, transposed	Jesus: "And of the Holy Ghost"
121	#15, m. 2, transposed	"Pray for us sinners"
122	#2, m. 2, transposed	Jesus: "And of the Holy Ghost"
123	#15, m. 2, transposed	"Pray for us sinners"
124-132	#22, mm. 14-15, transposed	1. "We desire to be like you in bravery here." 2. "We call and beseech for help."
133-134	---	---
135-137	#2, m. 11	Jesus: "I am going to my Father's"
138-140	#2, mm. 12-13	Jesus: "Where, later, you will see me again. May the (Holy) Spirit ever comfort and remind you."
141	#2, m. 2, transposed	Jesus: "And of the Holy Ghost"
142	#15, m. 2, transposed, partially inverted	"Pray for us sinners"
143-150	Figuration	Based on m. 142, b. 3-4
151-152	#4, mm. 17-18	"Oh, whom do we see! He is bringing a torch of Light."
153-154	#5, mm. 15-19	"Fellow believers, be happy. If I am sacrificed for Jesus' sake, I will be very glad indeed."

Measures	Movement in Oratorio	Text
155-156	#4, mm. 17-18	"Oh, whom do we see! He is bringing a torch of Light."
157-158	#5, mm. 15-19	"Fellow believers, be happy. If I am sacrificed for Jesus' sake, I will be very glad indeed."
159-162	#5, mm. 23-26	"The Creator whom I love, to Whom I swear, and Who keeps me preoccupied. When I am sacrificed, the following is my will. I will send no post-mortem curse from the grave."
163-166	#7, mm. 1-2	"Joseph Mukasa, the Protomartyr of his religion."
167-170	#10, mm. 13-14	"There he is teaching: Matthias Kalemba."
171-182	---	---
183-190	---	Based on notes of first chord, m. 1
191-203	#14, mm. 15-16, transposed	"Oh men that profess God, leap up! Hallelujah! I am leaping."

Untitled

Measures	Source	Text or Theme
1-2	Introduction	
3-11	Uganda Martyrs African Oratorio (hereafter UMAO), #1, m. 1	"Our Father who art in heaven"
12-13	UMAO, #1, m. 5	"All you my many brethren"
14-15	UMAO, #22, m. 14-15	"We desire to be like you in bravery"
16	UMAO, #1, m. 5	"Our Father who art in heaven"
17-20	UMAO, #22, m. 14-15	"We desire to be like you in bravery"
21-26	UMAO, #1, m. 5	"Our Father who art in heaven"
27-32	UMAO, #1, m. 25-26	"In the courtyard of that Father of ours"
33-35	UMAO, #4, m. 17-18	"Oh, whom do we see! He is bringing a torch of Light"
36-38	UMAO, #1, m. 25-26	"In the courtyard of that Father of ours"
39-42	Figuration	
43-46	Schuyler's list	"Cannibal" (altered)
47-49	Schuyler's list	"Negritude"
50-51	Schuyler's list	"Tanganyika"
52-55	Schuyler's list	"Tanzania"
56-57	Introduction	
58-61	UMAO, #2, m. 1	"In the name of the Father, and of the Son"
62-65	UMAO, #2, m. 2-3	"And of the Holy Ghost; Go and teach all nations"
66-69	UMAO, #2, m. 1	"In the name of the Father, and of the Son"
70-71	UMAO, #2, m. 10	"For I am departing, and saying goodbye, to return from whence I came"
72-73	UMAO, #2, m. 5	"This Gospel of peace"
74-75	UMAO, #2, m. 10	"For I am departing, and saying goodbye, to return from whence I came"
76-78	UMAO, #2, m. 5	"This Gospel of peace"
79-80	Schuyler's list	"Kwame Nkrumah"
81-82	Schuyler's list	"Usumburah"
83-84	Schuyler's list	"Zimbabwe"

Measures	Source	Text or Theme
85-86	*UMAO*, #3, m. 1	"Once upon a time"
87-88	*UMAO*, #2, m. 1	"In the name of the Father, and of the Son"
89-91	*UMAO*, #2, m. 1	"In the name of the Father, and of the Son"
92-93	*UMAO*, #3, m. 10	"Who are today great in heaven"
94	*UMAO*, #3, m. 10	"Who are today great in heaven"
95-98	Schuyler's list	"Negritude"
99-102	Schuyler's list	"Cannibal," altered
103-104	Figuration	
105-106	*UMAO*, #4, mm. 17-18	"Oh, whom do we see! He is bringing a torch of Light"
107-108	*UMAO*, #1, mm. 25-26	"In the courtyard of that Father of ours"
109-110	*UMAO*, #1, m. 5	"All you my many brethren"
111	*UMAO*, #22, mm. 14-15	"We desire to be like you in bravery"
112-117	*UMAO*, #1, m. 1	"Our Father who art in heaven"
118-121	Introduction-based	
122-123	*UMAO*, #2, m. 2	"And of the Holy Ghost"
124-125	*UMAO*, #2, m. 3	"Go and teach all nations"
126-127	*UMAO*, #2, m. 2	"And of the Holy Ghost"
128-129	*UMAO*, #2, m. 3	"Go and teach all nations"
130-133	*The Evil of My Tale*, mm. 129-130	
134-137	*UMAO*, #3, mm. 1-3	"Once upon a time, during the reign of Mwanga, let me tell you"
138-143	*UMAO*, #3, mm. 14-15	"Hallelujah, hallelujah, to the striplings resplendent with grace!"
144-147	*The Evil of My Tale*, mm. 129-130	
148-151	*UMAO*, #1, m. 1	"Our Father who art in heaven"
152-155	Schuyler's list	"Cannibal," altered
156-163	*UMAO*, #3, mm. 14-15	"Hallelujah, hallelujah, to the striplings resplendent with grace!"

Measures	Source	Text or Theme
164-168	*UMAO*, #22, mm. 7-8	"Oh Martyrs of Jesus sitting by Him Our Brothers; pray for us. Celebrated and blessed heroes, Now you are in heaven with God. Pray for us. Oh Brothers! We pray you for strength: pray for us. We desire to be like you in bravery here. Pray for us."
210-215	Introduction, altered bass	
216-218	Schuyler's list	"Negritude"

NOTES

1. Kyagambiddwa, English translations for *Uganda Martyrs African Oratorio*, 9-31.
2. Ibid.

Bibliography

"2,000 at St. Patrick's Attend Requiem for Philippa Schuyler." *The New York Times*, May 19, 1967. https://www.nytimes.com/1967/05/19/archives/2000-at-st-patricks-attend-requiem-for-philippa-schuyler.html

Agawu, Kofi. *The African Imagination in Music*. Oxford: Oxford University Press, 2016.

Aguirre, Julian. *Aires Nacionales Argentinos,* 3rd Edition. Buenos Aires: G. Ricordi & Co, 1930.

"Albert Schweitzer, 90, Dies at His Hospital." *The New York Times*, September 6, 1965. https://www.nytimes.com/1965/09/06/archives/albert-schweitzer-90-dies-at-his-hospital-doctor-won-nobel-peace.html

Anderson, Scott. *Lawrence in Arabia: War, Deceit, Imperial Folly, and the Making of the Modern Middle East*. New York: Anchor Books, 2013.

Anderson, Warren, revised by Thomas J. Mathieson. "Hymn: I. Ancient Greek." In *Grove Music Online*. Published online, 2001, updated 2013. https://doi.org/10.1093/gmo/9781561592630.article.13648

"Arab Influence on European Music." *Time & Tide: The British News Magazine* 46, No. 13 (April 7, 1965). Box 57, folder 5, Schuyler Family Papers, Schomburg Center for Research in Black Culture: Manuscripts, Archives, and Rare Books Division, New York, New York.

Arnold, Guy. *Africa: A Modern History*. London: Atlantic Books, 2005.

The Blockson Clipping File, Charles L. Blockson Afro-American Collection, Temple University Libraries, Philadelphia, Pennsylvania.

Brodeur, Michael Andor. "A Pioneering Black Composer Gets Her Due, 110 Years After Her Debut." *The Washington Post*, October 20, 2022. https://www.washingtonpost.com/music/2022/10/20/helen-hagan-samantha-ege-yale-music/

Brown, Rae Linda. Edited by Guthrie Ramsey, Jr. *The Heart of a Woman: The Life and Music of Florence B. Price*. Urbana: University of Illinois Press, 2020.

Canteloube, Joseph. *Anthologie des chants populaires français, groupés et présentés par pays ou provinces*. Paris: Durand, 1951.

Carminati, Lucia. "An Unhappy Happy Port: Fin-de-siècle Port Said and its Connections and Disconnections of Water and Iron." *International Journal of Middle East Studies* 54 (2022): 731-739.

Carr, John Dickinson. *The Burning Court*. London: Tandem Books, 1969.

"Chanson LXXXVII." In *Le Manuscrit de Bayeux: Texte et Musique d'un Requeil de Chansons*, 108. New York, New York: Columbia University Press, 1921.

"Children's Notebook - Philippa Schuyler, 1939-1940." New York Philharmonic Shelby White & Leon Levy Digital Archives.

"Children's Notebook - Philippa Schuyler, 1941-1942." New York Philharmonic Shelby White & Leon Levy Digital Archives.

Clark, John H. "New Books on Africa." *Freedomways: A Quarterly Review of the Negro Freedom Movement* 2, no. 3 (Summer 1962): 333-337.

Coles, Michael H. "Suez, 1956 – A Successful Naval Operation Compromised by Inept Political Leadership." *Naval War College Review* 59, no. 4 (Autumn 2006): 101-118.

Cooke, Peter. "Kyagambiddwa, Joseph." In *Grove Music Online*. Published online, 2001. https://doi.org/10.1093/gmo/9781561592630.article.49720.

"Danse de la Pleine Lune." Recorded by Marcel Thonnon and Anne Thonnon-Noury. Musiques et Danses du Congo Kivu-Uele. Arion, 1998.

Davis, Chester. "Miss Schuyler is Driven to Prove She Can Be Truly Superior." *Winston-Salem Journal*, July 5, 1966. https://www.newspapers.com/image/935713124.

Diagne, Souleymane Bachir. "Négritude." *The Stanford Encyclopedia of Philosophy, Spring 2023 Edition*. Edited by Edward N. Zalta & Uri Nodelman. https://plato.stanford.edu/archives/spr2023/entries/negritude/

Ehret, Christopher. *The Civilizations of Africa: A History to 1800*, 2nd edition. Charlottesville: University of Virginia Press, 2016.

Ericson, Raymond. "Philippa Duke Schuyler Plays Works for Piano Inspired by her African Tours." *The New York Times,* September 14, 1964. https://www.nytimes.com/1964/09/14/archives/musk-town-hall-recital-philippa-duke-schuyler-plays-works-for-piano.html.

Farraj, Johnny and Sami Abu Shumays. *Inside Arabic Music: Arabic Maqam Performance and Theory in the 20th Century.* Oxford: Oxford University Press, 2019.

Faulkner, Neil. *Empire and Jihad: The Anglo-Arab Wars of 1870-1920.* New Haven: Yale University Press, 2021.

Faupel, John F. *African Holocaust: The Story of the Uganda Martyrs.* New York: P.J. Kenedy & Sons, 1962; Reprint, Muriwai Books, 2018. Kindle edition.

Garrison, Lloyd. "Portrait of Nkrumah as Dictator." *The New York Times,* May 3, 1964. https://www.nytimes.com/1964/05/03/archives/portrait-of-nkrumah-as-dictator.html

Ginastera, Alberto. *Canción al arbol del olvido: para canto y piano.* Buenos Aires: Ricordi Americana, 1955.

Hebblethwaite, Benjamin, with editorial assistance of Bartley, et al. *Vodou songs in Haitian Creole and English.* Philadelphia: Temple University Press, 2012.

Helen Walker-Hill Collection. American Music Research Center, University of Colorado at Boulder, Boulder, CO.

Henderson, Willie. "Seretse Khama: A Personal Appreciation." *African Affairs* 89, No. 354 (January 1990): 27-56.

"His Save Our Surf Gave Waves a Break: John M. Kelly Jr. 1919-2007." *Honolulu Star-Bulletin,* October 5, 2007. https://archives.starbulletin.com/2007/10/05/news/story04.html

Holder, Nathan, illustrated by Charity Russell. *Where Are All the Black Female Composers? The Ultimate Fun Facts Guide.* Holders Hill Publishing, 2020.

Hulbert, Ann. *Off the Charts: The Hidden Lives and Lessons of American Child Prodigies.* New York: Vintage Books, 2019.

Huysmans, Joris-Karl, translated by Terry Hale. *La-Bas (The Damned).* London: Penguin Classics, 2001.

"The Iran Society." *Diplomatic Bulletin*, April 1, 1965. Box 57, folder 5, Schuyler Family Papers, Schomburg Center for Research in Black Culture: Manuscripts, Archives, and Rare Books Division, New York, New York.

Jacobi, Erwin R. "Schweitzer, Albert." In *Grove Music Online*. Published online, 2001. https://doi.org/10.1093/gmo/9781561592630.article.25204.

Jaegerhuber, Werner A. *Complaintes Haitiennes*, 2nd edition. Port au Prince, 1950.

Johnson, Paul. Unpublished transcriptions of Philippa Schuyler's *Damballa, Arirang*, and *Sakura*.

Kelly, Jr., John M. Folk *Songs Hawaii Sings: A Collection of Songs from Polynesia and Asia for Piano and Voice*. Tokyo: Charles E. Tuttle Company, Inc., 1962. Kindle edition.

Keysner, Catherine. "Genius in the Raw: The Schuyler Family and the Modern Mulatta." In *Artificial Color: Modern Food and Racial Fictions*. Oxford: Oxford University Press, 2019.

Klein, Howard. "Musical Tribute Paid to Schweitzer." *The New York Times*, January 15, 1965. https://www.nytimes.com/1965/01/15/archives/musical-tribute-paid-schweitzer-concerts-proceeds-given-to-his.html.

Kyagambiddwa, Joseph. *African Music from the Source of the Nile*. New York: Frederick A Praeger, 1955.

Kyagambiddwa, Joseph. *Uganda Martyrs African Oratorio*. Rome: Casimiri-Capra, 1964.

Lawrence, T. E. *Seven Pillars of Wisdom*. Hertfordshire: Wordsworth Editions Limited, 1997.

Le Fanu, Joseph Sheridan, edited by Kathleen Costello-Sullivan. *Carmilla*, Critical Edition. Syracuse: Syracuse University Press, 2013.

Library of Congress, Copyright Office. "Catalog of Copyright Entries, Third Series, Volume 14, Part 5, Number 1: Music, January-June, 1960." Washington, D.C.: Copyright Office, Library of Congress: For sale by the Supt. of Docs., U.S. G.P.O., 1961.

Library of Congress, Copyright Office. "Catalogue of Copyright Entries, Third Series, Volume 18, Part 5, Number 2: Music, July-December, 1964." Washington, D.C.: Copyright Office, Library of Congress: For sale by the Supt. Of Docs., U.S. G.P.O., 1967.

Lindsey, Lauren Michelle Brandon. "Werner Jaegerhuber's 'Messe Folklorique Haitienne': A conductor's guide." DMA diss., University of Southern Mississippi, 2012.

Madrid, Alejandro L. *Tania León's Stride: A Polyrhythmic Life*. Urbana: University of Illinois Press, 2022.

Markel, Howard. "Dr. Albert Schweitzer, a Renowned Medical Missionary with a Complicated History." *PBS NewsHour*, January 14, 2016. https://www.pbs.org/newshour/health/dr-albert-schweitzer-a-renowned-medical-missionary-with-a-complicated-history

Martin, James. "The Story of the Ugandan Martyrs." *America: The Jesuit Review*, June 3, 2011. https://www.americamagazine.org/content/all-things/story-ugandan-martyrs

Mason, Richard. *The World of Suzie Wong*, reprint. Cleveland: World Pub. Co, 1957; New York: Penguin Books, 2012.

Mitchell, Joseph. "Evening with a Gifted Child." *The New Yorker*, August 31, 1940, Issue 31. https://www.newyorker.com/magazine/1940/08/31/evening-with-a-gifted-child

Monterro, Felipa. "Terror in Angola." *American Opinion*, April 1963. Box 65, folder 3, Schuyler Family Papers, Schomburg Center for Research in Black Culture: Manuscripts, Archives, and Rare Books Division, New York, New York.

Moorehead, Alan. *The White Nile*. London: Hamish Hamilton, 1960; London: Penguin Books, 1963.

Music from Mozambique, Volume 2: Chopi Timbila, Two Orchestral Performances. Recorded by Francisco Banze and Ron Hallis. Folkways Records, 1982.

Music from Mozambique, Volume 3. Recorded by Ron Hallis and Gabriel Mondlane. Folkways Records, 1983.

Nasr, Seyyed Hossein, Editor-in-Chief. *The Study Quran: A New Translation and Commentary*. New York: HarperOne, 2015.

Nicolaides, A. "Early Portuguese Imperialism: Using the Jesuits in the Mutapa Empire of Zimbabwe." *International Journal of Peace and Development Studies* 2, no. 4 (April 2011): 132-137. http://www.academicjournals.org/IJPDS.

"On the Cover: Young Artist Abroad." *Musical Courier* CLIII, No. 1 (January 1956): 2.

"Original Girl." *Time* Magazine, March 25, 1946. https://content.time.com/time/subscriber/article/0,33009,888166,00.html

Othen, Christopher. *Katanga 1960-63: Mercenaries, Spies, and the African Nation that Wages War on the World*. Gloucestershire: The History Press, 2015. Kindle edition.

Overbea, Luix. "Visiting Concert Pianist Focuses Many Talents." Newspaper clipping, 1966. Box 57, folder 6, Schuyler Family Papers, Schomburg Center for Research in Black Culture: Manuscripts, Archives, and Rare Books Division, New York, New York.

Owens, Camille S. "'Fine Discords': Anarranging the Archives of Philippa Schuyler." *American Quarterly* 73, no. 2 (June 2021): 205-231.

"People Are." *Jet*, March 19, 1959. Accessed through Google Books.

"People Are." *Jet*, February 25, 1960. Accessed through Google Books.

Pereira, Ernie. "Nothing Could Stop Philippa." *Hongkong Sunday Tiger Standard*, January 11, 1959, 1 and 7.

"Philippa Schuyler's African Music Hailed at Town Hall." *The Pittsburgh Courier*, September 26, 1964. https://www.newspapers.com/article/128517031/the-pittsburgh-courier/.

"Philippa Schuyler: American Pianist Played for Monarchs and Desert Saint." *Musical Courier* CLIX, no. 6 (May 1959): 12.

Philippa Schuyler Collection. Special Collections Research Center, Syracuse University Libraries, Syracuse, New York.

Philippa Duke Schuyler-Concert Tours file. Series VII, Box 1, Alton Augustus Adams Collection, Center for Black Music Research, Chicago, Illinois.

"Philippa Schuyler, Pianist, Dies in Crash of a Copter in Vietnam." *The New York Times*, May 10, 1967. https://www.nytimes.com/1967/05/10/archives/philippa-schuyler-pianist-dies-in-crash-of-a-copter-in-vietnam-us.html

"Philippa Schuyler Triumphs in Cairo." *The Washington Afro-American*, January 4, 1966. Box 57, folder 6, Schuyler Family Papers, Schomburg Center for Research in Black Culture: Manuscripts, Archives, and Rare Books Division, New York, New York.

Pollard, Justin and Howard Reid. *The Rise and Fall of Alexandria: Birthplace of the Modern World*. New York: Penguin Books, 2006. Kindle edition.

Rose, Phyllis. "Prodigy and Prejudice." *The New York Times*, Dec. 10, 1995. https://www.nytimes.com/1995/12/10/books/prodigy-and-prejudice.html

Roufe, Gai. "The Reasons for a Murder: Local Cultural Conceptualizations of the Martyrdom of Gonçalo da Silveira in 1561." *Cahiers d'Études africaines* LV, no. 3 (2015): 467-487.

Sachs, Curt. *The Rise of Music in the Ancient World East and West*. New York: W. W. Norton & Company, Inc., 1943.

Salgado, Susana. "Aguirre, Julián." In *Grove Music Online*. Published online, 2001. https://doi.org/10.1093/gmo/9781561592630.article.00325.

Sams, Eric. "Cryptography, musical." In *Grove Music Online*. Published online, 2001. https://doi.org/10.1093/gmo/9781561592630.article.06915.

Schuyler Family Audio. Schomburg Center for Research in Black Culture: Moving Image and Recorded Sound Division, New York, New York.

Schuyler Family Papers. Schomburg Center for Research in Black Culture: Manuscripts, Archives,and Rare Books Division, New York, New York.

Schuyler, Josephine and Philippa. *Kingdom of Dreams*. New York: Robert Speller & Sons, 1966.

Schuyler, Philippa. *Adventures in Black and White*. Edited by Tara Betts. New York: 2Leaf Press, 2018. 1st edition: 1960.

Schuyler, Philippa. *African Rhapsody* or *Chisamharu the Nogomo*. February 2, 1965. Music Division, Library of Congress, Washington, D.C.

Schuyler, Philippa. *Around the World Suite*. January 27, 1960. Music Division, Library of Congress, Washington, D.C.

Schuyler, Philippa. *Eight Little Pieces*. New York: Mrs. George Schuyler, 1938.

Schuyler, Philippa. *Five Little Pieces*. New York: Mrs. George Schuyler, 1938.

Schuyler, Philippa. *Jungle Saints: Africa's Heroic Catholic Missionaries*. Rome: Casa Editrice Herder, 1963.

Schuyler, Philippa. "The Music of Modern Africa." *Music Journal* 18 (October 1960): 18, 60-63.

Schuyler, Philippa. *Nine Little Pieces*. New York: Mrs. George Schuyler, 1938.

Schuyler, Philippa. *Pianologue*. Circe Records, 1965.

Schuyler, Philippa. *Rumpelstiltsken para piano*. Buenos Aires: Ricordi Americana S.A., 1955.

Schuyler, Philippa. *Three Little Pieces*. New York: Mrs. George Schuyler, 1938.

Schuyler, Philippa. *White Nile Suite*. March 10, 1965. Music Division, Library of Congress, Washington, D.C.

Schuyler, Philippa. *Who Killed the Congo?*. New York: The Devin-Adair Company, 1962.

"Schuyler, Philippa." Folders 1-4, Record Group 18: Alumni Collection, Manhattanville College Library Special Collections, Purchase, NY.

"Schuyler, Philippa Duke." Box 13, Series 4 [13:4], file 35, Helen Walker-Hill Collection, Center for Black Music Research, Chicago, Illinois.

Sheehan, Peter. *Babylon of Egypt: The Archaeology of Old Cairo and the Origins of the City, revised edition*. Cairo: The American University in Cairo Press, 2010.

"The Shirley Temple of America's Negroes." *Look*, November 7, 1939. https://archive.org/details/sim_look_1939-11-07_3_23/page/n3/mode/2up

Sijpesteijn, Petra M. "The Arab Conquest of Egypt and the Beginning of Muslim Rule." In *Egypt in the Byzantine World, 300-700*, edited by Roger S. Bagnall, 437-459. Cambridge: Cambridge University Press, 2007.

"Society World." *Jet*, December 2, 1954. Accessed through Google Books.

Ssempijja, Nicholas. "Globalizing Catholicism Through Musical Performance: Kampala Archdiocesan Post-Primary Schools Music Festivals." Ph.D. dissertation, University of Bergen, 2011.

"St. Charles Lwanga and Companions, Martyrs of Uganda." Catholic News Agency, n.d. http://www.catholicnewsagency.com/saint/st-charles-lwanga-and-companions-martyrs-of-uganda-488

Stoll, Dennis Gray. Untitled review of *White Nile Suite*'s London premiere in "The Journal Reviews." Music Journal 23, no. 3 (March 1965): 75.

Streeter, Caroline A. "High (Mulatto) Hopes: The Rise and Fall of Philippa Schuyler." In *Tragic No More: Mixed-Race Women and the Nexus of Sex and Celebrity*. Amherst: University of Massachusetts, 2012.

"Success in Cairo." *West London Observer*, January 6, 1966. Box 57, folder 6, Schuyler Family Papers, Schomburg Center for Research in Black Culture: Manuscripts, Archives, and Rare Books Division, New York, New York.

"Super-Girl: Philippa Schuyler is a Musical Genius but Bobby-soxer at Heart." *Ebony* I, no. 5 (March 1946): 21-25.

Syahuka-Muhindo, Arthur and Kristof Titeca. "The Rwenzururu Movement and the Struggle for the Rwenzururu Kingdom in Uganda." Discussion Paper, Institute of Development Policy and Management, University of Antwerp, March 2016.

Talalay, Kathryn. *Composition in Black and White*. Oxford: Oxford University Press, 1995.

Talalay, Kathryn. "Philippa Duke Schuyler, Pianist/Composer/Writer." *The Black Perspective in Music* 10, no. 1 (Spring 1982): 43-68.

Tracey, Hugh. "Obituary: Ba Joseph Kiwele – Mrs. E.M. Dougall." *African Music: Journal of the International Library of African Music* 2(4) (May 1961): 102.

"Travelogue." *Jet*, October 27, 1955. Accessed through Google Books.

"Vatican to Canonize 22 Negro Martyrs." *The New York Times*, July 8, 1964. https://www.nytimes.com/1964/07/08/archives/vatican-to-canonize-22-negro-martyrs.html

Waito shepherd. "Shepherd's Flute Song." Recorded and edited by Lin Lerner and Chad Wollner. *Folk Music and Ceremonies of Ethiopia*. Folkways Records, 1974.

Walker-Hill, Helen. *From Spirituals to Symphonies: African American Women Composers and Their Music*. Urbana: University of Illinois Press, 2007.

Warburg, Gabriel R. "The Search for Sources of the White Nile and Egyptian-Sudanese Relations." *Middle Eastern Studies* 43, no. 3 (May 2007): 475-486.

Whitman, Alden. "Nkrumah, 62, Dead; Ghana's Ex-Leader." *The New York Times*, April 28, 1972. https://www.nytimes.com/1972/04/28/archives/nkrumah-62-dead-ghanas-exleader-nkrumah-former-president-of-ghana.html.

Zaratti, Alfonso. *Circle of Love*. Italy: Casamari Abbey Publishing Co., 1969.

Index

Africa. See specific countries and cities.
  Decolonization of: 135-136; 139
Aguirre, Julián, 34
Apedo-Amah, Georges, 124, 126
Arabic music, 7-8; 13-14; 15; 35; 41; 43; 45; 46; 64-65; 72-73; 80
Asia, 25-26; 64-65; 92; 100; 109; 111; 114; 117-118; 143; 145-147
Astrology, 10-11; 83; 111
  Horoscope-Numer-Tarot-Music system, 11-12

Blacking, John, 46
Blessed Martyrs of Uganda, 35; 44; 86-90
  Canonization of, 35; 86-87
  Death of, 86
  Kalemba, Matthias, 90
  Lwanga, Charles, 86
  Mukasa, Joseph, 86; 90
Books by Schuyler
  Adventures in Black and White, 1; 4; 36-37
  Jungle Saints, 9; 35; 41; 47; 53-54; 59; 82; 84
  Who Killed the Congo? 35; 94-96; 137
Botswana (formerly Bechuanaland), 138-139
  Khama, Seretse, 136; 138-139
  Williams, Ruth, 138
Buganda, 48; 86
  Music of, 43-44; 50; 62-63
  See also: Uganda

Cameroon, 39; 45
Catholicism, 4; 9-10; 22; 35; 38; 41-42; 44; 55; 57; 81-87; 111; 145; 147-148
  and the Church's stance on race, 83-84
  Blessed Martyrs of Uganda, 35; 44; 86-90

Drew, Msgr. Cornelius, 83
Convent School, Manhattanville College of the Sacred Heart, 5; 9; 15; 19; 43; 82-83
Jungle Saints (PDS), 9; 35; 41; 47; 53-54; 59; 82; 84
Kyagambiddwa, Joseph, 35; 39; 43-44; 47; 50-51; 62; 83; 85-88; 90; 130-131; 136; 139-142
  and Schuyler's conversion, 9; 81-84; 111
Stevens, Mother, 15-16
Zaratti, Fr. Alfonso, 83; 85
Cesana, Otto, 20
Chavez, Carlos, 20
Communism, 4; 81; 95; 138; 143-144; 146-147
Congo, 3; 6; 35-36; 39; 41; 45-46; 48; 51-53; 55; 59; 61; 94-96; 137-138; 143
  Independence of, 46; 94-95; 137
  Katanga, secession of, 46; 93-96; 137
  Music of, 46; 48; 51-52; 53; 59; 61
  Schuyler's concerts in, 45-46; 94
  Schuyler's reporting from, 6; 35-36; 41; 45; 55; 94-96
  See also: Lumumba, Patrice; Tshombe, Moïse; *Who Killed the Congo?* (PDS)
Copland, Aaron, 16; 123

da Silveira, Fr. Gonçalo, 54-55; 59; 63
Drew, Msgr. Cornelius, 83

Egypt, 7; 39; 42-43; 65-66; 70; 72; 74; 79; 105; 125; 127-130
  Alexandria, city of, 65; 69; 70; 74; 79
  Cairo, 43; 74; 122; 127-128; 134; 145
  Cairo Symphony Orchestra, 127
  Fortress of Babylon, 43; 65; 74; 79
  Nile River, 65-66; 80; 130-131

Port Said, 65; 72; 79

Elisabeth, queen of Belgium, 57-58

Ethiopia, 39; 42; 44; 47-48; 53; 130; 135
    Music of, 42; 47-48; 53; 130; 135
    Schuyler's travel to, 39; 42
    Selassie, Haile, emperor of Ethiopia, 42

George III, king of Toro, 45
Ghana, 39-40; 95; 136-137; 143
    Nkrumah, Kwame, 136-137; 139; 141; 143
Ginastera, Alberto, 29; 34

Haiti, 3-4; 7-9; 21-23; 37
    Schuyler's travel to, 21-22; 37
    Vodou traditions, 3-4; 7-10; 22-23; 25
Harlem, 15; 18; 83; 148
Hawaii, 25
Holt, Nora, 1; 8; 21

Islam, 7; 9; 42; 54; 67; 70; 83; 100; 104; 108-111; 114; 117; 119
    Schuyler's musical references to, 67; 100; 104; 108-111; 114; 117; 119
    Schuyler's study of, 7; 9

Jaegerhuber, Werner, 22-25
Jones, Arnetta, 18

Katanga, province of, 46; 91; 93-96; 137
Kelly, John, Jr., 25-28, 37
Kenya, 39; 136; 138
    independence of, 138
    Kenyatta, Jomo, 136; 138
    Odinga, Oginga, 136; 138
Kenyatta, Jomo, 136; 138
Khama, Seretse, 136; 138-139
Kingdom of Dreams (Josephine Schuyler and PDS), 85
Kiwele, Joseph, 46
    See also: Congo
Kyagambiddwa, Joseph, 35; 39; 43-44; 47; 50-51; 62; 83; 85-88; 90; 130-131; 136; 139-142
    interactions with Schuyler, 43-44
    African Music from the Source of the Nile, 44; 47; 62
    Uganda Martyrs African Oratorio, 35; 85-90; 139-142
Kyeyune, David, 87

Lambaréné, Gabon, 56
Latin America, music of, 15; 28-29; 33; 46
Lawrence of Arabia (1962 movie), 93
Lawrence, T.E., 3; 7; 79; 91; 93; 94; 96; 97; 100-101; 104-105; 107; 109-110; 112-114; 117; 119; 120; 131
    and Aqaba, 100; 107; 109; 117
    and Emir Feisal, 93; 105; 107-108; 119
    and Ottoman Empire, 92; 100-101; 104; 107; 109; 114; 117; 130-131
    Seven Pillars of Wisdom (Lawrence), 79; 91-93; 94; 96-97; 100-101; 104-105; 107; 109-112; 114; 117-119; 131
    and Auda Abu Tayeh, 100; 117
Lodge, Henry Cabot, 145
Lumumba, Patrice, 94-96; 137

Madagascar, 39; 46; 135
    Music of, 46; 135
    and Schuyler's heritage, 46
Mexico, 7; 20; 123; 126
Middle East, 8-9; 15; 35; 101; 110; 119; 128
    See also: specific countries and cities
Monterro, Felipa, 28; 135
    See also: Schuyler, Philippa Duke
Mozambique, 39; 46; 53; 55; 59-60
    Music of, 46; 53; 55; 59-60
    Timbila orchestras of, 60
Mupunzagutu, Chisamharu Negomo. 53-54; 59; 63
    See also: Mutapa Empire

Musical alphabet of Schuyler, 8; 12; 14; 30; 38; 99-100; 121; 136
Musical compositions by Schuyler
    African Rhapsody, 8; 35; 44; 47; 53; 58-61; 63
    see also: Chisamharu the Nogomo

Musical compositions by Schuyler *(cont'd.)*
    African Suite, 8; 35-37; 39; 44; 47-48; 51-53; 60; 63
        Sanga, 36-37; 47-49; 53
        Tweyanze, 36-37; 47-50; 55; 60; 62
        Fumitta Embogo, 36-37; 47-48; 50-52; 55; 60-63
    Arirang, 23; 26-27; 37
    Around the World Suite, 28; 36-37
    Carnival in Languedoc, 29-33
    Chisamharu the Nogomo, 35; 53; 55; 59; 64
        See also: *African Rhapsody*
    Christmas Eve, 16-17
    Cockroach Ballet, 7; 15; 17; 19
    Copyright of, 26; 28; 36-37; 60; 66; 78-80
    Criticisms of, 14; 21; 38; 53; 57; 60; 64; 66; 79; 123; 125-126; 128
    Damballa, 22-24; 37
    Death of the Nightingale, 7
    Encryption, use of, 8; 11-14; 35; 96
        See also: Musical alphabet of Schuyler
    Fairies Dances, 17
    Folk music, use of, 4, 7-8; 13-14; 21; 23; 25; 26-27; 28; 30-36; 130; 135
        See also: specific countries and styles
    Horoscope-Numer-Tarot-Music system, 11-12
    The Jolly Pig, 17-18
    Khanghai (alt. *Love Song from North Shenshi*), 26-28; 36
    Manhattan Nocturne, 20-21; 57
    Missing compositions, 22-23; 26-27; 29; 35-38; 134; 136; 145
    Musical alphabet, use of, 8; 12; 14; 30; 38; 99-100; 121; 136
    New Moon, 26; 37
    Nile Fantasy (alt: *Le Nil*), 35; 97; 122; 127-131; 134-136; 145
        Movement I: The Rebellion, 130-132
        Movement II: Inshallah, 130; 132-134
        Movement III: The Terror, 130; 132; 134
        Movement IV: The Road to Victory, 130; 133
        premiere of, 127-129; 132-134; 145
    Normandie, 29; 37; 148
        See also: *Suite de Normandie du Moyen-Age*
    Nubian Legend, 36; 66-67; 79
        See also: *Legend of the Mahdi*
    Patagonian Triste, 34; 36
    Program music, use of, 14-15; 16; 63; 126
    Rhapsodie togolaise, 37-38; 136; 145
    Rumpelstiltsken, 21
    Sakura, 23; 26; 37
    Seven Pillars of Wisdom, 8-9; 35; 38; 43; 59; 79; 91; 93; 96-101; 110; 112; 120-121; 123; 125; 129; 131-134; 136; 142; 144
        Prologue: Foundations of the Arab Revolt, 79; 96-97; 101
        Part I: Decay of the Ottoman Empire, 97; 104
        Part II: Fire and Reason, 93; 96-97; 107; 131; 133
        Part III: Blood, 92; 97; 107; 129; 133
        Part IV: The Evil of My Tale, 92; 97; 107; 109; 133; 142
        Part V: The Agonies, the Terrors, and the Mistakes, 96-97; 112; 132
        Part VI: Fortune Favored the Bold Player, 79; 93; 96-97; 114; 129; 133-134
        Part VII: The Final Stroke: Red Victory!, 97; 117; 129
        Epilogue: Disillusion, Death, and the Final Liberty of the Afro-Asian Peoples, 93; 98; 104; 115; 119-121; 134
    Sonata diabolique, 12; 37-38; 126
    Song of the Machine, 16-17
    Suite de Normandie du Moyen-Age, 29; 37
        The King of France, 29-30; 33; 36

The Poet's Love, 29; 33; 36
  See also: *Normandie*
Suite from the Arabian Nights, 18
Uganda Martyrs, 35; 44; 81; 87-88; 90; 136; 139-140
Untitled (final surviving work), 135-136; 140-142
Untitled (in seven movements), 21
Voodoo Festival (alt. *Festival in Port-au-Prince*), 8; 23-24; 36-37
Wanchai Road (alt. *On-Koto*), 26-28; 36
White Nile Suite, 7; 35; 43; 53; 64-66; 69; 72; 74; 78-80; 97; 121; 125; 129; 131-134
  alternate version of, 78-80
  Movement I: *Legend of the Mahdi*, 36; 65-70; 79; 129
    See also: *Nubian Legend*
  Movement II: *Alexandria*, 65; 70-71; 79; 129; 132
  Movement III: *Port Said*, 65; 72-76; 79; 129
  Movement IV: *Fall of Babylon*, 65; 74-79; 129; 132-134
Mutapa Empire, 53-54; 59-60
  See also: Mupunzagutu, Chisamharu Negomo

Négritude, 136; 139-141; 143-144
Nigeria, 6; 39
Nkrumah, Kwame, 136-137; 139; 141; 143

Odinga, Oginga, 136; 138

Pereira, Ernie, 27; 84
Pianologue (album, PDS), 23; 26-27; 29; 37; 48
Portugal, music of, 29; 46
Preminger, Marion, 56-57

Raymond, Maurice, 122-123
Rosewings, 81
  See also: Schuyler, Philippa Duke

Schuyler, George, 5; 149

Schuyler, Josephine Cogdell, 5-6; 9-11; 15; 20-21; 25; 27-28; 33; 36; 47-48; 55-56; 64; 80-85; 91; 93-94; 111; 122-127; 135; 143; 145-149
  as Schuyler's manager, 5; 25; 33; 47-48; 81
  death of, 149
  Kingdom of Dreams, 85
  and publicity, 56; 85
  and Schuyler's childhood, 5; 15; 20-21; 81-83
Schuyler, Philippa Duke
  Abortion, 123; 126; 129
  and Catholicism. See Catholicism.
  Childhood of, 2; 4-5; 7; 9; 15-21; 81-83
  and Communism, 4; 81; 95; 138; 143-144; 146-147
  as composer. See Musical compositions by PDS
  death of, 148-149
  and the occult, 9-12; 83; 85; 110-111; 122
    See also: Astrology; Tarot
  "Music of Modern Africa" article, 35; 39; 41; 44
  practice notes of, 83; 145
  pseudonyms of. See Monterro, Felipa; Rosewings.
  and racial prejudice, 9; 83-84; 139; 143; 148
  research on African music, 7-8; 35; 41-42; 44; 46
  as writer. See Books by PDS.
  and Vietnam, 6; 36; 41; 66; 145-148
Schweitzer, Albert, 3; 35; 53; 55-60
Selassie, Haile, emperor of Ethiopia, 42
Senegal, 39; 45; 139
Senghor, Léopold, 139
South Africa, 39; 46-47; 53; 84; 138
  apartheid in, 9; 46-47; 84; 138
  music of, 46
Stoll, Dennis Gray, 29; 38; 58; 64-66; 79; 123-128; 132
  compositions of, 64-65; 127-128
  divorce of, 124; 126
  review in *Music Journal*, 66

Stoll, Dennis Gray *(cont'd.)*
  romance with Schuyler, 29; 124-127
  and Schuyler's career, 29; 38; 64-66;
    123; 125; 127-128
Sudan, 7; 9; 39; 42-43; 65-67; 72; 83; 100;
    109; 130
  gender issues in, 42-43; 83
  Mahdist State in, 66-67
  music of, 43; 66-67; 100; 109; 130
  Omdurman, 65-67; 79
  Schuyler's travel to, 9; 39; 42-43; 66; 130

Talalay, Kathryn, 2-3; 85; 96
Tanganyika, 39; 53; 136-137; 139; 141-142
  See also: Tanzania
Tanzania, 39; 53; 136-137; 139; 141-142
  See also: Tanganyika
Tarot, 10-12; 83; 85; 110-111; 122
  Horoscope-Numer-Tarot-Music
    system, 11-12
  and *Seven Pillars of Wisdom*,
    110-111
Togo, 38-39; 59; 97; 145
Toro, 45; 48; 51; 138
  George III, king of Toro, 45
  See also: Uganda
Tshombe, Moïse, 95; 136-137
Town Hall, New York, 53; 55; 58; 59; 64;
    134
  Schuyler's recitals at, 53; 55; 59; 64

Uganda, 4; 7; 35; 39; 43-45; 47-48; 51; 53;
    59; 62; 65; 81; 83; 85-87; 130-131;
    138
  music of, 4; 7; 43-45; 47-48; 51; 53;
    59; 62; 86-87
  Schuyler's travel to, 39; 43-45; 47;
    62; 83
  See also: Buganda; Toro

Vietnam, 6; 36; 41; 66; 145-148
  Concerts in, 66; 145; 148
  Lodge, Henry Cabot, 45
  Schuyler as journalist in, 6; 36; 41;
    145-148
  Schuyler's death in, 148
  Schuyler's humanitarian work in,
    147-148
  racism in, 146; 148
Williams, Ruth, 138
WLIB, Schuyler memorial broadcast, 8

Young People's Concerts, 7; 16

Zaratti, Alfonso, 83; 85
  See also: Catholicism
Zimbabwe, 39; 53-54; 136-139; 141
  independence of, 137-138
  Zimbabwe African People's Union
    (ZAPU), 137-138

About the author

After stumbling across a brief mention of American composer Philippa Schuyler, Dr. Sarah Masterson embarked on a quest spanning the past several years to research and reconstruct Schuyler's piano music. Her 2022 world premiere recording of Schuyler's *Seven Pillars of Wisdom* received Third Prize in the 2023 Ernst Bacon Memorial Award for the Performance of American Music, and her 2024 album *Travelogue: Philippa Schuyler's Music for Piano* was funded in part by a generous Arts Project Support Grant from the South Carolina Arts Commission. The album includes world premiere recordings of several of Schuyler's compositions. Visit her online at www.sarahmastersonpianist.com.